# SOCIO-CULTURAL STUDY OF SCHEDULED TRIBES

## CASTES AND TRIBES OF INDIA-SERIES

1. Continuity and Change Among the Ahom/ **Nitul Kumar Gogai**
2. Ethnography of a Nomadic Tribe: A Study of Yanadi/ **N. Sudhakar Rao**
3. Mythos and Logos of the Warlis: A Tribal World View/ **Ajay Dandekar (Ed.)**
4. Naga Cultural Attires and Musical Instruments/ **A. Lanu Ao (Ed.)**
5. Socio-Cultural Study of Scheduled Tribes: The Pardhans of Maharashtra/ **S.R. Murkute**
6. The Banjara/ **S.G. Deogaonkar** and **Shailaja S. Deogaonkar**
7. The Kolam Tribals/ **S.G. Deogaonkar** and **Leena Deogaonkar Baxi**
8. The Korku Tribals/ **S.G. Deogaonkar** and **Shailaja S. Deogaonkar**
9. Tribal Dance and Songs/ **S.G. Deogaonkar** and **Shailaja S. Deogaonkar**

---

### About the Author

SHASHIDHAR RAMCHANDRA MURKUTE (*b.* 1934) has been working as Head, Department of Sociology at the Smt. Kesharbai Lahoti Mahavidyalya, Amravati (Maharashtra) for the last twenty five years. He obtained his M.A. as well as Ph.D. in sociology from Nagpur University. He also holds a Diploma in Library Science from the same university. He had been a Faculty Member on the Social Science faculty as well as a Member of the Board of Studies in Sociology of Nagpur University. Presently, he is a Member of the Board of Studies in Sociology of Amravati University.

Dr. Murkute has presented research papers at Regional, State and University level seminars and conferences.

*Castes and Tribes of India-2*

# SOCIO-CULTURAL STUDY OF SCHEDULED TRIBES

## THE PARDHANS OF MAHARASHTRA

S.R. MURKUTE

CONCEPT PUBLISHING COMPANY PVT. LTD.
NEW DELHI-110059

**ISBN: 978-81-7022-262-0**

First Published 1990

*Published and Printed by*

Concept
Since 1974

**Concept Publishing Company Pvt. Ltd.**
A/15-16, Commercial Block, Mohan Garden,
New Delhi-110059 (India)
*T* : 91-11-41101460
*E* : publishing@conceptpub.com, *W*: www.conceptpub.com

*To*

*My Father*

*Late Principal*

*Shri Ramchandra Balwant Murkute*

# Contents

# List of Tables

# List of Plates

## List of Photographs

# Foreword

It gives me great pleasure to write a foreword to this book written by my student Dr. S.R. Murkute who has been working as Head of the Department of Sociology in Smt. K.L. Mahavidyalaya at Amravati.

The Pardhans who are often called the minstrels of the Gonds are ethnically and culturally a part of the great Gonds and have been chiefly responsible for preserving and passing on of the mythology, rituals, folk-lore etc. of the tribe. Though foreign and Indian scholars have written about the Gonds, a cogent study of this tribe from Vidarbha had not been undertaken so far. I am glad that Dr. Murkute has studied the Pardhans from Yavatmal district which is the chief habitat of the Pardhans in Vidarbha.

Apart from studying their socio-cultural aspects he has also traced the social change which has set in the tribe since planned development started in the region. I am sure that this work will be a useful addition to the existing literature on the tribe and would be welcome by sociologists, anthropologists as well as by readers in general.

T.S. WILKINSON

# Preface

The tribal aborigines have always been attracting attention as adventurous people. As the author is born and brought-up in Vidarbha Region, he is well aware of and acquainted with the Pardhans, their ceremonial, artistic dances which they dance in festivals, their melodious instrumental music and plethora of rituals.

A perplexing problem pertaining to the Pardhans which poses a puzzle and baffles an anthropologist is, "How and why this, once highly honoured group of Gonds, had slipped to such a low social status of an out-law and comes to be termed and treated as untouchables by their own tribesmen?" The Pardhans feel that it is a punishment passed on to these poor patriotic people by the Raj-Gonds i.e., the ruling group of the Gond Tribals.

This book tries to peep in their social organisation, culture and seeks to find answers to many questions. As the book covers a vast area of study it was thought proper to restrict its scope to Yavatmal District which has the largest concentration of the Pardhans. (Nearly 65 per cent as per Census of India 1961 vol. X Maharashtra Part V-A Scheduled Castes and Scheduled Tribes in Maharashtra, Tables and Part B-B Scheduled Tribes in Maharashtra ethnographic notes). Since the Pardhans predominate the Yavatmal District, the study though confined to Yavatmal District, would represent the true picture of the core of the Pardhan Tribe spread all over Vidarbha.

Since 1951 social change started percolating in the life of these tribals because of the Government sponsored Community Development Programmes. Though all tribals could not change, many moved towards rapid acculturation. In informal discussion the villagers in Yavatmal District often say, "The Banjaras have progressed more as compared to Kolams, Korkus, Gonds and Pardhans". Some of them appear to have been lamenting over their slow progress. This encouraged the author to study the social changes in Pardhans. Hence, the question whether the Pardhans have changed or not, and the nature of change, if any, are also dealt with in this book.

Before I conclude this preface I cannot forget to mention

Dr.Y.B. Damle Retired Professor and Head of the Department of Sociology, Pune University; Shri R.K. Mutatkar, Professor and Head of the Department of Anthropology, Pune University; Shri V.B. Belsare, Librarian, Post Graduate Research Institute, Deccan College, Pune; Dr. V.V. Kulkarni, Librarian, Nagpur University, Nagpur and his colleague Smt. A Vaidya; Dr. M.Y.Qureshi Librarian, Nagpur University, Campus Library, Nagpur, Prof. Dr. S.G. Deogaonkar and Dr. Sau. Deogaonkar from Warora; Shri K.Y. Pande, Clerk, Govt. Post Graduate College, Chhindwara; Shri D.G. Joshi, Block Development Officer, Tamia (M.P.) for the help they rendered during my visits to Pune, Nagpur, Warora, Chhindwara and Tamia. The encouragement of Principal Shri R.N. Mundhada, Prof S.W. Nande and my other colleagues from Smt. Kesharbai Lahoti Mahavidyalaya, Amravati, need to be acknowledged.

During the last many years I have held innumerable discussions with Dr. T.N. Valunjkar, Professor of Sociology, P.G.T.D. Nagpur University, Prof. Dr. N.S. Vaidya, Prof. Dr. P.L. Bhandarkar, Prof. R.N. Ghode of Hislop College, Nagpur; Dr. V.M. Peshawe, Principal, Amolakchand Mahavidyalaya, Yavatmal; Prof S.G. Deogaonkar, Head of the Department of Political Science, Anand Niketan Mahavidyalaya, Warora; Prof. M.D. Deshpande, Shri Shivaji College, Amaravati; Prof. D.B. Kulkarni, Department of Chemistry and Prof. R.B. Chandrakar, V.M.V., Amravati, I will be failing in my duty if I do not make special mention of them.

Discussions with Prof. P.L. Bhandarkar; Dr. S.G. Deogaonkar and Shri M.G. Deshpande, Retired L.I.C. Officer were highly stimulating in raising new questions and new satisfactory answers and with their usual sharpness of intellect, they not only made a number of constructive suggestions but often raised critical issues in the light of which I could read and think.

It is my duty to express my gratitude towards all those respondents from Yavatmal District, particularly of Kelapur, and Wani Tehsils, and, the eminent and well known of Pardhans who rendered wonderful co-operation and spent their valuable time for me. I cannot forget the hospitality shown by Shri T.K. Janpadkar, Guruji of Pandharkawada who took trouble to see that my stay in various villages became comfortable. My special thanks are to Shri Venkatesh Atram of Kachanur, Wardha District, a Senate member of the Nagpur University and to Shri Rushi Meshram, an employee of Govt. Press, Nagpur, who encouraged me and relied on me while parting with the manuscripts in their possession for my study. I am also grateful to Shri S.V. Khapre, Photo-artist of Geography Department, V.M.V., Amravati; Shri P.B. Lad and M.S. Pimparikar student of Engineering College, Pune; and many others for the valuable help they rendered in drawing maps, plates etc.

I would be dishonest if I do not mention what my family members did for me. This work was more of a team work than an individual effort. My brothers Prof. A.R., Dr. V.R. and D.R. Murkute looked after the financial side when I was engaged in this work. Sau. Shailaja, my wife, Sau. Usha A. Murkute, Sau. Yashashri V. Murkute; Sau. Lata D. Murkute - (wives of my brothers;) Ku. Swati, Chi. Sunil and Ku. Vaishali - my children are those who patiently put up with all my whims and did not mind my negligence towards domestic duties.

The blessings of late loving father Shri R.B. Murkute; and my mother Sau. Manoramabai R. Murkute; my uncle Shri M.G. Deshpande, Retired L.I.C. Officer, Nagpur; were the motivating force behind my sustained efforts. Shri and Sau. Mohagaonkar Sub-Divisional Officer, Environmental Engineering Work, Sub- Division Shegaon; who always encouraged me in my efforts and toned up my zeal from time to time must be mentioned with gratitude.

I am proud that since I was a Post-Graduate student of the Department of Sociology, the then Head of the Department of Sociology, Hislop College, (Nagpur) Dr. T.S. Wilkinson, owes the credit of creating research aptitude and love for the subject in me.

I cannot forget his valuable guidance in my academic endeavour.

S.R. MURKUTE

# 1

# INTRODUCTION

The tribal people are an intrinsic part of our national life and with their rich cultural heritage have been instrumental in contributing to that complex amalgum which is termed as our national culture. An overview of the composition of our population will show that the figures are changing with the lapse of every decade. Let us start from the 1951 census and take stock of the situation.

According to the Census of 1951 the population of the Scheduled Tribes was 19,147,054, which was 5.3 per cent of the total population. After the Scheduled Tribes Lists (Modification) Order, 1956, tribal population rose to 22,511,845 or 6.23 per cent. The increase of 34 lakhs was due to the addition of certain groups after it was realised that these had been omitted from the earlier list.

According to the Census of 1961 the population of the Scheduled Tribes was 30,430,184 or 6.86 per cent of the total population.

As per Census of 1971 the total population of Scheduled Tribes was 3.80 millions in India's population of 54.8 million. This formed 6.94 or 7 per cent of the country's population which means the largest tribal concentration anywhere in the world is in India.[1]

Whatever may be the variation in the cultural life, geographic distribution and linguistic and racial affiliation of Tribal communities, their problems, which are common to all, centre round, isolation, illiteracy and economic backwardness.

The largest concentration of Scheduled Tribes in India is, in Andhra Pradesh, Assam, Bihar, Gujarat, Kerala, Madhya Pradesh, Madras, Maharashtra, Mysore, Orissa, Punjab, Rajasthan, West Bengal and Union territories.

This tribal population falls into four main zones. Three principal or main territorial zones are the North-eastern Zone, the Central Zone, the Southern Zone and one small isolated Zone.

1. The First, main North-eastern zone consists of the sub-Himalayan region and the hill and mountain ranges of North-

eastern India of the Tista valley and the Jamuna-Padma portion of the river Brahmaputra. This zone is inhabited by tribes like the Gurung, Limbu, Lepcha, Aka, Dafla Abor-Miri, Mishmi, Singpho, Mikir, Rabha, Kaçhari, Garo, Khasi, Naga, Kuki-Lushai, Chakma and others.

2. The Central zone which is separated from the North-eastern zone by the gap between the Garo Hills and Rajmahal Hills consists of the plateaus and mountainous belts between the Indo Gangetic Basin to the North and roughly the Krishna river to the South. The main tribes inhabiting this zone are the Santal, Munda, Oraon, Ho, Bhumij, Kharia, Birhor, Bhuiyan, Juang, Kandh, Savara, Gond, Baiga, Bhil, Koli etc.
3. The Southern zone may be said to consist of the part of Peninsular India which falls South of the river Krishna. This zone is inhabited by tribes like the Chenchu, Kota, Kurumba, Badaga, Toda, Kadar, Malayan, Muthuvan, Urali, Kanikkar, etc.
4. In addition to the above zones, mention may be made of a small and isolated fourth zone consisting of the Andaman and Nicobar Islands in the Bay of Bengal. The main tribes inhabiting this zone are the Jarawa, Onge, North Sentineleses and the Nicobarese. Numerically these are small tribes, though important anthropologically.[2]

**Scheduled Tribes of Maharashtra**

The President has (under powers conferred by Article 342 of the Constitution) declared certain tribes or tribal communities as Scheduled Tribes. As per Census of 1961 their population in Maharashtra is 2,397,159 (23.97 lakhs) which is slightly more than 6 per cent of the total population of State and 6 per cent of the total population of Scheduled Tribes in India.

The first order under Article 342 was issued by the President in 1950. Later on, was modified by the Scheduled Castes and Scheduled Tribes Orders (Amendment) Act, 1956.

As per the Census of India 1961 Vol. X Maharashtra Part V-A there are in all 40 Scheduled Tribes.[3]

They are:

(1) Andh, (2) Barad, (3) Bavacha, (4) Bhaina, (5) Bhattra, (6)

Bhil, (7) Bhunjia, (8) Binjhwar, (9) Birhul, (10) Chodhara, (11) Dhanka, (12) Dhanwar, (13) Dhodia, (14) Dhubla, (15) Gamit, (16) Gond, (17) Halba, (18) Kathodi, (19) Kawar, (20) Khairwar, (21) Kokna, (22) Kol, (23) Kolam, (24) Koli Dhor, (25) Koli Mahadev, (26) Koli Malhar, (27) Korku, (28) Koya, (29) Nagesia, (30) Naikde, (31) Oraon, (32) Pardhan, (33) Pardhi, (34) Patelia, (35) Pomla. (36) Rathawa, (37) Thakur, (38) Thoti, (39) Varli, (40) Vitolia.

From the administrative point of view Maharashtra State is divided into four divisions viz. Bombay Division, Poona Division, Aurangabad Division, Nagpur Division.

(Table 1.1 showing the distribution of Scheduled Tribes population by Administrative Division and Districts of Nagpur Division of Maharashtra).

Nagpur Division of Maharashtra State consists of Nine Districts viz. Buldhana, Akola, Amravati, Yavatmal, Wardha, Nagpur, Bhandara, Chandrapur and Gadchiroli.

Table 1.1 shows that there is no Scheduled Tribe or Tribal population in the five districts viz. Akola, Bhandara, Buldhana, Nagpur and Wardha in Nagpur Division. Even in the remaining districts viz. Amravati, Chandrapur and Yavatmal Scheduled Tribes are only in tehsils viz. Melghat (Amravati), Rajura, Gadchiroli and Sironcha (Chandrapur) and Kelapur, Wani and Yavatmal. The Scheduled Tribes population shown against those districts is therefore from those respective tehsils only, though the corresponding total population is shown for the entire district.

Here one thing should be made clear that the districts where tribal population is shown as nil e.g. Akola, Bhandara, Buldhana, Nagpur and Wardha districts, only because these districts or areas have not been included in the specified areas as scheduled areas, and hence no tribal population is shown in those districts. It does not mean that there is no tribal population in those districts.

The Table 1.1 shows that in Nagpur Division though only four districts out of nine have the tribal population, it claims the next higher percentage (4.27) of Scheduled tribe population to the total population compared to Bombay Division (12.35).

**Tribes of Vidarbha (Nagpur Division)**

Vidarbha area which is shown under the Nagpur Division for the Administrative purpose includes nine districts viz. Akola, Amravati,

TABLE 1.1: **Table Showing the Distribution of Scheduled Tribes Population by Administrative Divisions and Districts of Nagpur Division of Maharashtra State**

| State/Division/ District | Total population | Scheduled Tribes population | Percentage of Scheduled Tribes population to the total population |
|---|---|---|---|
| Maharashtra | 39,553,718 | 2,397,159 | 6.06 |
| Bombay Division | 13,662,321 | 1,687,229 | 12.35 |
| Poona Division | 10,360,282 | 213,359 | 2.06 |
| Aurangabad Division | 6,297,373 | 102,650 | 1.63 |
| Nagpur Division | 9,233.742 | 393,921 | 4.27 |
| **Districts** | | | |
| Akola | 1,189,354 | No Sche. Tribes | — |
| Amravati | 1,232.780 | 54,881 | 4.45 |
| Bhandara | 1,268,286 | No Sche. Tribes | — |
| Buldhana | 1.059.698 | No Sche. Tribes | — |
| Chandrapur (including Gadchiroli) | 1.238.070 | 183,431 | 14.82 |
| Nagpur | 1.512.807 | No Sche. Tribes | — |
| Wardha | 634.277 | No Sche. Tribes | — |
| Ytmal | 1.098.470 | 155,609 | 14.17 |

Bhandara, Buldhana, Chandrapur, Gadchiroli, Nagpur, Wardha and Yavatmal. Out of these eight districts only four districts viz. Amravati, Chandrapur, Gadchiroli and Yavatmal have tribal population. Out of the forty tribal communities of the State nineteen tribal communities belong to Vidarbha Area.

The remaining tribes (out of the forty tribes of the State) which have no tribal population in Vidarbha are as under:-

(1) Barad,
(2) Bavacha
(3) Bhil
(4) Chodhara
(5) Dhanka
(6) Dhodia
(7) Dulba
(8) Gamit
(9) Kathodi
(10) Kokna
(11) Koli Dhor
(12) Koli Mahadev
(13) Koli Malhar
(14) Nagesia

(15) Naikda
(16) Patelia
(17) Polma
(18) Rathawa
(19) Thakur
(20) Varli
(21) Vitolia

TABLE 1.2: **Table Showing Nineteen Scheduled Tribes of Vidarbha alongwith its Population**

(As per Census of India, Maharashtra 1961)

| S.No. | Name of the Tribe | Total Tribal population of the State | Population of the Tribe in Vidarbha, with Districts | |
|---|---|---|---|---|
| 1. | Andh | 60,261 | Yavatmal | 4,313 |
| 2. | Bhaina | 12 | Yavatmal | 12 |
| 3. | Bhattra | 3 | Yavatmal | 3 |
| 4. | Bhunjia | 6 | Amravati | 6 |
| 5. | Binjhwar | 24 | Amravati | 7 |
| | | | Chandrapur | 10 |
| | | | Yavatmal | 7 |
| 6. | Birhul | 22 | Yavatmal | 22 |
| 7. | Dhanwar | 40 | Yavatmal | 40 |
| 8. | Gond | 272,564 | Amravati | 4,398 |
| | | | Chandrapur | 166,266 |
| | | | Yavatmal | 85,803 |
| 9. | Halba | 5,430 | Chandrapur | 4,737 |
| | | | Yavatmal | 674 |
| 10. | Kawar | 2,915 | Chandrapur | 2,812 |
| | | | Yavatmal | 101 |
| 11. | Khairwar | 275 | Chandrapur | 275 |
| 12. | Kol | 53 | Yavatmal | 53 |
| 13. | Kolam | 43,788 | Chandrapur | 1,516 |
| | | | Yavatmal | 41,013 |
| 14. | Korku | 50,279 | Amravati | 50,279 |
| 15. | Koya | 33 | Chandrapur | 33 |
| 16. | Oraon | 1 | Yavatmal | 1 |
| 17. | Pardhan | 32,237 | Amravati | 60 |
| | | | Chandrapur | 7,145 |
| | | | Yavatmal | 22,280 |
| 18. | Pardhi | 21,417 | Yavatmal | 1,236 |
| 19. | Thoti | 109 | Chandrapur | 45 |

Above Table 1.2 shows that, only 8 tribes viz. Andh, Gond, Halba, Kawar, Kolam, Korku, Pardhan and Pardhi, out of the nineteen have more than one thousand population.

Out of these eight tribes the Gonds are more in number in Chandrapur Gadchiroli district, Korku in Amravati District, Kolams and Pardhans in Yavatmal district, Halba and Kawar in Gadchiroli

Chandrapur Districts.

It can therefore be concluded that Vidarbha is an area of tribal communities having more concentration of Gonds, Korkus, Kolams, Pardhans, Halbas and Kawars. But the tribal population of Halba and Kawar is very much less (5,430) and (2,915) as compared to Gonds, Korkus, Kolams and Pardhans.

TABLE 1.3: **Table Showing the Tribal Population of four main Tribes of Vidarbha**

(As per Census 1961)

| Tribe | Amravati | Chandrapur Gadchiroli | Yavatmal |
|---|---|---|---|
| Gonds | 4,398 | 166,266 | 85,803 |
| Kolams | Nil | 1,516 | 41,013 |
| Pardhans | 60 | 7,145 | 22,280 |
| Korkus | 50,279 | Nil | Nil |
| Total | 54,737 | 174,927 | 149,096 |

From the Table 1.3 it becomes clear that Gonds claim the first position; next come the Korkus which is mainly concentrated in Amravati District. Kolams come next i.e. at the third place but mainly concentrated in Yavatmal District. Though the Pardhans claim the fourth place in the tribal group of Vidarbha, it is yet the principal tribe of Yavatmal district.

Thus Yavatmal District is a district which claims sufficiently high percentage of tribal population. Chandrapur district claims the first place, Yavatmal second and Amravati third place respectively.

## Yavatmal District

As the title of the work reads, "Pardhans of Vidarbha; with reference to their social organization, traditions and social change", and as it has also been made clear in the preface about the scope of this research work, the study area has been mainly confined to Yavatmal District and that too Kelapur and Wani tehsils of the Districts where the Pardhans of Vidarbha have a largest concentration (69.11)[4] in the State; the author has dealt with the topographical situation as also the tribal population of the district in general and of the Pardhans in particular.

As has been stated earlier Yavatmal district has second position in respect of tribal population of Vidarbha and the Pardhans claim third place in respect of tribal population of the district.

*Geographical Situation*

The district of Yavatmal lies between 19°26′ N, and 20°42′ N Latitudes and 79°9′ E and 79°9′ E Longitudes. It has an area of 13,517 square kilometers and a population of 1,098,470 according to the 1961 Census figures distributed among 8 towns and 1,629 inhabited villages. The district forms 4.41 per cent of the total area of the state but has proportionately a lesser share of the population viz. 2.78 per cent.

The district is known as Yavatmal after the headquarters of the district. According to Aini-Akbari[5], it derived its name from "Yot Lohara", 'Yot' being an Urdu corruption of Yavat, the original name of the town Lohara, the name of the another village about 5 kilometers to its West. Subsequent to the merger of the village Lohara in the town, it came to be known as Yavatmal from Yavat, the original name of the town and Mal being a corruption of Mahal or Pargana town. It might also have been derived from Marathi word Mal being a plain and the town having been known as plains of Yavat or Yavat plains, i.e. Yavatmal.

*Administrative Evolution*

Largest of Berar districts, Yavatmal has been evolved by grouping together parts of the East Berar and Basim districts. Today, the district constitutes the South-Central districts of the Nagpur Division (Vidarbha) of Maharashtra State. The tehsils of Yavatmal, Darwha, Kelapur, Wun (or Wani as it has been re-named) of the East Berar districts were separated and grouped to form a new district in the year 1864. This district was originally named the South-East Berar and subsequently Wun district. In the year 1905, the tehsil of Pusad was transferred from the Basim district (now Akola district) to the Wun district and simultaneously the Wun district was re-named as Yavatmal district. The administrative headquarters, since the formation of the district in 1864, has however been at Yavatmal only.

With the reorganization of the States in 1956, the district was transferred from Madhya Pradesh to the then Bombay State. The district forms a part of Maharashtra State since 1st May 1960.

*Boundaries of the District*

Administratively, the district is bounded on its north-west by Washim, Mangrul Pir and Murtizapur tehsils of Akola district, on the north by Amravati and Chandur tehsils of Amravati district, on the north-east by Warora, Chandrapur and Rajura tehsils of Chandrapur district, on the South, it is bounded by the Kalamnuri tehsil of Parbhani district, Hadgaon and Kinwat tehsils of Nanded districts and by the northern tehsils of Adilabad district of Andhra Pradesh State.

*Geographical Boundaries*

Geographically, the river Penganga with its graceful meandering curves constitutes the southern boundary of the district from a point 3 km. west of Belura village in the Pusad tehsil, in the west till its confluence with the Wardha river, in the east in the village Jugad of Wani tehsil. The north-eastern and eastern boundaries run along the river Wardha from the village Sujan in Yavatmal tehsil about 6 km. south of the Pulgaon Railway Junction on Bombay-Nagpur main line railway, till its confluence with the Penganga. The rest of the boundary in the west as well as north is mostly one of the administrative convenience.

For administrative purpose, the district is at present divided into five tehsils, they are:

| | *Tehsil* | *Headquarter* |
|---|---|---|
| 1. | Darwha | Darwha |
| 2. | Yavatmal | Yavatmal |
| 3. | Pusad | Pusad |
| 4. | Kelapur | Pandharkawada |
| 5. | Wani | Wani |

*Climate*

The climate of this district is common with the neighbouring districts of North Deccan, is characterised by a hot summer and general dryness except during the South-West monsoon. The cold season from December to February is followed by the hot season from March to May. The period from June to September is the South-West monsoon season and October and November from the post-monsoon period.

*Scheduled Tribes of Yavatmal District*

Twenty two Scheduled tribes have been declared as such only for three talukas viz. Kelapur, Wani and Yavatmal. Out of them 16 Scheduled Tribes were reported in the notified area in the Census of 1961. It should be noted that because of the area restrictions, there are no Scheduled Tribes in Pusad and Darwha tehsils.

TABLE 1.4: **Table Showing the Total Population and Scheduled Tribes Population Figures of Yavatmal District**

(As per Census 1961)

| | | Total Population | Tribal Population | |
|---|---|---|---|---|
| Males | 557,010 | 1,098,470 | 77,315 | 155,609 |
| Females | 541,460 | | 78,294 | |
| Urban | 133,525 | 1,098,470 | 4,126 | 15,609 |
| Rural | 959,945 | | 151,483 | |

Table 1.5 shows that out of the sixteen tribal communities of Yavatmal Districts, the following communities viz. Kol, Dhanwar, Bhaina, Bhattra and Oraon, have their hundred per cent tribal population of the State to the district, while Gonds, Kolams and Pardhans have tribal population in thousands.

Though Yavatmal District is one of the districts which comes under the Scheduled area for tribes, the whole district does not come under scheduled area. Only Yavatmal, Kelapur and Wani tehsils have tribal population, while Darwha, Pusad tehsils have no tribal population.

Secondly, these three tehsils have been divided into eight Panchayat Samities. Yavatmal tehsil includes the three Panchayat Samities viz. Yavatmal, Kalam and Babhulgaon; Kelapur tehsil includes Pandharkawada, Ghatanji and Ralegaon; while Wani tehsil includes Wani and Margaon Panchayat Samities.

Amongst all the sixteen tribes of the Yavatmal district, Gonds claim the first place in respect of numerical strength (85,803) 31.48 per cent, while Kolams, the second (41,013) 93.66 per cent and

Pardhans, the third place (22,280) (69.11%). On the basis of the percentage of the tribal population of the district the Kolams come first and the Pardhan next.

Table 1.5: **Table Showing Tribal Population of the Individual Tribes of Yavatmal District Arranged on the Basis of the Strength of Tribal Population alongwith the Tribal Population of the State**

| Sr. No. | Name of the Tribe | Population of the tribes of Yavatmal District | Population of the tribes to the State |
|---|---|---|---|
| All Scheduled Tribes | | 155,609 | 2,397,159 |
| 1. | Gond | 85,803 | 272,564 |
| 2. | Kolam | 41,013 | 43,788 |
| 3. | Pardhan | 22,280 | 32,237 |
| 4. | Andh | 4,313 | 60,261 |
| 5. | Pardhi | 1,236 | 21,417 |
| 6. | Halba | 674 | 5,430 |
| 7. | Kawar | 101 | 2,915 |
| 8. | Kol | 53 | 53 |
| 9. | Bhil | 49 | 572,122 |
| 10. | Dhanwar | 40 | 40 |
| 11. | Birhul | 22 | 32 |
| 12. | Bhaina | 12 | 12 |
| 13. | Binjhwar | 7 | 24 |
| 14. | Bhattra | 3 | 3 |
| 15. | Korku. | 2 | 50,279 |
| 16. | Oraon | 1 | 1 |

*Source*: Census of India, *Scheduled castes and Tribes*, Vol. X 1961.

Of these two most important tribes of the district the author has selected the Pardhan tribe for the study, because one, Dr. Bhausaheb Mandeokar, has already worked on the Kolams of the said District.[6]

Hence the next important tribe, to the Kolams (93.66%) having the largest percentage of concentration (i.e. 69.11) viz. the Pardhans, on which no special study has been undertaken so far by anybody, has been selected for this work.

## A General Review of the Population of Pardhan Tribe

Pardhan is a scheduled tribe in Andhra Pradesh, Madhya Pradesh and Maharashtra.

The President has, under Article, 342 of the Constitution

declared certain tribes or tribal communities as Scheduled Tribes. The first order under Article 342 was issued in 1950.

This order of 1950 was modified by the Scheduled Castes and Scheduled Tribes order (Amendment) Act, 1956.

Pardhan Tribe according to the Scheduled Tribes list is enumerated in three States viz. Andhra Pradesh, Madhya Pradesh and Maharashtra.

In Andhra Pradesh, tribal communities alongwith Pardhans are enumerated in the districts of Hyderabad, Mahubnagar, Adilabad, Nizamabad, Medak, Karimnagar, Warangal, Khammam and Nalgonda.

Other important tribal communities of the Andhra State are Andh, Bhil, Gonds including Naik Pod and Raj Gonds and Kolams.

Pardhans are particularly located in Hyderabad and Adilabad.

In Madhya Pradesh, tribal communities alongwith Pardhan and sub-tribes of Pardhan viz. Pathari and Saroti are enumerated in following districts of the State. Pardhans particularly in:

(1) Bastar area : Chhindwara, Seoni, Mandla, Raigarh and Surguja districts.
(2) Baihar tehsil of Balaghat district.
(3) Betul and Bhainsdesh tehsils of Betul district.
(4) Bilaspur and Katahora tehsils of Bilaspur district.
(5) Durg and Sanjari tehsils of Durg district.
(6) Murwara- Patan and Sihora tehsils of Jabalpur district.
(7) Hoshangabad and Sohagpur tehsils of Hoshangabad district.
(8) Harsul tehsil of Nemar district.
(9) Bindra, Nawagarh Dhamtari and Mahasamund tehsils of Raipur districts.

Other important tribal communities of the Madhya Pradesh are Agariya, Andh, Baiga, Bhil, Gond, Kol, Kolam and Korku.

In Maharashtra State, Pardhan tribe is not enumerated in two divisions viz. Bombay and Poona of the State. It is only in Aurangabad and Nagpur Division. In Aurangabad Division it is in all the districts viz. Aurangabad, Parbhani, Bhir, Nanded and Osmanabad.

In Nagpur Division out of nine districts, only four districts viz. Amravati, Chandrapur, Gadchiroli and Yavatmal districts have Pardhan population. Pardhans alongwith sub-tribes Pathari and Saroti are mainly in Melghat tehsil of Amravati district, Gadchiroli and Sironcha tehsils of Chandrapur district and Kelapur, Wani and Yavatmal of Yavatmal district.

TABLE 1.6: **Table Showing Pardhan Population of India**

(According to Census 1961)

| State | Total Population | Male | Female |
|---|---|---|---|
| Andhra Pradesh | 9,701 | 4,539 | 5,162 |
| Madhya Pradesh | 50,226 | 25,043 | 25,183 |
| Maharashtra | 32,237 | 16,109 | 16,128 |
| Total | 92,164 | 45,691 | 46,773 |

Maharashtra claims the second place on the basis of numerical strength of Pardhans in India.

According to Census of India, 1961, Andhra Pradesh constitutes of twenty districts, of which only two districts viz. Hyderabad and Adilabad have Pardhan population (9,701) and that too much concentrated in Adilabad district (9,344).

In respect of Madhya Pradesh the Pardhan population is mainly in Bhopal, Jabalpur, Bilaspur and Raipur Divisions. Out of the seven divisions of the State, viz. Gwaliar, Rewa, Indore, Bhopal, Jabalpur, Bilaspur and Raipur, two divisions viz. Gwaliar and Rewa have no Pardhan population. Indore division has only 35 persons in East Nimar district, similarly in Bhopal Division, Hoshangabad and Betul districts, have the entire Pardhan population of Bhopal division. In Jabalpur division, except Sagar and Demoh districts all other districts viz. Jabalpur, Narsinghpur, Mandla, Chhindwara, Seoni and Balaghat have Pardhan population. Seoni and Mandla districts have higher concentration (16,189) and (14,715) respectively.

Out of 43 districts of Madhya Pradesh, 15 districts have Pardhan population.

In Maharashtra, out of 4 divisions viz. Bombay, Poona, Aurangabad and Nagpur only two divisions viz. Aurangabad and Nagpur with five and four districts respectively have Pardhan population and that too much concentrated in Yavatmal district of Nagpur Division, (22,270).

**Pardhans of Maharashtra and Vidarbha**

As has been stated earlier, the Pardhan tribe is not enumerated in

MAP NO. I.

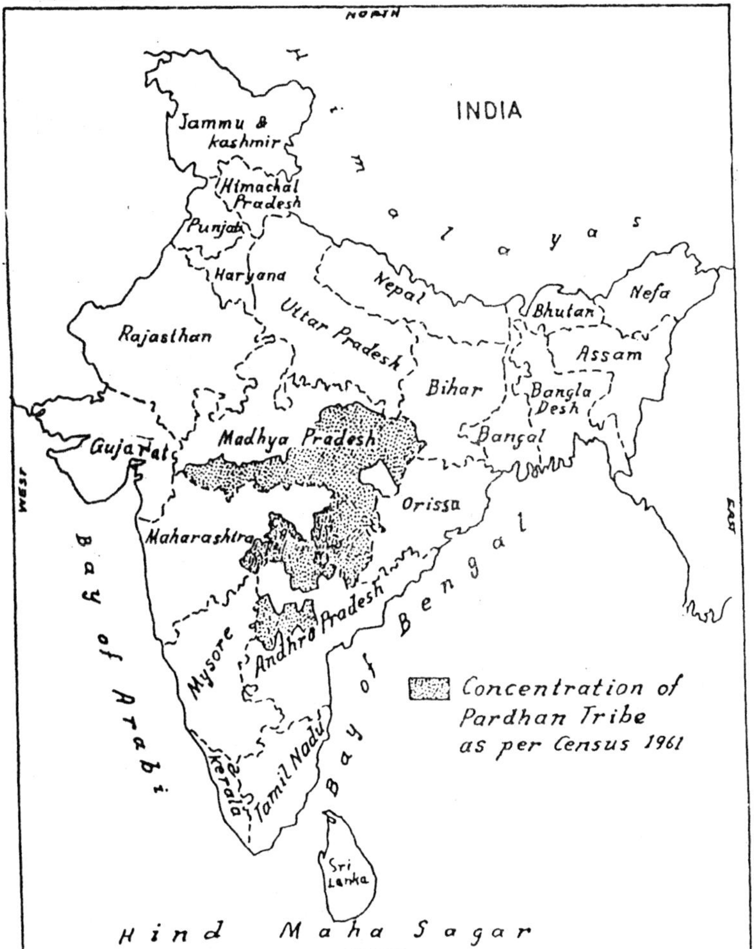
NORTH
INDIA
Jammu & kashmir
Himachal Pradesh
Punjab
Haryana
Rajasthan
Uttar Pradesh
Nepal
Bihar
Bhutan
Nefa
Assam
Bangla Desh
Bangal
Gujarat
Madhya Pradesh
Orissa
Maharashtra
Mysore
Andhra Pradesh
Kerala
Tamil Nadu
Sri Lanka
Bay of Arabi
Bay of Bengal
Hind Maha Sagar
WEST
EAST
SOUTH
Concentration of Pardhan Tribe as per Census 1961

all the four divisions of the State, but only in two divisions viz. Aurangabad and Nagpur.

TABLE 1.7: **Table Showing Pardhans Population of Maharashtra State According to Sex and Location i.e. Rural/Urban**

(Census 1961)

| Area | Pardhan total population | Males | Males Rural | Males Urban | Females | Females Rural | Females Urban |
|---|---|---|---|---|---|---|---|
| AREA - MAHARASHTRA | 32,237 | 16,109 | 15,542 | 567 | 16,128 | 15,568 | 560 |
| AURANGABAD DIVISION | 2,752 | 1,382 | 1,371 | 11 | 1,370 | 1,361 | 9 |
| NAGPUR DIVISION | 29,485 | 14,727 | 14,171 | 556 | 14,758 | 14,207 | 551 |

In Aurangabad division, the Pardhans are located in all the districts viz. Aurangabad, Parbhani, Bhir, Nanded and Osmanabad. Their population is comparatively very less to Nagpur Division. Pardhans of the State are mainly concentrated in the Yavatmal district of Nagpur Division.

The Pardhans' population of Maharashtra State according to the sex and location i.e. Rural/Urban as per Census 1961 is shown in Table 1.7.

From Table 1.8 one point about the tribal population of the Pardhans gets clear that in respect of Urban population of Pardhans, Yavatmal District has the highest number. They are more in number in Yavatmal District (22,280). Next comes Chandrapur District (7,145).

TABLE 1.8: **Table Showing Pardhans Population in State, Divisions and Districts; alongwith Location i.e. Rural and Urban**

(Census: 1961)

| State/Division District | Pardhan Population | Rural | Urban |
|---|---|---|---|
| MAHARASHTRA | 32,237 | 31,110 | 1,127 |
| **Aurangabad Division** | 2,752 | 2,732 | 20 |
| Aurangabad District | 2 | 1 | 1 |
| Parbhani District | 237 | 237 | — |
| Bhir District | 142 | 142 | — |
| Nanded District | 2,196 | 2,177 | 19 |
| Osmanabad District | 175 | 175 | — |
| **Nagpur Division** | 29,485 | 28,378 | 1,107 |
| Amravati District | 60 | 60 | — |
| Yavatmal District | 22,280 | 21,261 | 1,019 |
| Chandrapur District (Including Gadchiroli) | 7,145 | 7,057 | 88 |

Concentration of the Pardhan population in Maharashtra State is shown in Map No. 2 showing the four divisions i.e. Administrative boundaries of the State indicating the corresponding numbers to the districts viz. 1 to 7 for Bombay Division and so on.

## Historical Background

Prior to the advent of the Aryans, the tribal groups of people inhabiting this land were known as non-Aryans or Anārya. With an aim to abode here the Aryans aggressively attacked the Non-Aryan possessions to conquer and acquire them for themselves. The Non-

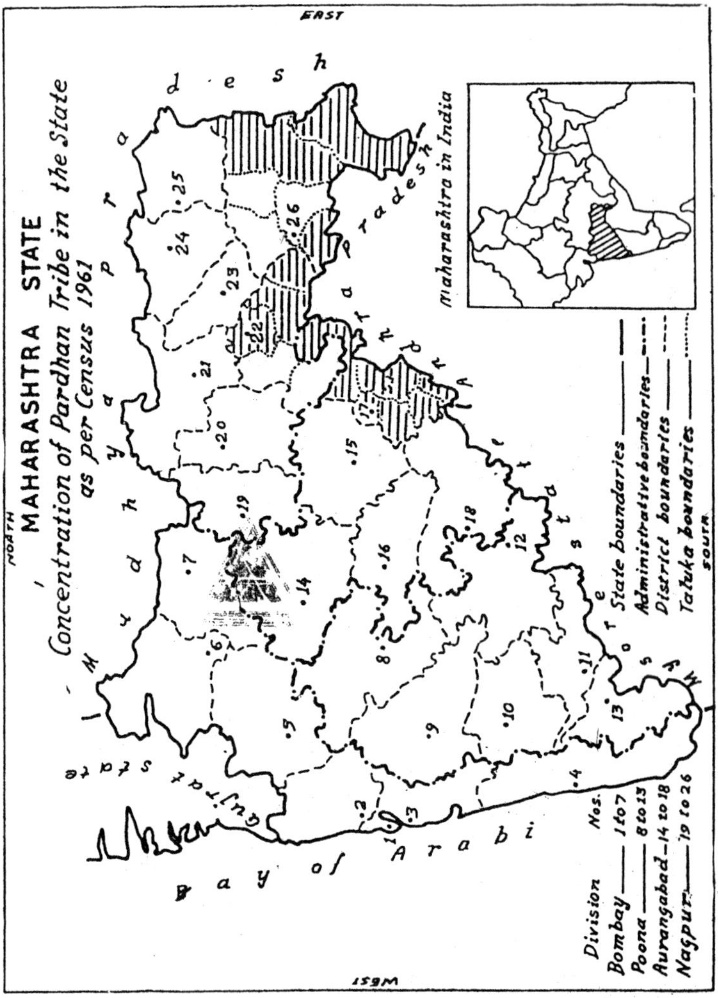
MAHARASHTRA STATE
Concentration of Pardhan Tribe in the State
as per Census 1961
NORTH
SOUTH
EAST
WEST
Madhya Pradesh
Andhra Pradesh
Gujrat State
Mysore State
Bay of Arabia
Maharashtra in India
Division Nos.
Bombay — 1 to 7
Poona — 8 to 13
Aurangabad — 14 to 18
Nagpur — 19 to 26
State boundaries
Administrative boundaries
District boundaries
Taluka boundaries

MAP NO. 2.

**Maharashtra State, its divisions and district numbers:**

| | Divisions | | Districts | District Nos. |
|---|---|---|---|---|
| 1. | BOMBAY DIVISION | 1. | Greater Bombay | 1 |
| | From 1 to 7 | 2. | Thana | 2 |
| | | 3. | Kolaba | 3 |
| | | 4. | Ratnagiri | 4 |
| | | 5. | Nasik | 5 |
| | | 6. | Dhulia | 6 |
| | | 7. | Jalgaon | 7 |
| 2. | POONA DIVISION | 8. | Ahmadnagar | 8 |
| | From 8 to 13 | 9. | Poona | 9 |
| | | 10. | Satara | 10 |
| | | 11. | Sangli | 11 |
| | | 12. | Sholapur | 12 |
| | | 13. | Kolhapur | 13 |
| 3. | AURANGABAD DIVISION | 14. | Aurangabad | 14 |
| | From 14 to 18 | 15. | Parbhani | 15 |
| | | 16. | Bhir | 16 |
| | | 17. | Nanded | 17 |
| | | 18. | Osmanabad | 18 |
| 4. | NAGPUR DIVISION | 19. | Buldhana | 19 |
| | From 19 to 26 | 20. | Akola | 20 |
| | | 21. | Amravati | 21 |
| | | 22. | Yeotmal | 22 |
| | | 23. | Wardha | 23 |
| | | 24. | Nagpur | 24 |
| | | 25. | Bhandara | 25 |
| | | 26. | Chandrapur (including Gadchiroli) | 26 |

Aryans were mainly the aborigines. The fear of losing throne and position of ruling chief was always lurking in the minds and hearts of Raj Gonds (Ruling class of the Gond Tribe). They, therefore, preferred to avoid the troubles adhereing, to the strategy of surrender and save their position and possession, by accepting the servitude of the Aryan lordship. But the other Gond groups viz. Pardhans, Dalave, Mokashi etc. who had bravery in their blood, brawn and brain and also fight to-finish power and powers in their sinewy shoulders were not inclined to such strategy of surrender to servitude. They decided to defend by shedding the last drop of their blood in fight with the Aryans. This was against the advice of the Raj Gonds, who wanted to save their position and possessions any way.

MAP NO. 3.

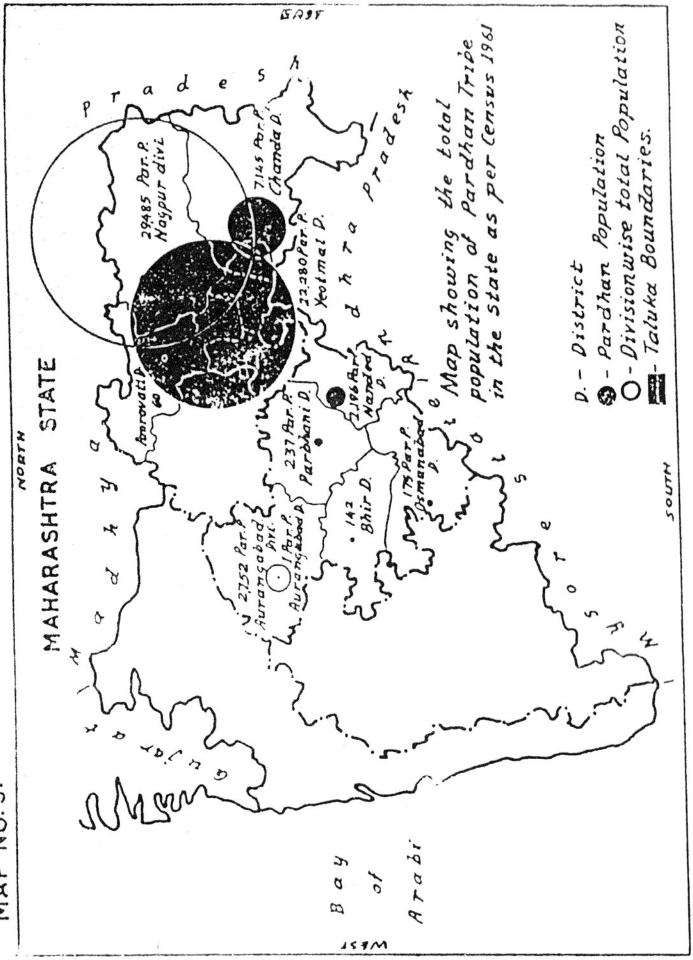
MAHARASHTRA STATE
NORTH
EAST
SOUTH
WEST
Madhya pradesh
Andhra pradesh
Gujarat
Bay of Arabi
29485 Par. P. Nagpur divi.
7145 Par. P. Chanda D.
22280 Par. P. Yeotmal D.
Amravati D.
237 Par. P. Parbhani D.
2,196 Par. Nanded D.
174 Par. P. Osmanabad D.
142 Bhir D.
2,752 Par. P. Aurangabad divi.
1 Par. P. Aurangabad D.
Map showing the total population of Pardhan Tribe in the State as per Census 1961
D. - District
- Pardhan Population
- Divisionwise total Population
- Taluka Boundaries.

These other Gond groups defined the Raj Gonds and separated themselves from them. The Raj Gonds, therefore, boycotted them (the other groups) and outlawed from the tribe. These other sub-sects kept on struggling and fighting with Aryans as and when occasion arose. But due to meagre manpower, mean military material and odd organization, they could not stand against the superior strength of the well-organized Aryans. They were, therefore, ultimately defeated and the Aryan conquerers treated them as slaves. This gave rise to a separate community of the Dasyus-the-salves-who were declared outlawed and were later secluded and treated as untouchables. Thus, these honour loving patriotic people, who forcefully fought the aggressive Aryans, defying their supremacy and for defending and protecting independance of their rule and region, became outlawed untouchables and secluded from the other Gond groups of the entire tribe. The Raj Gonds solemnly surrendered to the Aryans, handed over all their possessions to them and accepted their servile, 'Yes-Men'. Becoming friendly with the aggressive Aryans, they started oppressing the people of the own class and creed. All other Gond families were treated untouchables, by the Raj Gonds. Factually, this type of seclusion and untouchability was a prejudiced one. There is no solid or basic reason for it, nor it is founded on any strongly accountable and justificable principle. No sub-sect of the Gonds is superior to other. Their blood is one and the same. Their culture and creed are one and the same. Their surnames, ways of worship and of wedding and matrimonial procedure and many other customs have not a little difference. On the contrary their devotion towards the society and social practices is same and similar. Hence the superior-inferior complex or touch and touch me–not tradition amongst these aborigines–Adivasis are a crooked custom and a later enforcement in the community. Not only that, but the higher morals and social vices are being maintained and practised today among these very subsects who are termed and treated as inferiors.

The Pardhans hold that their outlawed position was created due to their defiance to the aggressive Aryans to whom the Gond ruling class had surrendered. It appears that it may be a truth, but not the whole truth. The Aryan aggression appears to have divided the homogeneous solid Gond group into superior-inferior or subjects. History tells us that the powerful Gond Kingdoms were in existence even during the medieval period. They were so prospering that even the Rajput rulers had established friendly, social and matrimonial relations with them. The famous Rani Durgawati of Gadha Mandla was a Rajput princess, married the Gond rulers Dalpatshah. The Pardhans and other subsects of the Gonds were still in service under the Gond rulers in good position and all their social religious traditions were maintained and continued. The remote Aryan aggression appears to have subduded them i.e. other Gond groups but had not deprived them of their tribal territory, customs, traditions and faith.

Like the Aryan aggression in the past, we find from the history that there was a second similar but more severe aggression on the tribal Kingdoms by Muslim invadors after they established themselves in Northern India. Many a small Gond rulers had surrendered to these Muslim attacks and accepted the servitude and even conversion to Muslim faith. This is evident from the fact that even to day some of the Gond ruling families have their names and way of life according to Muslim customs e.g. the powerful Gond ruler, "Bakht Bulandshah" of Nagpur and also that of Deogad of Chhindwada district (M.P.)

It was the most powerful and prosperous Gond Kingdom of Gadha Mandla that had given a tough-to-finish defence to the Muslim (Mougal) aggression under the leadership of brave Rani Durgawati. Rani Durgawati preferred martyrdom to Muslim conversion and servitude. The Muslim invasion had always been like an attack of a dreadful dragon and moved like a massacring machine. On the fall of Rani Durgawati, her kingdom was annexed to Mougal empire and crueal attrocities and forceful conversion were let-loose on the tribal subjects of Rani Durgawati. It therefore, appear that the tribal population migrated to nearby thick forest regions to save themselves from massacre and Muslim conversion.

From these hidings some of them moved towards the Satpuda region of Chhindwada, Seoni and Betul and thence to the plain of Nagpur and Wardha Districts. But a bigger group of them migrated through Bastar forest to adjacent area of Aheri, Sironcha, Gadchiroli and Chandrapur of Chandrapur District. They had established their rule in Chandrapur district; and the descendants of the then Gond rulers are still living in Chandrapur. After the downfall of the Gond rulers the various Gond tribals spread over the adjacent regions for maintenance and livelihood. The Pardhans especially, appear to have moved to the nearby Yavatmal District and presently have settled on both banks of the Painganga river. This may account for their thick settlement in Kelapur; and Wani tehsils of Yavatmal District of Vidarbha and Nanded, Osmanabad and Adilabad region of old Nizam State (Now Andhra Pradesh).

A majority, almost 65 per cent of the Pardhans of Vidarbha are in Kelapur and Wani tehsils of Yavatmal District. It is for this reason that the study has been concentrated on the Pardhans of Yavatmal District.

The information of 1981 census regarding the detailed classification and other statistical information of the Pardhans from Vidarbha in general and that of the Yavatmal District and its tehsils in particular, where the said tribe has the highest concentration has not been published and hence is not available.

1971 CENSUS*

| State /District | Persons | Males | Females |
|---|---|---|---|
| **Maharashtra State** | | | |
| 1. Pardhan | 3,985 | 2,039 | 1,946 |
| 2. Pardhan, Pathari, Saroti | 46,925 | 24,164 | 22,761 |
| 3. Gond or Rajgond | 2,306 | 1,230 | 1,076 |
| 4. Gond (including Naik Pod and Raj Gond) | 17,432 | 8,782 | 8,650 |
| 5. Gond including Arrakh or Arrakh, Agaria, Asur, Badi Maria or Bada Maria, Bhatola, Bhimma, Bhuta, Koilabhuta or Koilabhuti, Bhar, Bisonhorn, Maria, Chota Maria, Dandami Maria, Dhuru or Dhurwa, Dhoba, Dhulia, Dorla, Gaiki, Gatta or Gatti, Gaita, Gond Gawari, Hill Maria, Kandra, Kalanga, Khatola, Koitar, Koya, Khirwar or Kucha Maria, Kuchaki Marin, Madia (Maria), Mana, Mannewor, Moghyaor Mogia or Monghya, Mudia (Muria), Nagarchi, Nagwanshi, Ojha, Raj, Sonjhari Jhareka, Thatia or Thotya, Wade Maria or Vade Maria | 312,060 | 157,316 | 154,744 |
| 6 Kolam | 52,431 | 25,688 | 26,743 |
| 7. Kolam including Mannervarlu | 3,630 | 1,803 | 1,827 |
| 8. Korku, Including Bopchi, Monasi, Nihal or Nahul and Bandhi or Bondeya | 67,742 | 34,445 | 33,297 |
| Pardhan, Pathari and Saroti | | | |
| Yavatmal District | 32,338 | 16,435 | 15,903 |
| Chandrapur District | 14,581 | 7,729 | 6,855 |
| Amravati District | 3 | — | 3 |
| | 46,925 | | |

* Letter from the Government of India to the Author-Letter No. MS/MISC/5756/ dated 29th September, 1979.

Though the population of the Pardhans of Vidarbha (including-Pardhans, Pathari and Saroti) as per Census is shown as 46,925, Pathari and Saroti are shown as sub-sects of the Pardhan tribe in the above letter. There is no reference of Saroti in the book *Tribes and Castes of Central Provinces of India* by R.V. Russell and Hiralal. In Vol. IV. Hiralal and Russell have stated that, "The tribe have several endogamous divisions of which the principal are the Raj Pardhans, the Ganda Pardhans and the Thothi Pardhans. The Raj Pardhans appear to be the descendants of alliances between Raj Gonds and Pardhan Woman. The Thothia subtribe are said to be the descendants of illicit unions, the world Thothia meaning 'Maimed', and the Gandas are the offspring of intermarriage between the Pardhans and members of that degraded caste. Russell and Hiralal also refer to a curious grouping found in Chanda where the tribes are divided into the Gond Patharis and Chor or thief Patharis."[7]

TABLE 1.9: **Table Showing Increase in the Population of the Pardhans in Maharashtra State and Yavatmal District During the Last Ten Years.**

Pardhans in Maharashtra State

| | Total | Male | Female |
|---|---|---|---|
| 1961 | 32.237 | 16.109 | 16,128 |
| 1971 | 46.925 | 24.164 | 22.761 |
| Increase over 10 years | 14.688 | 8,055 | 6.633 |
| Percentage Increase | 45.6% | 50.0% | 41.1% |

Pardhans in Yavatmal District

| | Total | Male | Female |
|---|---|---|---|
| 1961 | 22.280 | 11,119 | 11,161 |
| 1971 | 32.338 | 16.435 | 15,903 |
| Increase over 10 years | 10.058 | 5,316 | 4,742 |
| Percentage Increase | 45.1% | 47.8% | 42.5% |

As stated earlier the detailed classification and other Statistical information of the Pardhan of Vidarbha being not available in the Volume form, and though the population figures for year 1971 are given in Table 1.9, the information received from the Government of India; Director of Census Operations Letter No. MS/MISC/5756 dt 29th September, 1979 the base of Census of 1961 has been taken for this work.

In the Yavatmal District there are in all 16 tribal communities. Out of these 16 tribal communities Kolams claim first (41,013) and

Pardhans second (22,280) position of the tribes in the State.

Out of the three tehsils of Yavatmal District, viz. Yavatmal, Kelapur and Wani only two viz. Kelapur (9,159) and Wani (8,249) having 69.11 per cent of Pardhan population in the State are really representing the majority of the Pardhan tribe.

TABLE 1.10: **Table Showing the total Population and Pardhans Population of the Yavatmal District**

(As per Census 1961)

| Yavatmal | Males | Females | Total |
|---|---|---|---|
| Total Population | 557,010 | 541,460 | 1,098,470 |
| Total Tribal Population | 77,315 | 78,294 | 155,609 |
| Total Pardhans Population | 11,119 | 11,161 | 22,280 |
| Population of Pardhans of Yavatmal Tehsil | – | – | 4,872 |
| Population of Pardhans of Kelapur Tehsil | – | – | 9,159 |
| Population of Pardhans of Wani Tehsil | – | – | 8,249 |

## REFERENCES


1. Perspective on Tribal Development and Administration: Papers and proceedings of the workshop held at NICD Hyderabad April 1974.
2. *The Adivasis*; The Publications Division, Ministry of Information and Broadcasting, Government of India, 1955, pp. 23-24.
3. *Census of India 1961*, Vol. X Maharashtra Part V-A. –Scheduled Castes and Scheduled Tribes in Maharashtra Tables, 1964, pp. 216.
4. Scheduled Tribes in *Maharashtra Census of India*, 1961; Vol-X Maharashtra Part V-B, Scheduled Tribes in Maharashtra; Ethnographic Notes. Published by, the Maharashtra Census Office, Bombay, 1972, p. 235.
5. *Yavatmal District Gazetteer of India*. Maharashtra State Yavatmal District 2nd Ed. 1974 Bombay.
6. Dr. Mandeokar, *Kolam* (Marathi) by Seva Prakashan Amravati, 1966.
7. Russell, R.V. and R.B. Hiralal, *Tribes and Castes in Central Provinces of India*, Vol. IV, p. 354.

# 2

# The Pardhans–Their Origin

Among the important tribal communities which are recognized as aboriginal tribes, the Gonds, the Kolams, the Korkus, the Bhils and the Pardhans of Vidarbha have maintained the frame and form of their traditional customs and ways of life. Their traditional customs differ somewhat in accordance with the region of inhabitance, contacts with other local societies and the prevailing circumstances. The traditional deviation may also be attributed to the acculturation process among the tribes of independent identity. These tribals are known as the Adivasi Aborigines, and now the, "Scheduled Tribes". The term Scheduled Tribe connotes such primitive tribal people, who for their protection, educational, social, economic and political rights need-special and separate considerations or concessions and hence have been included in a particular schedule by the Government of India.

Even to-day, the cultural customs and original traditions of tribes are taken as the base for identification and classification. Really speaking, notable differences can be observed among the traditional customs of the Kolams, the Korkus and the Bhils, while the Raj-Gonds and the Pardhans are not quite distinct, separate and independent tribes.

Raj-Gonds and Pardhans are the titles traditionally transferred to the families and progeny belonging to the pedigree of persons holding two principal posts or positions i.e. "A ruling chief or king and an administrative chief or Minister", in the Gond Tribe. Later these were passed off as names of these family groups and treated as two separate sub-sects or tribes among the Gonds. Raj-Gond and the Pardhans are not independent tribes but may be said to be the branches or two sub-sects of the principal tribe "Gond".

A prevalent theory is, that among the Gonds, an intelligent individual who had the capacity to know all the professional jobs was deputed to the duty of governing the tribal establishment and was appointed as a chief or the prime administrator and was called

Pardhan. Paradhan means the Prime Minister. The word "Pradhan" in Sanskrit language means, "above all", "greatest among all" or "Supreme Superior".[1] Due to common usage and difficulty in proper pronunciation of the Sanskrit word Pradhan, (Pradhan means Principal or Chief) it may have come to be pronounced as, "Pardhan or Paradhan", and the same pronunciation seems to have continued.

The Pardhans are known by a number of different names. The Gondi word for Pardhans is *Patadi*[2] (Pata means a song and Patadi is a person who has preserved the memory of the heroic past of the Gond Raja in his songs and epics.) Another Gondi word for Pardhans is *Pana*.[3] The origin of Pana has been traced to "Pahuna", a visitor". Pardhan means one who eats other peoples' rice-Para-"others" and Dhan-Rice. Another derivation is from Par-"Embankment" and Dhan-Rice, which implies that the first Pardhan was born on the embankment of a rice field.[4]

Among themselves, the Pardhans accept, *Palal*[5] as their caste but in tribal society they were known as the Pardhans. The word Palal comes from the word "Pala", which means, "ripe, or intelligent or wise." Palal is a word in Pardhan language and means "Name or Fame". In some parts the Pardhans are known as "Palangals", the meaning is, "a seer, a searcher, a highly learned man".

**The Pardhans in Mythology, Legend and Literature**

The Pardhans made their first entry into the literature with the publication of Rev. Stiphen Hislop's papers relating to the Aboriginal Tribes of the Central Provinces, which were edited by Sir R. Temple and printed by him in 1866.[6] Hislop on the basis of the oral source of a Pardhan priest tells a Gond myth of the creation of the world and the origin of the Gonds and their liberation from a cave through the divine hero Lingo, in which they were shut by God Siva. Hislop's paper discusses the legend of Lingo, a long and remarkable account of the origin of the Gond race.[7] For Gond tribals and tribal societies, Lingo is a God.

The creation of the world, the origin of mankind, the establishment of the Gond tribe and separation of the Pardhans from the original race give the account which follows the lines already familiar to anthropologists through the researches of Hislop.

The version of the legend, lacks freshness in Hislop's story, but the author thinks that many of the old myths are, like ancient pictures slowly losing the richness of their colour and are often overlaid by later and anterior work.

Pardhans in other legends are described variously. R.V. Russell and Rai Bahadur Hiralal have given a different legend, which they ascertained in the course of their study, *Tribes and Castes of the Central Provinces of India*, the legend runs as follows:

A Gond and his wife, the two, lived in Barahangarh. They had six sons. The Gond and Gondin went Bekiw-Chaurdongri, to the flat ground below the forest to cut the grass and made a field. When the filed was ready, they sowed rice in it. When the rice was almost ready, they made a platform to guard the crop. Every night they went to sleep there. At that time the Gondin was pregnant, the day of the birth of a child approached. When the rice was ready, they began to reap it. When half of the field was cut, on that very day, on the border of the field, Gondin gave birth to a child. The Gond said, "Let us make a pile of rice in a winnowing-fan and put the child to sleep in it". When the Chhatti day came they gave the child its name. The six brothers said, "We, who have been born in the house, have names of the house, but this boy, who was born outside should take his name from outside. And so saying they gave him the name Pardhan, because he was born on the embankment of the rice field". And because he was born outside, the brothers decided that he should not live or eat inside. As the boy was born when the half of the field was cut, they decided to give him half the share of a brother. Since he was put to sleep in a winnowing-fan, the Gonds, always give the Pardhans their Sukhdan in a winnowing-fan. 'He is our brother, it is true, but we will not give him full brothers' share. And when anyone dies, he will sit with us and receive a turban with the others, but he cannot eat with us or go inside our houses', say the Gonds.

Since that day, there are Pardhans among the Gonds. The Pardhans get half a share, for the Pardhans and the Gonds have the same parents.

At first the Gonds used to play on Bana. However, as per another legend one day the seven Gond brothers were worshipping their God. He (God) did make his appearance, so the youngest of them made a musical instrument out of a string and a piece of wood and played on it. The God was pleased with his music and came down to be worshipped, and hence the Pardhans as the decendants of he youngest brother continue to play on Kingri or Lyre, which is their distinctive instrument.

The great Gond race has given birth to many cadet branches. The Pardhan is one of them. The Pardhans claim themselves to be belonging to the Gond group of the Aborigines. But the Gonds very vehemently deny it and disown them with disregard. The Pardhans are also known by various names such as Palal, Patadi, Pana, Pathari, etc. deriving the word from Gondi dialect. They had been advisors and administrative chiefs of the Gond rulers. Later, they served the Gond tribals as minstrels and bard poets. They were engaged to perform traditional "Puja" or worship their tribal deities on ceremonial and matrimonial functions and festivals. They were, therefore, regarded as tribal priests and referred to with respect and reverence in the past. They were invited to invoke deities, to offer sacrifice to deities and distribute the sacred food (Prasad) to the community colleagues. The Pardhans learned the mystic hymns and traditional mythology of the tribal history and recited them at ceremonial and festive functions. They sang social songs on their harps, Kingari, Kindri or Kingree. They were therefore, given honour by the community on all such occasions.

The Pardhans assert their ancestry to Lunar Lineage,[8] as do the Gonds. They claim (though the Gonds do not approve of it) that, geneologically they go to the Gond group of the tribal Aborigines. They hold that in the remote past the Gonds were a homogenious unit, having honest harmony in holding the social frame, form and culture of the ancient Aboriginal inhabitants of this land. To achieve this triumph, tribal testimony and territorial trade they had to do division of labour, distribution of duties to selected section of the people and reinforce rigid regimental regularity of working to run the regime. Thus the count of capability and capacity of craft, classification of sub-sections came into existence. This gave rise to sub-sects, such as, administrative agents, agricultural activists, ferocious fighters, hunters, tactful traders, riteous religious ritualists etc. These classes were co-ordinative, cooperative and concurring. They were conductive and conduced to conduct the community towards the common cause for amenity or against calamity. They fostered and followed the feeling of unity and diversity. Later through ages following faithfully the same occupation dutifully over generations with will and skill, the class came to be contemplated as a caste.

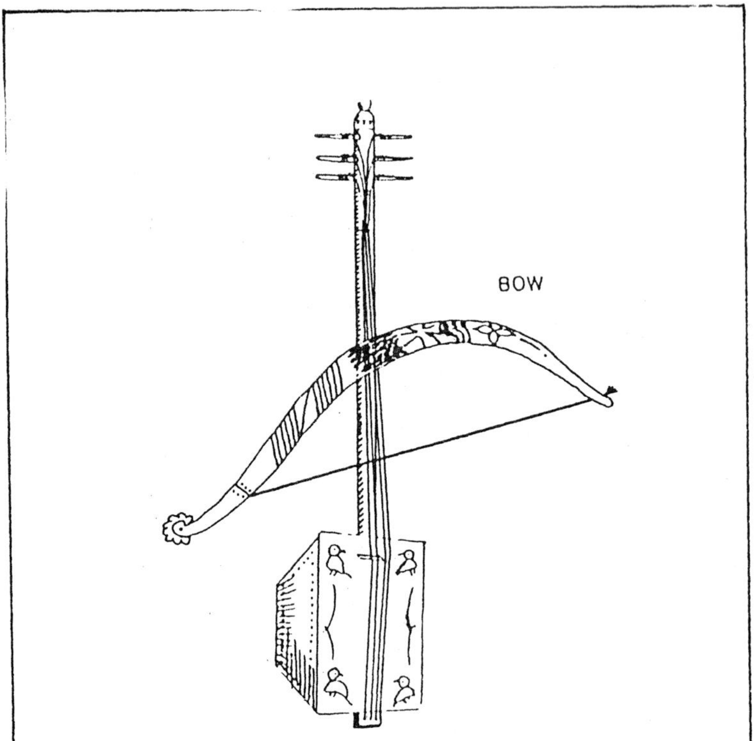


1. Pardhan's Kingri and Bow made of Antelope's Horn. Kingri is the main instrument used by the Pardhan Bards while singing the Ballads of the Gond Patrons.

2. A Kingri-Artist playing on the instrument.

The Pardhans postulate that the various subsects, the Koiturs, (Koitoors) the Pardhans (Paradhans), the Dalawa (Dalva), the Madias (Madiyas), the Burads (Boorads), the Mokasi (Mokashi), etc. are all the integral ingredients of the composed compound community– The Gond. They came to be nomenclated and are now known by the professions they perform for the tribal triumph. They seem separate but are set out from one and the same social source of Gonds in the ancient past. They are the limbs of the same body inhaling the same breath of faith, culture and custom and have the same skin cover of tribal tradition.

Elderly persons of the tribe, whose word was regarded with respect as command for their age and experience in life were placed at the higher post and position of the rulers of the tribal settlements and termed as Rajas. Their kith and kin formed a royal family over the ages. Such royal families gathered together to form a group of their own and called themselves as Raj Gonds (Raja Gonds). Later the concept of conceit caught hold of their conscience and puffed with superiority sense they secluded themselves from the main-stream and settled separately from other units of the tribe. They therefore, came to be called as Koiturs. The term Koitur is derived from "Koisthana", (the Gondi dialect meaning to cut or to separate). The Marathi word "Koyata" an instrument for cutting is similar to it. Koiturs are thus the group of Gonds cut away and separated from the integral Gond community.[9]

Talented and intelligent individuals were given governance of the tribal settlements and appointed as administrative advisers of the ruling chiefs. They were thus ministers, the Pardhans, prime or principal heads of administration. Their relations and families were later recognised as Pardhan Gonds. Person having stout and sinewy shoulders hudded in their blood, formed a fighting force for the tribal settlement. Such a section of the society came to be known as–"Dalvi Gonds". The word Dal, connotes a fighting force. Still others who accepted agricultural assignments settled at places of their performance to produce food for the community, they, with their families, friends and helping fellowmen formed a settled group of grain growers and were on that count called as "Mokashi Gonds".

Yet advanced adventurous and hunters happened to hold their dwelling on hill and hillocks to find and fetch flesh for the community and save the settlements from savages, they later created a class of their own through generations, formed their family groups and were nomenclated as "Madia Gonds". 'Mod' means tree or forest and Madia thus means forest dweller. Among the stationary settlers some sought an occupation other than agriculture. They cut bamboos from the woods and prepared from their fibers, baskets and varied vessels large and small for storage of grains and goods, fodder and other materials of livelihood of the tribals. They went from settlement to settlement for their trade and earned their maintenance. These trading tribals were termed as "Burad Gonds".

Thus the great Gond group of the Aborigines got vivisected into different developed professional sub-sections and were named differently from the occupational assignments offered to and accepted by them for the tribal welfare, development and prosperity. This social system ran smoothly and all assembled annually or even occasionally to share together the solemnity of the society festivals, functions and ceremonial celebrations as one compact community.

The Pardhans, propound, propose and pose also to be the propagated progeny of the pedigree, pertaining to Pardhan Gonds. Like Koitur Gonds, they also boast of their belonging to Lunar lineage and called themselves as "Chandal Pallal", i.e. direct decendants of Moon dynasty.[10] Seniors and superiors among them acquired and accepted appointments as administrators and advisers, governors and ministers of Gond rulers. Other intelligent and industrious individuals collected and compiled good, great and glorious events, achievements of the Gonds and composed praising and poignant, periscopic poems on patriotic persons, historic happenings, heroes, heroines and marvellous myths of the mythology. They committed them to memory and presented them vehemently at the royal residences, cerimonial celebrations and festive functions. Yet some others studied astrology, occultism and mystic learning and served the society by foretelling future evil events and means to meet them for solace and safety. Still others mastered music and pleased people with melodious performance on their harps (Kingri) at social, matrimonial, ceremonial and festive functions.

For all these qualities, (the administrative ability, lofty learnings, attracting art, poetic performance, dedication to deity meditation, future foretelling etc.) this class of the people was held in high honour, commanded commendable confidence and respect and was placed in prime prominence and pious position alike the Brahmins among the Hindus. It was maintained and freely fed by the tribals on these counts.

As the progressive aggression of the Aryans advanced to attack the Aboriginal tract, the Gond rulers and their royal regiments retorted them for some time but had to resort to retreat as they could not stand the superior archery of Aryan army. Ultimately the Gond rulers surrendered to the superiority and supremacy of the Aryan aggressors and sought servile servitude under them, to save their position and possessions as a mandatory. The patriotic Pardhans denied and defied this desperate decision of their ruling chiefs. They opted to offer opposition to the Aryan offenders. Despite the ruling chiefs they mobilised men and means for a mutiny in tricky and tactful guerrilla style. This hurt the honour of the egoistic ruling class and they exiled them (Pardhans) and banned their entry into their (Gonds) regions. The patriotic Pardhans preferred to dwell in desolate destination. They were humiliated, hated and hunted like harmful hyenas by the Gond royals. They were declared out-laws, and other tribals were taught to treat them untouchable severing all social connections with them i.e. Pardhans. Thus the pure patriotic people proved to be poor Pardhans of the present period.

The plea of Pardhans pleading their out-law position as argued above, may stand to reason so far as the conditions and circumstances causing and concerning it but the historical happening referred to, does not seem to be of such as an ancient antiquity as the Aryan aggression on the Aborigines. Regions of Gond rule and regime had spread wide from Sagar to Chandrapur and their kingdoms were prospering and flourishing during the medieval period. They were so strong and influential that even Rajput rulers had established effective friendly relations with them. Even then the Pardhans continued to be in their services on various posts and jobs. The plight of the Pardhan patriots as claimed by them might be a making of the Muslim march on the Gond Government, wherein to avoid mass massacre many a monarch surrendered, subdued to servitude and even courted conversion. A few, like the heroic queen Durgawati of Garha-Mandla defied and defended the dreadful dragons of marching Muslims and met martyrdom. It is likely that the protesting people had to hide in hills and helplessly migrate to thickest forests to save their life, honour and culture.

**Pardhans as Portrayed in Scholarly Works**

The origin of the Pardhans is shrouded in mystry. All that we know about their origin is based on certain legends; some prevalent these days, and some long forgotten.

It may now be taken for granted that the Pardhans are a branch of the great Gond tribe. They are the musicians of the tribe, retaining in their memories and constantly recounting the glorious history of the ancient Gond Kingdoms.

To Hislop, the Pardhans were mainly priests. In "Mahadeo Hills", he says, "the highest Pardhans act as Pujaris and the lower as crude musician. Pardhans perform the important function of negotiating marriages of the Gonds, a duty which they still perform to the best of their ability.[11]

Daltan has given a brief summary of Lingo Legend and says, "It is obviously derived from Hindu teachers of wild imagination that it cannot be regarded as embodying any true Gondi traditional lore." Daltan in his book has said nothing about the Pardhans but was attracted to somewhat Hinduized tribes of Central Provinces.[12]

The Legend of Lingo has also been given by J. Forsyth in his book,[13] and also been reproduced by various other writers such as R.V. Russell and Shamrao Hivale.[14]

The Pardhans are the minstrels/bards and servants of the Gonds. At any rate they now speak Hindi dialect. They are found mainly in Madhya Pradesh and Berar. They depend much on Gonds for their economic life, who look down on them as social inferiors, they i.e. Gonds treat them i.e. Pardhans as impure. The Pardhans eat almost any kind of food including beef, pork and flesh of rats and mice. They practise levirate. They are averse to hard work in the fields and prefer to earn their living as singers and musicians of the Gonds.[15]

There are only a few members of this most interesting tribe allied to, but distinct from, Gonds in Bastar. There is a Pardhan Pujari for the shrine of Lingo Pen at Semurgaon, and Pardhan minstrels and Priests are to be found in Muria villages. Pardhan boys and girls are admitted to membership of Ghotul.[16]

The Aborigines apparently had no regular tribes, as it is evident from names which were merely equivalents of "Man" as distinguished from other animals, in their respective language. For instance those calling themselves Korku, derive the names from Kor i.e. a "man", "Ku" being the plural suffix. Similarly, the biggest tribe

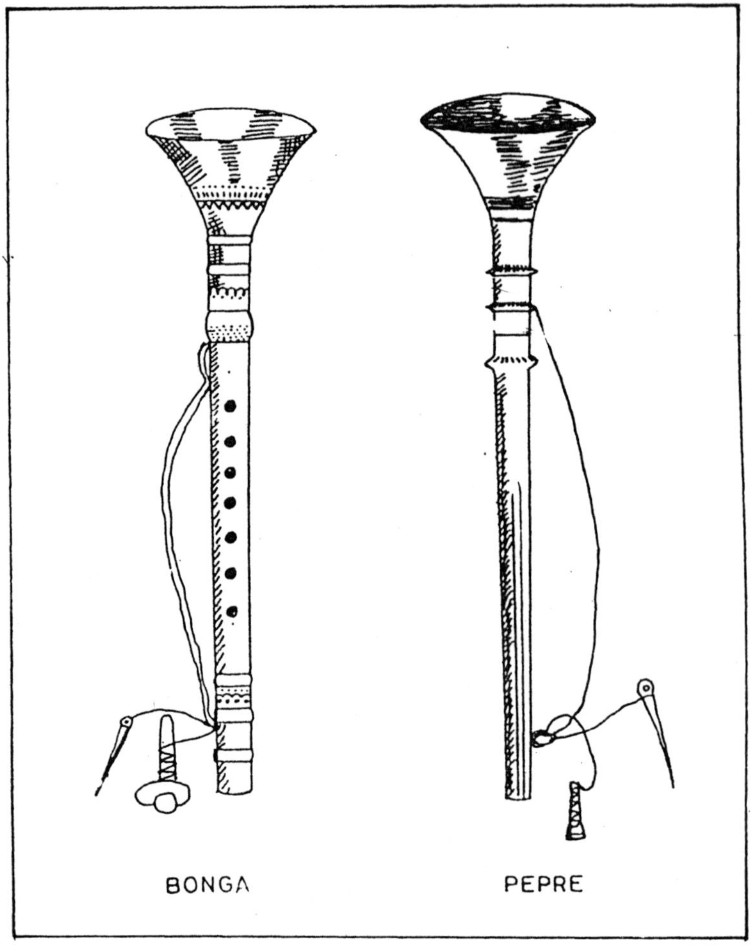


3. i. Bonga is the Wind Instrument played at the festival and religious functions by the Pardhans.
   ii. Pepre.

4. A Pardhan playing on Bonga. Bonga is a Wind instrument akin to Shenai.

in Central India is Gond' and in Gondi language is known as Koitur, which means "man".

The structure of the Gond tribe shows that the Gonds have contributed a number of occupational groups such as Agarias or Iron-workers, the Gowaris or Graziers, the Ojhas or Soothsayers, *the Pardhans or Priests and Ministrels.*[17]

> "The Tribes and Castes of Central Provinces of India", Russell and Hiralal describe them as "an inferior branch of the Gond Tribe whose occupation is to act as the Priests and minstrels of the Gonds".[18]

Hiralal and Russell says that Pardhans play on Kingri and give brief account of their origin and describe some of their endogamous divisions. But its account of Pardhan religion entirely misses the point of sacred character of the Bana. Bana is the sacred musical instrument of the Pardhan. The Gondi word for Pardhan Bana is Kikri. The Kingri or Kindri or Kingari is an entirely different type of instrument, made with Gourds and played with one finger.

Shamrao Hivale in his book, *The Pardhans of Upper Narbada valley*, states that the Pardhans of Dindori – a Tehsil of Mandla District of Madhya Pradesh– however, do not know the Legend of Lingo and to them Lingo is simply a God dwelling in the fine mountains of the same name on the far side of Narbada river.[19]

P.N. Bose (who wrote an account of Chhattisgarh in 1890) says, "The Pardhans form a small caste. Their social status is considered lower than that of other Gonds. The Agarias appear to form a sub-section of them, as also the Patharis who correspond to the Ghats of the Rajputs. The village Baiga does not often belong to Pardhan caste. The name Pardhan appears to be of Sanskrit origin signifying "Chief" and it is rather strange that the caste should be held in such a low estimation".[20]

"Like Andhs, the Gonds and Pardhans have a larger extent than in the Central Provinces. Although they are really of the same tribe, the two are distinguished at any rate by name. The Pardhans are the Bards and Musicians of the Gonds and are considered to occupy a lower position than the Gonds. Together they form 10 per cent of the population. In Wani (Wun), a Tehsil in Yavatmal District Pardhans are considered to be even lower than the Mahars and one class of them will remove night soil. The Gonds have three divisions–the Raj Gonds, Dedwes and Mokasis, the name of the last may possibly be derived from the fact that they held land on privileged tenure under Chanda King, and they rank higher even than the Raj Gonds, who will take food at their hands. The Dedwes are the lowest sub-division and will take food from either of the other two. Besides these sub-castes which are endogamous, the Gonds are also sub-divided into sections who worship different number of Gods, and no two persons who have the same number of Gods, may marry with each other. The worshipper of four, five, six, seven and even twelve Gods are locally distinguished, the last not being known in Central Provinces (Madhya Pradesh). The people in the tribe speak Gondi among themselves, but can talk in Marathi with outsiders and they dress like the Kunbis. they are tenants and labourers and a few are Patels of villages".[21]

Like the Andhs, the Gonds and Pardhans have adopted Hindu dress and customs to a larger extent than in Madhya Pradesh. Although they are really of the same tribe, the two are distinguished at any rate by name.[22]

There are a number of forest sub-tribes or castes (in small numbers) who appear to have been subjugated by the Gonds. They are inferior to them in social rank and used to perform the usual village services extracted from subject races, though (during the last many decades they have now taken to agriculture), many of them by taking to agriculture have greatly raised their status. In features and general physique they bear a strong resemblance to the Gond type. The chief sub-tribes are as follows:

The Pardhans are said to be, formerly the musicians and Bards attached to Gond families of distinction. In many Gond villages the Bhumak is a Pardhan. Pardhans also perform priestly functions like blessing the cattle and fields. Now as a caste their occupation is spinning and weaving. In former days they were able to recite the genealogies of the Gond chiefs and sing ballads in praise of their valour. Some still follow the (their) ancestral profession of village musicians and a few can (may) relate tales of ancient days though in a faltering manner. Locally they are equated with 'Dheds' (Mahars) as a caste whose touch is pollution.[23]

*In the Tribes and Castes of Bombay* the Pardhans have been stated as a sub-division of Mahars.[24]

Similarly, the book on *The Baigas*, shows Pardhan as a caste of musician.[25]

### Gogia Pardhan and Rajnengi Pardhan

Gogia Pardhan is a branch of Pardhan tribes of Central Provinces whereas Rajnengi Pardhan is a group of Pardhan type living in Mandla District, Madhya Pradesh and its neighbourhood.[26]

### Bards and Craftsmen Associated with Aboriginals

In the greater part of the literature on Gonds of Central Provinces, the Pardhans are described as the priests of Gond. This denomination is definitely misleading, while in places where Aboriginal culture is in decay, the position may become obscure, the Pardhans of Adilabad and the adjoining area of the Central Provinces cannot by any stretch of imagination be endowed with priestly functions. Pardhans are the hereditary Bards of the Gonds and the songs and stories which they preserve by oral transmission are the most important dispositions of Gond tradition. Their presence at many religious rites is obligatory but at these they function only as musicians never as priests. As bards and guardians of traditions, the Pardhans play a vital role in Gond culture.

The most important professional instrument of the Pardhan is his "Kingri", a string instrument with three cards and a square wooden round box covered by a skin membrane. On this fiddle (Kingri) Pardhans play during certain phases of Persa Pen rites and accompany themselves with singing hymns or reciting epics. At festivals it is usual that the most important Pardhans play on Kingri while younger ones blow trumpets and beat drums. There is hardly much room for doubt that the origin of the Pardhans has an intimate association with Gonds. Culturally they belong to the aboriginal sphere, but their racial roots seem to be elsewhere. Even at a glance most of the Pardhans are easily distinguished from Gonds.

The Gond system of exogamous phrateries and clan also rules Pardhan society, and each Gond has a family Pardhan (Rota Patari) of own clan, who plays at certain social functions and is entitled to traditional gifts from his patron as well as to share immovable property left by any member of the family.

Often the family Pardhan does not live in his patron's village, and today this would indeed be impossible as most Pardhans stand to more than one Gond in the relationship of Rota Patari, and their Patrons are scattered over several villages. But this may only be recent development and when each Gond clan occupied its own land, the Pardhans of the same clan probably also lived close at hand. Though closely connected with the Gonds in the most sacred rites, the Pardhans are not accorded with social status. Gonds do not partake in their food or grant them entrance into the interior of their houses. With the infiltration of Hindu ideas this distinction tends to deepen and the Pardhans are now in danger of being classed with the outcastes of Hindu society. In predominately Aboriginal areas however, they are not subject to any appreciable disability, they mix freely with Gonds even to the point of bodily touch and sit in the close verandah of Gonds houses like any other visitors. Many Gond villages contain houses of Pardhans. Now-a-days good many Pardhans have taken to agriculture and work on the fields like other labourers. But this is not their traditional profession, and even to-day there are numerous Pardhans who live only on what they receive from Gonds as wages for their performance and on the fees due to them in their capacity as family Pardhan.

In dress Pardhan men are distinguishable from Gonds but the women as a rule wear a Choli of the type customary among all the lower Hindu castes and their lower head is often marked with a red caste mark.

On social occasions like marriages and funeral-rites, they follow practically every detail of the Gond pattern. They worship the same Gods as Gonds and attend almost all of their religious ceremonies but without ever taking the role of the officiating priests.

All Gonds do not have Pardhans as hereditary bards. In some clans and families a function similar to that of the family Pardhan is performed by another tribe bards and minstrels–the Totis. Hiralal and Russell describe the Totis as a sub-tribe of Pardhans.[27] The mode of life of the two (castes), tribes and their peculiar relationship to Gonds are no doubt identical, but in Adilabad, Pardhans' own language is Marathi. Totis speak Gondi as their mother tongue and claim an association with the Gonds older than that of any Pardhan. The physical type of Totis seems to be slightly more primitive than the average Pardhans and their pigmentation is much darker

In social scale they (Totis) rank lower than Pardhans. Gonds say Pardhans beg from them and Totis beg from Pardhans. The stories and the songs recited by Totis are similar even in a verbal identity. Though same as those of the Pardhans it is said that tne speciality of the Totis are stories of 'Gond Bhima'. Totis too always carry with them the Kingri–the three-stringed fiddle and blow trumpets on ceremonial occasions.[28]

The Pardhans play an important and necessary part of the Gond social system. The Pardhans are the only people who have preserved through their songs the memory of Gond hero and heroines, the story of the origin of the Gond race, its wandering, its woes and triumphs. Very few Gonds know these songs, and it is customary to call in the Pardhans on select occasions when the villagers gather to hear the Pardhans' song on their Kingri.

For a long time it was thought that the Pardhans were the hereditary priests of the Gonds and presided over the latter's religious ceremonies. It has been stated by Shri Setu Madhaorao Pagdi that Pardhans have nothing to do with the religious ceremonies of Gonds. Pardhans seem to have been looked down upon by the Gonds as shrewd fellows whose work was to act as general advisors to Gonds in all matters, to act as messengers and negotiators in marriages and other affairs and sing ballads and other songs. They were thus bards, advisors and general companions who were admired for their shrewdness by Gond chiefs. Secondly, they (Pardhans) were regarded as inferior to the Gonds by the Gonds themselves who consider themselves to be the patrons of the Pardhans. All the Gond clans have their Pardhan bards who are supposed to know Gond Myths in general and the history of the family of the patrons i.e. Gond family in particular.

Pardhans preserve the memory of their great hero-Hirasuka Pardhan. Hirasuka seems to have been the advisor of the Gond chief. The Gond heroine Manko, to escape from ill-treatment at the hands of her husband takes shelter in his i.e. Hirasuka's house. Further when she wandered in wilderness, Hirasuka sent Pardhans to bring her back. The Gonds, it thus appears could not think of affairs without their Pardhans. If the Gond desired to marry a girl he would call his Pardhan to the house of the father of the girl and Pardhan would start the negotiations. Thus Pardhans have made themselves necessary without becoming their priests.[29]

The hereditary bards and chronicler occupy an important position in many Indian communities and in his article, "The Institution of Bards in Western India" Dr. Dave has given an account of the peculiar relationship between the Bhats and Rajput patrons. The role of the Pardhans in Raj Gond society provides a striking parallel and the occurrence of practically the same social configuration among an Aboriginal tribe and an advanced Hindu caste presents the student of Indian ethnology with an intriguing problem.

Pardhans are found in many Districts of Central Provinces as well as in Hyderabad, everywhere they are closely associated with Gonds. Yet the distribution of Gonds and Pardhans does not apply to several Gond Tribes such as Hill Marias of Bastar who lack the association with Pardhans. Certain features of relationship between Gonds and Pardhans have been mentioned already by Hislop as well as Russell and Hiralal, but the first detailed description of a section of the Pardhan community is contained in Shamrao Hivale's book *The Pardhans of Upper Narbada Valley*.[30]

Pardhans have increased since 1891 from 9,170 to 12,165. The increase is mainly due to Hindu Pardhans having now returned themselves as following the animistic religion compared with 1881, they have increased by 1,137. Originally they were of Gond division and they are described as hereditary priests of the tribe; but of very low social status.

Prof. C. von Furer-Haimendorf considers Pardhans a caste of hereditary bards and musicians closely attached to Raj Gonds and described in Gondi as Patari and in Marathi and Hindi as Pardhan.[31]

### The Relation of Gonds and Pardhans

There is a close connection between the Gonds and the Pardhans which is illustrated by the popular tribal proverb:

> "Gond aur Pathari (Patari) an ga,
> Marthan Sarthan ta ek sath dhuti ma tangthan"

It means we are Gonds and Patharis and when we die and rot, we are hung up together in one fish kasket.

This is a very interesting saying, suggesting that whatever happens here, after death the departed souls of both tribes live together in one world. This is further emphasized in Kunda ceremony when symbols of the dead are offered to Bara Pen. On this occasion the offering of both Gonds and Pardhans are tied together with the saying, "We are of the same tree" and the priest exclaims, "O you ancestors, all of you are of the same family. Lie down together in one place".

The most interesting connection between Gonds and Pardhans is that they have the same clans, a fact that leads to the fundamental economic relationship between them that will be dealt with in a separate Chapter. Gonds and Pardhans have the same mythology, indeed the majority of the Gonds owe what little they know about the legendary origin of the world and the genesis of their own tribe to the Pardhans. The two tribes have the same religious practices. They observe the same festivals. The Pardhans often officiate as geneologists of the Gonds. The Pardhans are also known sometimes as Diwan and this suggests that once the Gond Raja kept Pardhans as Ministers and not only as their minstrels and geneologists. When Gonds and Pardhans sit together at marriages or such ceremonies, they behave as if they belong to the same family. They very well mix together and address one another by family terms as father, mother, uncle or aunt as the Gonds do among themselves.

A Gond does not treat a Baiga or an Agaria on this level although they have been neighbours for centuries. In some parts Gond avoids the Agria and goes to him when he needs his axe or sickle sharpened. He calls the Baiga to free the village of disease or to drive a man-eating tiger away; but he looks down upon him and hardly ever meets him socially. But the Pardhan is in every way his younger brother and like any younger brother ubiquitous and privileged. The Gonds recognize their connections with the Pardhans and often stress their unity; but they will not marry them and although the Pardhans will take cooked food from the Gond, the Gond does not return the compliment. The Gond considers the Pardhan to belong to a lower social order than himself. In order to emphasize his superiority he will not let a Pardhan sit on his bed, for this would be regarded as a sign of familiarity and might lead to intrigues between Pardhan men and Gond girls who are often fascinated by the wit and poetry of the younger brother.

But there certainly is a limit to this connection. The Pardhan is very different from the Gond both in his physical character and in temperament. The Pardhan is romantic, the Gond is businessman. The Pardhan's devotion to his *Bana* (the sacred fiddle or Kingri) fills his life with poetry and the stout and steady Gond looks dry and arid as compared to him. The Gond has the power of sticking to a job and of accumulating wealth. There are many Gond farmers even to-day who are substantial men of business employing many servants and owing large properties. This almost is unknown among the

Pardhans. To the Pardhan a song is more important than a sack of grain, and this is ultimately true even though the Pardhan insists on getting what he can from the material world.[32]

LEGENDS ABOUT GONDS AND PARDHANS

Legend of the creation of the world; the origin of mankind; creation of the Gonds and their imprisonment by Mahadeo; the birth and history of 'Lingo'; establishment of the Gond tribe and separation of the Pardhans from the original race i.e. the Gonds, as related by Rev. S. Hislop, and R.V. Russell and Rai Bahadur Hiralal in their book, *The Tribes and Castes of Central Provinces of India*, Vol. III 1916 is as follows:

**Legend of the Creation as Related by Rev. S. Hislop**

In the beginning there was water everywhere, and God was born in a lotus-leaf and lived alone. One day he rubbed his arm and from the rubbing made a crow, which sat on his shoulder; he also made a crab, which swam out over the waters. God then ordered the crow to fly over the world and bring some earth. The crow flew about and could find no earth, but saw a crab, supporting itself with one leg resting on the bottom of the sea. The crow was very tired and perched on the crab's back, which was soft so that crow's feet made marks on it, which are still visible on the bodies of all the crabs at present. The crow asked the crab where any earth could be found. The crab told that if God made its body hard, the crab could find some earth. God made its back hard, as that still remains. The crab then dived to the bottom of the sea, where it found Kenchna, the earthworm. It caught hold of Kenchna by the neck with its claws and the mark thus made is still to be seen on the earth worm's neck. Then the earth worm brought up earth out of its mouth and the crab brought this to the God, which God scattered over the sea and patches of land appeared. The God then walked over the earth and a boil came on his hand, and out of it Mahadeo and Parwati were born.

**Creation of the Gonds and their Imprisonment by Mahadeo**

From Mahadeo's urine numerous vegetables began to spring up.

Parwati ate these and became pregnant and gave birth to eighteen threshing-floors of Brahmin Gods and twelve threshing-floors of Gonds Gods. All the Gonds were scattered over the jungle and they behaved unlike the good Hindus.

Mahadeo then decided to get rid of the Gonds, he invited them all to a meeting. When they sat down, Mahadeo made a squirrel from the rubbings of his body and let it loose in the middle of the Gonds. All the Gonds began to chase it, hoping for a meal. They seized sticks and stones and clods of earth and their uncombed hair flew in the wind. The squirrel dodged about and ran away, and finally, as directed by Mahadeo, ran into a large cave with all the Gonds after it. Mahadeo, then rolled a large stone to the mouth of the cave and shut up all the Gonds in it. Only four remained outside, and they fled away to Kachikopa Lohagarh, or the Iron cave in the Red Hill and lived there. Meanwhile, Parwati perceived that the smell of the Gonds, which had pleased her, had vanished from Dhawalgiri. She desired it to be restored and commenced a devotion. For six months she fasted and practised austerities. Bhagwan (God) was swinging in the swing. He was moved with Parwati's devotion. He sent Narayan (the Sun) to see who was fasting. Narayan came and found Parwati and asked her what she wanted. She said that, she missed her Gonds and wanted them back. Narayan told Bhagwan, who promised that they would be given back.

**The Birth and history of "Lingo"**

Continues Hislop, yellow flowers of the tree Pahindi were growing on Dhawalgiri. Bhagwan sent thunder and lightning, and the flower conceived. First fell from it a heap of turmeric and saffron. In the morning the Sun came out, the flower burst open and the Lingo was born. Lingo was a perfect child. He had a diamond on his naval and a Sandal-wood mark on his forehead. He fell from the flower into the heap of turmeric. He played in the turmeric and slept in a swing. When he became nine years old, he felt that there was no one like him, and he would go where he could find his fellows. He climbed a needle-like hill, and from far off he saw Kachikopa Lohagarh and the four Gonds. He came to them. They saw, he was like them, and asked him to be their brother.

After the earth was fixed in place Bhagwan formed the fifty-two Gods of the Gondwana, after which he gave the order for Raja Inkar to be born. Because of this, Raja was born from the word of Bhagwan. He was like fire. He had to stand one cubit and a quarter above the ground, had he touched it the earth would have been burnt to ashes. Bhagwan wanted to give the Raja a wife and he created Akaina. She stood before Bhagwan with folded hands and said, "why have I been made? I am very hungry. Show me some way to earn my living". "Go", said Bhagwan. 'You are to be the wife of Inkar. Live with him and take your pleasure with him and he will care for you'. The girl went to Inkar and stood before him with folded hands. "You are my lord and master, enjoy me and keep me as your woman". But this displeased the Raja and he opened his mouth to swallow her. "O Raja! if you swallow me, how will the mankind be created?". 'But how can I enjoy your body? If I touch you, you will be burnt to ashes, we must have intercourse with our eyes'. So, when their eyes met the woman conceived and after a year she gave birth to sixteen boys.

On goes the Legend, of these, one died, eight went to upper world and became *Dut* (Doot) and *Bhut* (Bhoot), six went to Bindraban and turned into animals and one became the Raja Himachal. This Raja went to the mountains and began to do penance. From time to time he would rub off some of the dirt from his body and make into images. One day he made a beautiful image of a girl. He called this image Parwati. As he named her, she suddenly came to life. When she was twelve years old the seat of Mahadeo trembled and he left his heavenly abode and came in search of her.

When Mahadeo found Parwati, he took her to Kailas and made a hut for her there on the mountains. He prepared a garden with three hundred and sixty beds of flowers and a strong fence all around. He said to his wife, "do not touch any of these flowers". Then he went away into the dark Kajliban to get wood to make a plough. But in his absence Parwati looked at the flowers and said in her mind, "why did he tell me not to pick them?". One day, she picked one flower, then another until at last she picked the flowers from every one of the three hundred and sixty beds. She dressed herself in flowers and slept on flowers. Its sweet smell entered her body eternally and she conceived. In due time, she had two daughters viz. Angarmati and Pichlo. Angarmati was a Hindu and Pichlo was a Gond.

From Pichlo, the fifty-three lakhs Gondwana were created and from Angarmati fifty-two lakhs Hindwana. Parwati was very upset when she saw so many children and her sorrow bothered Mahadeo, and he came home quickly to see what had happened to his wife. When he tried to get into his house he found it crammed with children and there was no place for him to sit. So he went to the jungle and made a great trench eighty hands long. He took the fifty-three lakhs of Gonds and put them in the trench and covered it with a long flat stone. He appointed Madan Pat to look after them and protect them from wild animals. The fifty-two lacks of Hindus he sent away telling them to lookafter themselves for he thought they were well capable of doing so. He kept Pichlo and Angarmati in the house.

Now, the fate of Gond children worried Bhagwan and his throne began to tremble. "If these children die, he thought I will be cursed". So he created five kinds of trees, Barro, Dumar, Pipar, Thuba and Bharela and planted them near the trench. These trees gave abundant milk and both the Hindus and the Gonds were able to drink the milk for twelve years. The two girls Angarmati and Pichlo were now also twelve years old and had begun to go with little earthen pots to fetch water. One day after they had bathed and were about to lift up their pots and go home, Angarmati shouted to Pichlo, "Be careful, don't touch my pot". Pichlo said, "why not?". Angarmati replied, "Because I am a Hindu and you are a Gond". Pichlo replied, "Have we not the same parents?". How then can we be different? Tell me, otherwise there will be endless quarrels between us." So saying she broke Angarmati's pot and began to fight. Bhagwan heard the noise and quickly went down to the stream to pacify them. "Why are you quarreling?". Pichlo said, "Because she told me not to touch her pot". Bhagwan said, "But she is right". You are really a Gond. At that Pichlo began to weep loudly. "If I am a Gond then show me where my own people are living". Bhagwan took the little girl to the great trench and showed her the children living there. She was very annoyed and broke the stone by killing its guard Madan Pat. Pichlo stood at the edge of the trench weeping and the fifty-three lacks children began shouting, "who are you?" "I am your sister Pichlo". Come out of the trench and possess the land. It is yours, "O sister! we cannot come out unless whoever put us here helps to escape". Bhagwan came and told them to come out, but they said, "How can we come out when we are naked. Are you going to give us clothes? Bhagwan was troubled about this and he went down to the under-world where the four great cobras lived. Their names were Hansadhari, Baradhari, Sisdhari and Shes-Nang. From them, he begged for twelve lakhs of bullock-carts laden with cloth. The Cobras said "How are we to give you cloth?". "If you do not give, said Bhagwan, I shall sit down and die here". Then said the cobras, "If you go to Jahaldip and ask Dhur Nangin and Basmotin Kaniya they will give you the cloth. Bhagwan went to them and they gave him what he wanted. He came back by a great train of twelve lakhs of bullock-carts laden with cloth and began to distribute them to the children. When he began distributing, he gave more to the first eighteen, he gave less and less until at last when all but two had received a share, he only had one and a quarter cubits left. He threw this bit of cloth into the trench. One of the children grabbed it and tying it on as a loin cloth ran away from others. They all shouted, "catch him, catch him", but Bhagwan said, let him be alone. He will be called Nanga Baiga. He will live in the great mountains and will rule over the forests. Whenever you are in trouble he will come to help you. One last child remained and he was naked. They cried, "catch him and throw him away". But he climbed out and began to run. Bhagwan said let him go. He will live in the jungle and will be called *Ban Manus* (Jungleman). He will live on wild fruits and you will never see him. If a pregnant woman crosses his foot-prints she will get a dumb child like him. Then said Bhagwan again, "Go away and live happy in the world".

Out of the fifty-two lakhs of Hindus there arose Kawar Raja who ruled in Graha-Mandla. He had a bamboo bow and a bamboo arrow. With this one arrow he could kill a hundred thousand men. The fiftythree lakhs of Gonds came to his kingdom, but when they heard about his arrow they turned back and went instead to the kingdom of Phuljhar. When they reached the boundary they found two flowers of many colours growing under a Saga tree. When they saw the flowers they tried to pick them but failed. Then they tried to destroy the flowers, at that moment from one flower, Motijhar was born and from the other Aginjhar. As their eyes met Aginjhar gave birth to Bara Pen and then Dulha Deo and all other Gods. Last of all was born Narayan Deo who stood aside in a corner. Once the Gods were born Motijhar and Aginjhar disappeared. The fifty-three lakhs of Gonds crowded round the Bara Pen and asked him who he was. "I am the great God of fifty-three lakhs of Gonds. Worship me and serve me". But they refused to believe that he was their God. We will not trust you unless you help us to conquer Garha-Mandla. Bara

Pen went down to the under world and said to four cobras, "Look I am relying on your strength, when Kawar Raja comes out riding on his horse, break the earth beneath him and get hold of the four legs of his horse". Then Bara Pen went secretly to Garha-Mandla and finding the great bamboo bow whose name was Kari Surung, he folded his hands and bowed before it. "Listen to me, O Kari Surung!' I will always serve and worship you. If you do what I wish, you will be honoured first and I afterwards. When the Raja shoots you from his bow, fall short and do not injure anyone. But the bow replied, no Bara Pen I can't do this. It is the bow that is responsible and as the bow shoots me I have to go. Bara Pen summoned all the Gods and they turned themselves into culmborers. They got into the wood of the bow and ate its inside so that it was very weak. Then Bara Pen returned to the Gonds and said, "come let us attack the fort now".

The army got ready for the assault and their leaders blew loudly on their hunting horn. When the Kawar Raja heard the noise he prepared to fight. He rode out on his horse and made it stand on a platform of sandal-wood. Then drew his bow, and when he fired it, it broke in half and the arrow fell short. Bara Pen took the form of a dwarf and ran to it and picked it up. Then the Raja took his sword and tried to make his horse jump into the air towards the Gond army, but as he did so the earth broke and the cobras caught the horse's legs from below. Then the woman came out of the palace and fell at the feet of the Gonds saying, "Let our bangles be unbroken and we will leave this kingdom". So they allowed the people to leave it and go away.

Afterwards from the Gonds was born Dudesal Sai. He became a great Raja and built a fort in his own name. He had three queens viz. Karka, Kunja and Kare. Kare's son was Raja Dalpat Sai.

His four sons were married and while their wives were still pregnant, the children were taken from the womb by Bara Pen in anger because the royal family had given up worshipping him. Bara Pen said to Dalpat sai, "Have your four grandsons sacrificed to me or I will devour your sons". 'What do you desire? I want *rot malida* (a kind of sweet made of ghee, wheat, flour and gur)'. So the woman of the Gondwana put their frying-pans on the earth to make *rot malida*. While a woman was sitting before the fire and cooking, she said to the rest, don't touch it, but the others said, "It is not only your God but belongs to us also". With that eighteen of the women caught hold of the frying pan and it broke into eighteen pieces. Bara

Pen went to Durgawati Rani and Kare Rani and told them what had happened. They said, "This means that the brothers have separated into eighteen houses. Now, O Bara Pen, you must take sacrifice from each house". Bara Pen said, "I will no more take food from these broken units, but instead I will have a bearded goat".

The Gonds of the Gondwana were worried about this. They thought that the Gods might later be angry and destroy them. They sent someone to fetch Nanga Baiga from his mountain. The man reached there and said to the Nanga Baiga, come and speak to Bara Pen on our behalf. The Baiga said, I have nothing to offer him. I have not even a chicken. What can I do? Now the Nanga Baiga had six sons and six daughters and he said in his mind, I will take my own children and offer them to Bara Pen. He put his sons in a great basket and started off for Gondawana. But as he went Bhagwan saw him and was afraid. He sprinkled water and the Pankas were created. O Panka, take goats and go to Gondawana, the Gond Gods demand goats for sacrifice. Bhagwan went and from the water in his left hand he created the Basors. Go, O Basor, and take these pigs to Gondawana, the Gond gods would have them for sacrifice. He tapped his bow and arrow and the Dhanwar was created, Go, O Dhanwar, take these chickens to the Gondwana, The Gond Gods would have them for sacrifice.

The Panka, Basor and Dhanwar were going along the road with their animals. When they met Nanga Baiga, they asked him where he was going and he told them that he was going to offer his sons to Bara Pen in sacrifice. But they said, "If you give your beautiful children, how will world be populated and where there will be Baigas to keep the earth steady with their nails". Let your sons go and take these animals instead. Nanga Baiga sent his sons home and went on to Garha-Mandla with others. The Gods were standing their a cubit and a quarter above the ground, they would not touch it for the earth was impure. When he saw this Nanga Baiga went to the under-world and brought the Surhi cow from there. He plastered the earth at Garha Mandla with her dung and then the Gods stood on the earth and Nanga Baiga in the name of all the Gonds offered them goats, pigs and chickens in sacrifice.

But now, the Gonds found that they had no grain to eat. so Nanga Baiga went down below the under-world where the great cobra lived. On her head were the twenty-one kinds of grain. Nanga Baiga flattered her and made her laugh and she gave him grain and he brought it back to Garha Mandla.

Nanga Baiga cut a Saja tree and set it up outside the fort. He made a platform of mud round it and dunged it with the dung of the Surhi cow. Then he began to make sacrifice. For the great bow and arrow of the Kawar Raja he offered a black goat and sacrificed a speckled goat for Bara Pen. But when he offered them rice, they refused to eat it as a sign that the Gods were displeased. The Gonds came and made every kind of offer to please the Gods. They promised them every sort of gift, but they took no notice. The youngest of the eighteen brothers had gone to hunt and now he returned. Play on your Bana and perhaps that will please the Gods, said the others. He sat down and began to play crying, 'O Bara Pen, O Narayan Deo' and as he said these words Sarso Mata and Sarada Mata took possession of his throat and revealed to him the name of all the gods of the Gondawana. As he played for the first time, from his Bana came sweet music and the Gods began to eat. But the other brothers at once said, "little brother, do not touch us, lest the Gods get angry with you. Do not come into our houses, but go on playing on your Bana'. They sent someone to go and tell the youngest brother's wife not to touch the pots of the other seventeen wives and then they said to the youngest brother, "Now you are a musician". You are born behind our backs and so we will call you Pathari". The boy's music pleased the Gonds so much that they gave him many presents of cattle, money and pots. He said, why are you giving me this? If the Gods are pleased with you, should not we also be pleased? In the house elder women also were giving presents to the youngest daughter-in-law. Now you will always be called Rajnengi Pathari. But when they gave the boy his water in a separate pot and his food in a separate plate, he began to cry. Why do you trouble about this boy? We drink from an earthen pot worth one piece but to you we gave water in brass-pot worth five rupees. We sit on a string cot worth four annas, but we give you a hempan sack worth five rupees. We will always give you cows and buffaloes from our shed, a horse which we ourselves have mounted, vessels from which we have eaten and ornaments for half your body. Every year we will give you one rupee.

There was also a trouble with the boy's wife. She had gone to fetch water. When the other women saw her coming, they said, "Sister, put your water in your own room, for your husband is coming drunk and he will be very thirsty". Then, gradually they explained to her that she must not touch either pots or enter the kitchen. The poor girl wept bitterly and left the house.

Next morning, the younger brother sat for his *Dan* (Charity) and was given what had been promised. There are eighteen brothers, go and get Dan from them all. The charity received in coins and kind will be so much that you will not be able to count them in your house. The boy then made his Bana in the shape of a bow and decorated it with bells and peacock feathers. From that day, he became a singer and a begger, yet he was always a poor.

## REFERENCES


1. Hivale, Shamrao, The Pardhans of the upper Narbada Valley, *Man in India,* Geoffrey Cumberlege. Oxford University Press, 1946.
2. Bodhankar, Anantrao, *Gondi-Marathi Hand Book,* Director Govt. Printing Press, Maharashtra State, Bombay, 1964, p.48.
3. Hivale, Shamrao, The Pardhans of upper Narbada Valley, *Man in India* Geoffrey Cumberlage, Oxford University Press, 1946, Chapter I-Introduction.
4. *Ibid.*
5. Mandaokar, Bhausaheb, "Festivals and ceremonies of Pardhans; (Marathi)", *Nanda-Deep,* edited by, Dr. Sarojini Babar. Lok Sahitya Prakashan, Pune, 1972, p.127.
6. Hislop, Rev. Stephen, Papers relating to Aboriginal Tribes of Central Provinces, Nagpur, 1866.
7. Russell, R.V. and Hiralal, *The Tribes and Castes of Central Provinces of India*, London, 1916, Vol. III.
8. Masram, Rushi, Typical cultural references of Aboriginal tribes: (Unpublished article in Marathi) (Secretary, Maharashtra Adiwasi Seva Mandal, Nagpur) 1971.
9. *Ibid.*
10. *Ibid.*
11. Hivale, Shamrao, *The Pardhans of upper Narbada Valley*, Published for *Man in India* by Geoffrey Cumberlege, Oxford University Press, 1946. Appendix 1, p. 51.
12. Dalton, E.T., *Descriptive Enthology of Bengal Calcutta*, 1972, p.282
13. Forsyth, J., *The Highlands of Central India,* London, 1871, p.197.
14. Russell, R.V. & Hiralal, R.B., *Tribes and Castes of the Central Provinces of India*, Vol. III, 1916. London, Reprinted 1975. p.51.
15. Stephen, Fuchs, *The Aboriginal Tribes of India*, Mac-Millan India, 1973, pp., 161-162.
16. Elwin, V., *The Muria and their Ghotul*, Oxford University Press, Indian Branch 1977, pp. 13-14.
17. Hiralal Rai Bahadur, The Aborigins of Central India, *Man in India*, vol. II. Mar. & June, No. 1 & 2, 1922, pp. 12-32.
18. Russell R.V. & Hiralal, R.B., *The Tribes and Castes of Central Provinces of India*, London, 1916, Vol. IV, p.352.
19. Hivale, Shamrao, The Pardhans of upper Narbada Valley' Published for *Man in India*, Geoffrey Cumberlege, Oxford University Press, 1946, p. 7
20. Sects & Castes Chhattisgarh: Notes on its Tribes, *J.A.S.B.* Vol. LIX, 1890,

p.284.

21. Brown, C. & Russell, R.V., *Central Provinces District Gazetteers*, Yavatmal District, vol. A. Descriptive, Calcutta, 1908, p.70.
22. *Maharashtra State Gazetteers*, Yavatmal District, Second Edition, 1974, Bombay, pp. 207-208.
23. Begdie, L.F. and Nelson, A.E. *Central Provinces District Gazetteers*, Chanda District, Allahabad, 1909, p. 107.
24. *The Tribes and Castes of Bombay*, Vol. III, Bombay, 1922, p.252.
25. Elwin, V., *The Baigas*, 1939, p. 535.
26. Elwin, V., Specimens of oral literature of Middle India: Myths of Middle India, Oxford University Press, 1949, *Gogia Pardhan*, p. 496, *Rajnengi Pardhan*, p. 498.
27. Russel, R.V. and Hiralal, R.B., *Tribes and Castes of Central Provinces of India*, Vol. IV, London, 1916, p. 354.
28. Furer Haimendorf, Von Christoph, *The Raj Gonds of Adilabad : A Peasant Culture of the Deccan- Myth & Rituals*, Macmillan & Co. Ltd., 1948.
29. Pagdi, Setu Madhaorao, *Among the Gonds of Adilabad*, Popular Book Depot, 1949, Chapter VII "The Pardhans", p.69.
30. Furer Haimendorf, Von Christoph, *The Pardhans: The Bards of the Raj Gonds*. The Eastern Anthropologist; a quarterly record of Ethnography & Folk culture, Vol. Nos. 3 & 4, 1951, pp. 172-184.
31. Furer Haimendorf, Van Christoph, *The Gonds of Andhra Pradesh*, Vikas Publishing House, Bombay, 1979, p. 24.
32. Hivale, Shamarao, *The Pardhans of upper Narbada Valley*, Geoffrey Cumberlege, Oxford University Press, 1946.

# 3

# The Clan–Social Organization, Sagas & Totem

Although tribe, caste, sect, racial group and class are the various types and orders of social groups found in India, it is the tribe and the caste which dominate the scene, the former primitive communities and the latter the Hindu Society. Society is a web of social relationships and social organization is the particular system of social relationships. In this system of social relations, i.e., the groups are individuals. The mutual relationship between individuals are controlled and regulated by institutions and associations. Hence institutions and associations, along with individuals and groups form a part of the social organization. Social organization may refer also to the sum-total of cultural institutions and their inter-relationships including the body of the unorganized activities characteristic of the group. Thus the social organization, "includes and comprehends the cultural institutions and their inter-relationships in addition to the unorganized activities of the group". To quote Reuter and Hart, "By social organization is meant the totality of cultural institutions and their inter-relationships together with the body of the unorganized activities".[1]

Elliott and Merrill describe "Social organization "as a state of being, a condition in which the various institutions in a society are functioning in accordance with their recognized or implied purposes".[2]

Social organization has usually been taken as a synonym for social structure. Thus social organization of a small group or a tribe is the organization of inter-related roles at a particular time within it as expressive of certain permanent or semi-permanent structural principles. As such social organization would consist of the inter-relations, between a particular type of groups viz. those groups which make social life possible. The clan, marriage and family are the examples of such groups. Groups of people engaged in economic pursuits comprise the economic organization of the tribe and groups like the Panchayats constitute its political organization. The former sustains, the latter controls and regulates the social organization. The inter-relation between the three would present the total pattern of tribal organization. Religion and religious groups are both social as also regulative.

Indeed no aspect of the social and ritual life of the Tribal communities is explicable without an understanding of its basic structure. The invariable and permanent elements of this structure are exogamous patrilineal descent groups known in Gondi dialect *Saga*. The phratries or Saga are firmly rooted in Tribal mythology, and their establishment as the principal exogamous units is described in myth which form a part of the spiritual heritage of all the tribals in general and of the Pardhans in particular.

Tribal opinion unanimously regards *Kalikankali*[3] as the ancestress of almost the entire Gond people. The myths recorded in, "*The Gonds of Andhra Pradesh* by Haimendorf in Chapter 11 about the origin of Gond and their Gods, and how the Gond Gods-emerged from the cave into four batches and this division into four groups laid the foundation for the basic structure of Gond and Pardhan tribe." The myths do not offer any explanation for the division of the original Gods into four groups but all Gonds and Pardhans agree that these groups consisted of Seven, Six, Five and Four brothers respectively and consequently the phratries, which have no names, are described and termed as, Yerwen, Sarwen, Siwen and Nalwen Saga i.e. Seven-wen, Six-wen, Five-wen and Four-wen phratries in the book *The Gonds of Andhra Pradesh* by Haimendorf and translated freely as Seven brother, Six brother, Five brother, and Four brother.[4] Dr. M.P. Buradkar in his thesis, "*Social Organization of Gonds*, says, "The Gonds are among those aboriginals in India who have maintained their primitive clan organization. The clans among them are grouped into exogamous phratries. Each of these phratries is designated by the number of Gods, its members are supposed to worship such as Seven Gods (Yerung Penk) Six Gods (Sarung Penk) Five Gods (Saiyung Penk) and Four Gods (Nalung Penk).[5]

The social group wider than and next to the family in the social structure of the Pardhan tribe is the clan. The clan consisting families, members of which bear the same clan-name. Members of the clan believe that they have been descended from a common ancestor. The clan being patrilineal, a man passes his clan name on to his children. A woman keeps for her father's clan-name till she is married. The clan among the Pardhans are mainly of four kinds. They are totemic, titular, territorial and eponymous. The first two kinds constitute the majority. The other two are limited in number.

(A) A Totemic clan bears the name of an animal, plant, fruit, a natural phenomenon or object such as Bāgh (Tiger) Gōha (Large Lizard) Tekām (Teak Tree) Loha (Iron) Tirgām (fire) etc.
(B) A titular clan derives its name from some personal peculiarity or adventure of the founder of the clan. The name of the titular clan may also refer to the office the ancestor of the clan is supposed to have held. Such clans for example are Khandēte (Swordman), Pedām (Village Headman) Subhedār (Military Rank) Lochantia (Salt Licker) etc.
(C) A territorial clan is known after some locality where the ancestor of the clan lived. It also sometimes refer to the early settlement of the clan, from where it has migrated to its present locality. Such clan are Māhānadiā, Jainpuriā etc.
(D) An eponymous clan bears the name of a famous ancestor, a saint, a legendary hero or a chief. Such clans are very few among the Pardhans.

The clan organization of the Pardhans of Vidarbha constitutes the first two kinds of clan.

Since the Pardhan economic and religious system depends on the community of clans between the Gonds and the Pardhans, the Clan organization of the latter closely resembles that of the Gonds, and in its main out-lines is based upon it. In detail, however, and especially in the development of local sub-clans, there is considerable divergence. Hivale, in his book, *Pardhans of Upper Narbada Valley*, has listed five groups of clans among the Pardhans of Patangarh. (Mandla District of Madhya Pradesh). There, as per the restriction on marriage i.e. exogamy, members of the each first four groups must marry outside their clans, and group of clan is observed strictly but there is some vagueness among the Pardhans about the matrimonial relations towards the members of the other group. The relations of the fifth group have not been determined. The group contains 17,10,13,7 and 15 clans respectively.[6]

In respect of the clan organization of the Pardhans of Vidarbha, it can be inferred that the Pardhans strictly observe the restriction of clan i.e. of Saga system in respect of marriage relations.

The concept of Saga i.e. God on which the clan system of the Pardhans is based has been given below.

In all there are five clan groups of the Pardhans in Vidarbha viz;

1. Four 'Saga' group
2. Five 'Saga' group
3. Six 'Saga' group
4. Seven 'Saga' group and
5. Twelve 'Saga' group

The first group viz. the four God Saga Contains 51 clans. The rest, five, six, seven and twelve contain 18 (Eighteen) 27 (Twenty seven), 28 (Twenty eight) and 7 (Seven) clans respectively. They are as follows:

*First group of 'Saga' i.e. the 'Saga' of 4 Gods Having 51 Clans*

1. Bādām
2. Bhidām
3. Chudām
4. Dāwām
5. Dasedām
6. Derām
7. Dhārnām
8. Dimdām
9. Dopām
10. Ghātte-
11. Gushrām
12. Gudrām
13. Jārām
14. Kadpam
15. Kerām
16. Kowe
17. Kudām
18. Kunjām
19. Kusrām
20. Mādkām
21. Madpachy
22. Māldām-
23. Mangām
24. Matte
25. Muchal
26. Nahakam
27. Naitam
28. Neti
29. Odam
30. Pacam
31. Parchaki
32. Patam
33. Peram
34. Pidpam
35. Pusam
36. Pusram
37. Sedmaka
38. Sedmaki
39. Sidam
40. Sidkam
41. Sonam
42. Sudam
43. Taram
44. Talande
45. Tedam
46. Tekam
47. Udam
48. Varal
49. Vedram
50. Wasam
51. Watti

*Second Group of 'Saga' i.e. Saga of 5 Gods Having 18 Clans*

| | | |
|---|---|---|
| 1. Ade | 7. Iskapa | 13. Kursange |
| 2. Anhak | 8. Istam | 14. Poreti |
| 3. Arka | 9. Jugnak | 15. Poyam |
| 4. Dhikram | 10. Kadti | 16. Soyam |
| 5. Gawande | 11. Kinaka | 17. Surpam |
| 6. Ghodam | 12. Kumre | 18. Uram |

*Third Group of 'Saga' i.e. Saga of 6 Gods Having 27 Clans*

| | | |
|---|---|---|
| 1. Aahram | 10. Kudmethe | 19. Tumram |
| 2. Atram | 11. Kumre | 20. Udye |
| 3. Gedam | 12. Markam | 21. Uike |
| 4. Katlam | 13. Parteti | 22. Urveti |
| 5. Kodape | 14. Pawale | 23. Vadey |
| 6. Kohashale | 15. Pendor | 24. Veladi |
| 7. Kohawade | 16. Salam | 25. Verkade |
| 8. Koram | 17. Todsam | 26. Wate |
| 9. Kotnak | 18. Toral | 27. Yerme |

*Fourth Groups of 'Saga' i.e. Saga of 7 Gods Having 28 Clans*

| | | |
|---|---|---|
| 1. Alam | 10. Karsange | 20. Ranwati |
| 2. Bhalavi | 11. Katange | 21. Sarate |
| 3. Dadanja | 12. Kokade | 22. Sayam |
| 4. Dhurwe | 13. Korwati | 23. Tadam |
| 5. Inwati | 14. Madavi | 24. Vansidam |
| 6. Irpati | 15. Masram | 25. Vedma |
| 7. Jugnak | 16. Marskol | 26. Velka |
| 8. Kannak | 17. Pandram | 27. Wadve |
| 9. Karpati | 18. Purkam | 28. Wadiwa |
| | 19. Pusnak | |

*Fifth Group of 'Saga' i.e. Saga of 12 Gods Having 7 Clans*

| | |
|---|---|
| 1. Harekadapa | 5. Raisidam |
| 2. Harekumra | 6. Tora |
| 3. Mandali | 7. Vedi |
| 4. Marapa | |

No clear division among the Pardhans of Yavatmal district is observed in their clan organization into phratries, although groups of clans regard themselves as saga i.e. as related to each other. But there does exist the classification of clans according to the number of Gods worshiped that has been recorded in area under investigation.

The following are the groups of clans together with few totems recorded by the author during the data-collection in Yavatmal district. Each of the groups consists of clans that are related to one another and cannot intermarry. Each member must marry outside, not only his own clan, but his own group. The Pardhans of the Yavatmal District are not very clear about whether, he can marry a member of any of the clans in the other groups.

The main clan groups according to Saga in Yavatmal District are as follows:

*Four (4) Gods Clan: Totem-Tortoise*

| | *Name* | *Totem* |
|---|---|---|
| 1. | Chikram | (A species of hawk) |
| 2. | Keram | – |
| 3. | Kusram | – |
| 4. | Kowa | (Monkey) |
| 5. | Naitam | ( Dog ) |
| 6. | Pusam | – |
| 7. | Markam | (MangoTree) |
| 8. | Parchaki | – |
| 9. | Shadmake | – |
| 10. | Tekam | (Teak Tree) |
| 11. | Talandi | – |
| 12. | Sidam | (Louse) |

*Five (5) Gods Clan: Totem-Crane*

| | *Name* | *Totem* |
|---|---|---|
| 1. | Ada or Ade | – |
| 2. | Kinake | (Leaves of Ki tree) |
| 3. | Kumare | – |
| 4. | Surpam | – |
| 5. | Ghodam | (Ghode-Nil) |
| 6. | Poyam | – |
| 7. | Iskap or Iskape | – |

*Six (6) Gods Clan: Totem-Tiger*

| | *Name* | *Totem* |
|---|---|---|
| 1. | Atram | – |
| 2. | Rajgadkar-Gedam | – |
| 3. | Kudmeta | – |
| 4. | Kotnalika | (Leaves of Kot tree) |
| 5. | Pendam or Pendor | (Anus) |
| 6. | Salam | ( Sal fish) |
| 7. | Todsam | – |
| 8. | Marappa | – |
| 9. | Uika | – |
| 10. | Tumram | – |
| 11 | Yerma or Yarma | (She Buffalo) |
| 12. | Toria | – |

*Seven (7) Gods Clan: Totem Procupine*

| | *Name* | *Totem* |
|---|---|---|
| 1. | Alam | – |
| 2. | Dhurwa | (Chief) |
| 3. | Kanaka | ( From eye) |
| 4. | Karpati | – |
| 5. | Kursange | (Deer) |
| 6. | Maraskota | (Axe) |
| 7. | Meshram | – |
| 8. | Jugnakha | (Leavs of Jugai Tree) |
| 9. | Soyam | – |
| 10. | Madavi | ( Tree ) |
| 11. | Bhalavi | – |
| 12. | Purke | – |

The principal function of the clan was to regulate and keep restrictions on matrimonial relations i.e. marriage on basis of Saga. Under modern conditions the importance of the clan in all respects (except to some extent other than those ritual and regulation of marriage) is clearly on the decline and the present system of land tenure combined with the state laws of inheritance leaves little room for the right of the clan to prevent the diversion of the property of any of its members to persons outside the circle of clan-members.

The survey of the clan organization of the various sections of the Pardhan community inhabiting the Vidarbha area, particularly in

Yavatmal District discloses certain characteristics. Firstly, the organization of the clan survives among these people only for the purpose of regulating marriages. Secondly, the majority of the clans, found among the Pardhans and Gonds are identical in names.

## REFERENCES

1. Reuter and Hart, *Introduction to Sociology*, McGraw Hill Book Co., New York, 2nd Ed., 9th impression, 1935, p. 143.
2. Elliott and Merrill, *Social Organization*, (4th Edition) Harper and Row Publisher, London 1950.
3. Furer Haimendorf, Christoph Von, *The Gonds of Andhra Pradesh*. Vikas Publication House, Bombay, 1979, pp. 180-84.
4. *Ibid*, p. 80.
5. Buradkar, M.P., *Social Organization of Gonds*, unpublished Ph. D. Thesis. Nagpur University, Nagpur.
6. Ferreira, John V., *Totemism in India*. Oxford University Press. 1965, p. 144.

# 4

# Marriage

There is no definition which adequately covers all the types of human marriage. It is an institution of society which can have very different implications in different cultures. Broadly speaking, however, marriage may be defined as, "a socially sanctioned sex relationship involving two or more people of the opposite sex, whose relationship is expected to endure beyond the time required for gestation and the birth of children". The social sanction of most cultures would imply a stable relationship, hence marriage is not co-existensive with sex life and excludes relationships with prostitutes or any other sexual relationship which is viewed as causal and not sanctioned by custom, law or church.

Biologically the institution of marriage and the rearing of children from the lengthy period of dependence of children on their parents and the need for prolonged parental care and training.

Socially, however, there are added to the sexual and parental ideas of marriage other elements; marriage is given the hallmark of social approval; it becomes a legal contract, it defines the relationship between husband and wife and between parents and children; it has to be concluded in a public and solemn manner; sometimes receiving; as a sacrament, the blessings of religion, and as a rite, the good auspices of magic. Marriage is rooted in the family rather than the family in marriage.

This section on marriage is chiefly devoted to two significant aspects, namely (1) the traditional feature of marriage institution among the Pardhans, and (2) the changing aspects of marriage due to impact of urbanization and contact with other communities.

The marriage ceremony among the Pardhans is considered to be an affair of the entire tribe, and not of a family. The entire tribal community takes interest in the observance of the rites and ceremonies connected with a wedding. This was so due to their nomadic and co-operative, collective way of life. The marriages are generally settled during the Holi festival. The proposals regarding the marriage of girl or boy are first referred to the traditional leader who happens to be the chief of the tribal council through the members or the council and the direct negotiations regarding the marriage between two parties are not considered to be proper. The main reason for this may be that the failure in marital relations or disputes arising out of marital discords are then consequently referred to Panchayat for its resolution. Thus the council plays a very significant role in the settlement of marriages. The practice of arranged marriages is widely accepted among the Pardhans. About the choice of partner too boys and girls had absolutely no say in the matter. It was reported that the selection of the suitable match was completely the decision of the elderly people of the family and the traditional leader of the tribe. Some of the young respondents have gone up to the extent of saying, "even if the elderly people select a blind girl for the bridegroom, he has to marry her". This shows that the practice of arranged marriage is the accepted value among the Pardhans.

The father of the girl or boy approaches the traditional leader or the members of council with a proposal of marriage. The father of the girl or boy accompanied with the traditional leader calls upon the concerned family for marital negotiations. It is customary at the time of the first approach to ask the party concerned, from where you have come? They have to furnish the information regarding the original place of the residence to which the family belonges so as to understand their family and historical background. It appears that such questions are posed to trace out of the nature of original place and their relationship. At the time of the settlement of marriage, the father of the boy alongwith the relations, accompanied by the members of the tribal council reach the place where the girl stays and offers her coconut hair oil, vermilion, some sweets, which is symbolic of the fact that the marriage has been settled. The bridegroom party has to supply sufficient coconut oil to all the female members of the bride's party and it was reported by the respondents that inadequate supply of oil often led to conflict and clashes among the parties concerned. This is generally the cause for quarrels between the two parties, as reported by the respondents.

The practice of dowry is very such dominant among the Pardhans. After the settlement of marriage, the father of the bridegroom has to pay the minimum amount of Rs. 12 to Rs. 70 or even more to the father of the girl (bride). It varies in different localities and places. This is known as bride-price. It is also considered as the expenses towards the marriage of the bride.

One of the characteristics of the bride-price is that the whole amount is not paid when the marriage is first settled. A certain portion usually one half is paid to the bride's parents at the time of the settlement of marriage, the balance being paid at the time of marriage ceremony. The dowry amount is not fixed but it cannot be less than Rs. 12 and ranges between Rs. 70 or more depending upon the economic condition of the bridegroom's party. At the same time the bridegroom's father has also to hand over the requirement of number of liquor bottles to be offered to his party by the bride's father. It is customary that the father of the bride has to offer a particular number of liquor bottles to the party of the bridegroom as agreed upon by both the parties. Liquor constitutes one of the major expenses in the marriage ceremony of the Pardhans.

As stated earlier, marriage being a community affair, no formal invitations are extended to the members of the tribes, but all participate in it as a matter of right and tradition. In the past, the day of the wedding used to be fixed by the traditional leader, usually after the Holi festival. The Pardhans celebrate marriages on any week day excepting Monday, Tuesday and Saturday which are considered to be inauspicious by the members of the tribe.

It may be noted here that in the past the entire marriage ceremony was performed under the supervision of the traditional leader generally the priest or pujaris but now-a-days it is performed even without the priest.

One of the characteristic features of the Pardhans marriage ceremony is that it is marked with the quarrels, clashes and conflicts among the members of the tribe and with the Pardhans, and others who had come to participate in marriage. One of the reasons for quarrels is heavy drinking habit. Drinking liquor on festive occasions has become very common among the Pardhans. On such occasions women also join their husbands in drinking. At times such quarrels acquire a severe nature and the entire tribe gets involved into it. The entire scene is really worth observing when the people are under the influence of liquor. Drinks are a must in the marriage ceremonies of the Pardhans.

Marriage ceremony of the Pardhans traditionally continues for a couple of days i.e. for 5 days. The details of the marriage ceremonials are briefly as below.

**Five Days Programme of Pardhan Wedding**

| Name of the rite and ritual | Particulars of the Performance |
|---|---|
| **1st Day**<br>1. *Khar-chang* (offer of dowry) | The groom's party ceremoniously sends the articles of dowry offer (fixed at the time of settlement) to the bride's house. Unless they are received as proposed, the bride's party does not proceed further with the wedding functions. |
| 2. *Kharchang-Yer Arumal* (To tie fist of the bride) | Bride's body is besmeared with turmeric powder ointment and she is given the first ceremonial bath with hot water chanting auspicious hymens all the while. |
| 3. *Nahanorang Udmal* (Bathing the Bride and groom) | Bride and groom are given ceremonial bath simultaneously but separately in their respective pandals. |
| 4. (a) *Pichi Normal*<br>(b) *Pichi Tournal* | Turmeric roots are grinded into powder by women, then its paste is first applied to their divine deities and then to the bride and then to the groom. |
| 5. *Nahan* (Bath) | Bride and groom are given a second auspicious bath ceremoniously. |
| 6. *Munda* (Pandal Raising) | A green pandal is errected, made of the green branches of the *Jamun* (Black berry) *Pippal* (Buman) and Moh trees. |
| **2nd Day**<br>1. *Kharcha-Samān* (Dowry-Materials) | The articles of the dowry received, are carried in a ceremonial procession to the bridal pandal, while the female folk sing the song "Akashi Mandap, Dharatee Bohale : (sky |

| | |
|---|---|
| | is the pandal and earth below is the wedding platform). |
| 2. *Nahān* (Bath) | In their respective pandals the bride and the groom are given bath by married couples. In the Pandal (The bride or groom) is seated on a wooden platform in the middle of the pandal and on either side of this platform sitting arrangement is made for the married couples. On one side of the couples belonging to odd number deity class sit while the opposite side is occupied by the couples pertaining to the even number of deity class. Couples on either side approach the bride (or groom) one after another and bathe her (or him) by pouring water. |
| **3rd Day** *Bondhe-Kimāl* (Advising the bride and the groom) | In their respective pandals the parties assemble to meet the bride or groom (as the case may be) sing and songs describing the past life, past memories and qualities of the bridegroom and also songs containing advice to her/him in respect of leading the future life as a married couple. |

Among the Pardhans, the number 4 has a great and unique importance because of its denoting the number of the great Gods of Pardhans viz. Lingo, Jango, Hirajyoti and Manko. Hence the 4th day is most important in the Pardhans marriage ceremony.

| | |
|---|---|
| **4th Day** 1. *Nahān* (Bath) | The community people gather in the pandal and give an auspicious bath to the bride/groom with great pomp and fanfare. |

2. *Kidnap*

There was a custom amongst the Pardhans people to kidnap the bride and the groom and conceal her/him in a secret place. Hence a strict vigilance is kept on them during the day. The custom is however abolishing now a days.

3. *Angnāl* (Shaving the groom)

The groom's hair is ceremoniously shaved and his sister collects the shaved hair in her new saree offered to her for the purpose.

4. *Mundā-*

The males of the bridal or groom's party bring a big branch of the Moh tree in a ceremonial procession and worship it-cautiously and invoke their divine deities dwelling thereon to the wedding ceremony. The opposite party tries to create trouble and difficulties in their worship. They try to burn the Munda (tree branch) upside down by the force of black magic hymns chanted secretly. When the Munda reaches the marriage pandal it is tied to a post of the pandal and worshipped with the traditional technique. The women sing the folk lore and dance around it. Feast is given to the party after midnight, on the finish of the function.

5. (a) *Gaymanshi-Chowk*

After the feast, the bride is dressed in her 'Chorok' i.e. the wedding attires. She then stands on a raised platform with rice held in her right fist, people approach her one by one and apply *tilak* (red-mark) on her forehead and sing traditional songs.

(b) *Mithusmal* — The groom is also adorned likewise in his wedding dress and traditional songs are recited.

6. *Shig-Yetmal* — The bride is taken to the groom's Pandal in a ceremonial procession singing songs by the bridal party after midnight of the 4th day and reach there in the early morning. They stop on the outskirts of the groom's village, or at a distance from the Pandal in the same village.

**5th Day**

1. *Bride's arrival* — On this day the actual marriage takes place. In the ancient times the Pardhans performed the marriage function on a barren land. Then the custom changed to performing it under a lonely tree. Now-a-days however it is performed in the groom's pandal. Reaching the groom's place in the early morning the bridal party sends word to the groom's party, calling for the palanquins to carry the bride to groom's pandal. They then take her to the groom's pandal in early morning of the 5th day. When they reach there, the groom's party receives them with respect and honours them. The groom's people wash the bride's feet in a metal dish and females of both parties sing songs, containing romantic satire and even

obscene meaning. They also perform various folk dances namely Sehla, Ghera, Dhemsa, Faqunare etc. The function ends in shouting aloud "Pilli Sata, wata, Dhangyanna rou re Jamosa" (The rat died foul smell spreads around, leave for scheduled place).

2. *Sama Kimal* (Marriage meet)

The Wedding function starts with the offer to the bride of the gifts to be given by the groom to her. The bride then enters the pandal and approaches the groom who opens out her closed fist with his one hand only. He then puts on her finger an iron ring and ties a Garsory of black *beeds* (Mangal sutra) round her neck. (At this juncture the groom has to face some tests taken by the bride and her people and she chooses to wed him only on his withstanding these tests to her satisfaction. This denotes that the girl chose her husband on testing him to her satisfaction).

3. *Tarher Kanyadan* (offering the daughter)

Both the Parties assemble together in one place. The priest sits in their middle and declares the wedding as done, whereupon the assembly showers Akshata (Juwar grains coloured yellow with turmeric powder) on the bride and the groom. Women sing the traditional auspicious wedding song of five verses, peculiarly pertaining to the occasion.

4. *Acceptance of the Bride*

The groom then holds the hands of the bride as a token of his accepting her as his beloved. The guests applaud it by clap of hands in joy and express their approval of the couple. Then starts the wedding procession, in a pecular chain of hand holding. The groom holds the finger of the priest, the bride holds the groom's finger, and a leading woman holds her finger. Then the rest of the party follow holding one another's finger forming a long chain at the end of which are two women with earthen lamps on their heads. This procession accompanied with music of the flute, Kingri and drum sounding, goes round several posts of the pandal. The procession stops if the finger chain breaks and again continues on completing it.

5. *Chudure usare pitle Korale usmall*
(Poor sparrow taking leave)

The bridal party takes leave of the poor sparrow, the bride. Then newly wedded couple–the bride and the groom are seated on the top of the members of the bridal party and they bless them. While this function is in process the pathetic songs are sung and sad notes of pathos are played on flutes and drums. Every and all partaking, shed tears white parting from the bride. In the end the bride sits on the top of her father, takes his leave, then goes to her father-in-law and sits in his lap.

6. *Bhetuni* — The groom with his bride goes to his father-in-law and mother-in-law, bows to them and to all elderly persons of the bridal party and takes their parting leave. The bridal party then returns back to its residence.

**6th Day** — On the 6th day the groom party gives a bath to the new couple wiping off the turmeric ointment on their bodies and the couple is made free. This ceremony takes place in the groom's pandal.

1. *Pichi Usmal* (Wiping off the wedding ointment)

2. *Deo-Devi* (Worship of family deities) — The new couple then worships the family deities of both the bride and groom, then the couple is introduced to all the members of the groom family. The couple is then made conversant with the family traditions and ancestral history. Sweets are offered to family deities and that sacred oblation is distributed to all as Prasad (blessing).

**Changing Aspects of Marriage Among the Pardhans**

In a marriage ceremony of Shri Soyam of Matharjun (Kelapur tehsil) it was observed that some of the aspects of traditional pattern of marriage are in the process of change and at the same time new practices are being adopted by these people. The contacts of urban area seem to have provided intensive and extensive opportunities for social interaction to the members of this tribe and consequently new patterns are being accepted by these people.

*Age at Marriage*

The practice of child marriage has been reported among the Pardhans. During field investigation a few cases of child marriage were noticed.

However, child marriage is not common among the Pardhans

Some of the Pardhans reported that in the past the tribe being nomadic, the marriages were settled at an early age during socio-religious festivals when all the members of the tribe used to assemble on a common place and then move about for their economic activities. Thus earlier marriages were celebrated at the age of 13 to 14 years for the bride, and 16 to 20 years of for the bridegroom. Most of the marriage unions are settled at the developed age (15 to 20 years) and particularly when the girl attains puberty.

### *Participation in Marriage*

As the marriage ceremony was exclusively the affair of the entire tribe, the outsiders i.e. other tribes and castes had no room in their marriage ceremonies excepting the physical presence, because the out-lawed position and the stigma of untouchability on the Pardhans But due to the impact of industrialization and urbanization there has been a noticeable change in this respect in recent days, with appreciable participation of others in the marriage ceremonies. This is one of the changing aspect of the marriage among the Pardhans.

It is reported that these days there is good participation of outsiders in the marriage ceremonies of the Pardhans.

Some of the outsiders participate in the marriage of the Pardhans only for enjoying liquor. Their participation seems to be confined to that activity only. This is the latent reason of their participation. To some extent participation of other caste people in the marriage ceremonies of the influentials of the tribe is due to frequent contacts with them.

### *Some New Patterns*

The Pardhans have been adopting some of the new patterns in their marriage ceremonies. In the past formal invitations were not extended to the members of the tribe. They used to participate in it as a matter of privilege and tradition. At present formal invitation cards are also printed, to be given to the outsiders and also to the persons of the community. This is reported to be a new pattern. Secondly, the marriage ceremony among the Pardhans has become a costly affair. It is due to the inclusion of more pomp and show due to the interaction with other caste groups and impact of urbanization. Such as hiring of loudspeaker, inviting the photographer to snap photographs of the important rituals of the marriage ceremony. One still more new pattern these people have taken to, is the practice of giving gifts to the bride and bridegroom. The announcement of the nature of gift and the name of the giver is made on the loudspeaker. Some of the respondents have said, this practice has been taken from the other caste groups of the area. Thus the Pardhans have been adopting some new practices in the marriage ceremony.

**Pardhan's Marriage Ceremony (with Songs)**

Marriage is a social institution. As such it may be defined as 'A relation of one or more men to one or more women which is recognised by customs or law and involves certain rights and duties both in the case of the parties entering the union and in the case of the children born of it". These rights and duties vary among different people and cannot, therefore, all be included in general definition, but these must of course, be something which they have in common. Marriage always implies the right of sexual intercourse, society holds such intercourse allowable in the case of husband and wife, and generally speaks with even regards of it as their duty to gratify in some measure the other partners' desire. But the right to sexual intercourse is not necessarily exclusive. It can hardly be said to be so, from the legal point of view, unless adultery is considered an offence which entitles the other partner to dissolve the marriage union; and this is by no means always a case.

At the same time, marriage is something more than a regulated sexual relation. It is an economic institution, which may in various ways affect the property rights of the parties. It is the husband's duty, so far as it is possible and necessary to support his wife and children, but it may also be their duty to work for him. As a general rule he has some power over them, although his power over the children is in most cases of limited duration. Very often, marriage determines the place which a newly born individual is to take in the social structure of the community to which he or she belongs, but this cannot, as has been sometimes maintained, be regarded as the chief and primary function of marriage, considering how frequently illegitimate children are treated exactly like legitimate ones with regards to descent, inheritance, and succession. It is finally necessary that the union, to be recognised as a marriage, should be concluded in accordance with rules laid down by customs or laws whatever these rules may be. They may require the consent of the parties themselves or of their parents, or of the parties as well as of their parents. They may compel the man to give some consideration for his bride, or the parents of the latter to provide her with dowry. They may prescribe the performance of a particular marriage ceremony of one kind or other. And no man and woman are regarded as husband and wife unless the conditions stipulated by custom or law are complied with.

Like other tribes Pardhans do not seek advice from the priests for settling the date of marriage. Since ancient times, the marriage ceremonies among the Pardhans, generally, take place during the spring season e.g. during the months of Phalguna (Chaitra and Vaishakh) every year. The function takes place either on the 5th or 9th day after the Amavasya (Dark Night) of these months. So it is the unwritten custom amongst the Pardhans to celebrate marriage ceremonies on these dates every year, which go on for continuous five days. Folk dances and folk songs fill their lives with joy and humour.

The folk-lores of the Pardhans, during these marriage-celebrations, are not merely a thing of humour or entertainment, but also of a great social importance. A good deal of advice to the bride and the bridegroom is imparted through folk-songs–an advice concerning customs, clan-rituals, religious rites, culture and life, and what not. So the marriage ceremonies are of great social and religious importance to them.

Long ago, there was a peculiar custom of "Lamjaade" i.e. the bridegroom, who had to live in the family of his father-in-law. According to this custom, the bridegroom had to stay at his father-in-law's house, until he was proved to be worthy of earning his own livelihood and also of winning the heart of his would be bride. When the father of a marriageable girl was fully satisfied in accordance with those conditions, the date of marriage was to be declared and the marriage used to take place. But now-a-days this custom is absolutely abolished.

## Settlement of Marriage

After the disappearance of the aforesaid custom, the Pardhans sought another way of settlement of marriage. People from the bridegroom's party take their marriageable boy with them and go to the place where the expected bride resides. Old-folk of the village gather together and in the assembly they ask the following questions to the boy in folk-verses:

"Jaati Ro Baati Riyore Dada?
Jaati Ro Batti Bhidi ro Dada"?

*Meaning*: O, young man which caste you have come from? Which class do you belong to? Let us know about it.

This custom is known as *Bhidi*. The boy answers the question and explains what class he does belong to and what caste he has come from. Apparently, the answer too, is given in folk-verses. For example:

"Chandekar, Bhondekar, Neet Navaral Kummekar
Jaati Re (Name of the class) Ana Riyore Dada!"

*Meaning*: I am not a vagabond. I belong to a respectable family of so and so class from Chanda District, who has ability to marry a girl of yours!

These questions and answers are of a customary type. Preparations of those are done well before. A boy is compared with a copper-pot, while the girl with an earthern pot. It means that a boy is free to marry for several times, while the girl once only!

After these formalities, 3 questions are put to the boy:

1. Niwang Bachole Penk Mandang?
   (How Many deities have you?)
2. Bona Vijja Andi?
   (Whose son are you?)
3. Bona Paal Utti?
   (Whose milk have you drunk? i.e. who is your mother?).

Unless these three questions are answered, the marriage cannot be supposed to be settled among the Pardhans. It is because these questions bear some basic facts, those have much importance in the functioning of marriage-engagements.

It will not be out of way to explain the intention hidden behind those questions. Let us go thoroughly through the reasons.

The Pardhans are divided into two chief classes, namely "Deo-Saga" (Section).

These two Sections among them–equal number Deo-Section consists of those having 2,4,6,8,10,12,16, etc. number of deities; and unequal number Deo Section consists of those who belong to 3,5,7,9,11,13, etc. number of deities.

Thus, a class belonging to equal number Deo Section is regarded as one kind of "Beeja-Gotra". Marriages amongst the same Beeja-Gotra are strictly prohibited. Hence they seek matches from another Beeja-Gotra. Thus, the intention behind the aforesaid question indicates that marriages do not take place among people belonging to the same "Beeja-Gotra".

Secondly, it is also notable that marriages do not occur among those "Milk-Class" i.e. a boy cannot marry a girl from such class, which his mother comes from!

The Pardhans used to regard a girl from the same class as his "sister" and from his mother's class as his "Mother". Apart from these Gotras, marriages generally take place among the others. But now-a-days this custom has been disappearing and marriages have been taking place among the nearest kinsmen such as the daughter of a maternal uncle or of an aunt.

When marriage is settled, first of all the girl is adored with the Kum-Kum by the bridegroom. On this occasion the Tribe-chief calls upon both in a meeting. From the maleside Rs. 12 (Rs. 10 for Arti and Rs. 2 for Gonazadi) are charged by the Chief, while Re. 1 from the femaleside as a charge against calling the meeting. In this very meeting it is also decided that, what ornaments, clothes and grains are to be given by the bridegroom for the bride. In Vidarbha, 2 Kudavas of Jawar or Wheat (approximately 20 kgs.); 7 Kudavas of "Belda" i.e. pulse, rice etc; silverornaments, 5 sarees including yellow coloured Khenda and a Aaji-Bondri are generally given by the bridegroom for the bride. All these things are kept ready five days before the marriage and are to be sent to the bride.

## 1st Day of the Marriage Ceremony

Since the day, those things being sent to the house of the bride, the Five-Day-Marriage-Ceremony commences. *Kharchang* – this custom is known as Kharchang custom being performed on the 1st day of the marriage. On the 1st or the 5th day, of Vaishakh, the bride is adored with the "First Bath of Kharcha" i.e. with the yellow coloured turmeric. This is known as "Kharchata Yer Arumal". There is a faith in the Pardhans that after this Bath the girl changes into a woman! On the very day the fist of the bride is tied with the chanting of some Mantras! Then the bride and the bridegroom are adored with the 1st Bath in their respective pandals. This custom is known as "Nahanorang Udmal". On this occasion a lovely folk-song is sung by the ladies-

"Yer Dehabi Lata De
Jaati Re Baati Miyale Sango
Yer Dehaki lata de!
Jaati (of so and so Kul) Dheke Miyyale Sango!
Yer Dehaki lata De! 1

Ladina Verode Sango! Yeni Pohe Mata De!
Ladana Yerode Sango! Gadhal Pohe Mata De 2

Yeni Pohe Mata Te Sango! Gango Pongi Lata De!
Gadhal Dube Mata De Sango! Dob Sache Mata De 3

Mune Mune Navati! Paja Paja Tavari
Tavarita Niy Zalake Mata De! Bhabhidare
Ladina Verode Sango! Yeni Pohe Mata De 4

*Meaning:* (1) Which class or Gotra does this beauty come from? Lo, she is busy in bath. Do you know, she belongs to such and such class. She is busy in playing with water.

(2) Aye, darling! Look towards this beautiful girl. She takes bath in such a style, as if a majestic elephant is swimming. And lo! that young man is playing like a donkey in that muddy pond!

(3) For this magnificent elephant, i.e. bride, the Holy Ganges has appeared here; while that donkey (bridegroom) is hopping-dopping in the muddy pond.

(4) The beautiful bride goes ahead, and lo! the oil in the lamp begins to dance because of her attraction. She is taking her bath, with the grace of an elephant!

Before Nehanoran, the bride and the bridegroom are adored with turmeric, which has been ground by all the ladies of the tribe. While grinding the turmeric, a meaningful folk-lore is sung.......

*Jatta Maloni Arata*

Bad ladina Rota O, Nawoni Yaya O!
(So and so) Ladina Rota O, Nawoni Yaya O!
Jatta Maloni Arata O, Nawoni Yaya O!
(So and so) Ladina Rota O, Nawoni Yaya O!
Kaishar Zurani Arata O, Nawoni Yaya O!
(So and so) Ladina Rota O, Nawoni Yaya O!
Zarana Zurani Arata O, Nawoni Yaya O!

*Meaning:* Thus the grinder is sad! which beauty does this grinder belong to? It belongs to such and such beauty. Thus the grinder is sad!

Which beauty does this groom belong to? It is, too, sad! Oh mummy, it belongs to such and such lady! It has become very pale in her love!

See, how this thing has also been pale and sad in her love!

All the things, belonging to the girl seem to have become restless with the idea of her departure from that house. Every person is sad in the house.

*Pichi Normal*

Pichi Norale Wala Wo Ange Wo, Pichi Norale Wala Wo
Nee Manata siriyale Ange; Dadana manata Waya Wo!
Damoo Jode Kisi Ange, Niwa Siriyal Tatti Wo!
Niwa Manata Siriyal Ange; Dadana Manata Wayo Wo!
Jatta Dhondite Udandi Wo; Zape To Zape Kulkandi Wo!
Niwa Manata Siriyal Ange, Tammuna Manate Wayo Wo!
Niwa Ladok Sherandoona Ange, Walle Ladokindi Wo!
Jati Bati Miyani Ange; Pichi Norale Wala Wo!

To Grind the turmeric

*Meaning:* Oh, dear Sister-in-law! Come here to grind the turmeric. Here is your sister of your choice, but my brother has no fancy for her. Oh! you have spent every penny to find her, but my brother does not like her. You were pondering over with drowsy eyes near the grinder, while grinding, but my brother did not care for her, whom you have brought with an earnest choice. Oh, sister-in-law. How much did you love your brother-in-law! You have come from a dignified family. You ought to have come for grinding turmeric in my marriage.

Then comes the next stage of adoration with turmeric. First the ladies take the turmeric powder with them, make it wet with water and adore the deities of the clan. Then the balm of turmeric is applied to the bride and the bridegroom.

*Pichi Tarumal*

Dadare Dada Indale Baiwo! Dore To Dadane Mutale
Baiwo//
Pahilo to Pichi Natendor Melyane! Doosar Pichi
Natendor Bhimane//
Tisaro to Pichi Natenda Yayane! Pajada Pichi
Shiwarya Bhowaryane//
Dadare Dada Indale Baiwo! Bore to Dadane Mutale
Baiwo//

To Adore Turmeric.

*Meaning:* This innocent sister would cry out oh Dada! Whom would she call? First of all she would call the Chief Deity of the village, whom the turmeric would be adored with! Then would come Bhimdeo of the village. Thirdly the deity of the town, and at last the turmeric would be offered to the guards-Shiwarya-Bhawarya of the village! "Dada, oh Dada" would be sister's call, whom would she call?

After having adored with turmeric, the bridegroom nas to put on the ornaments, mainly used by ladies and also a Knife! He has to wear silver ornaments in his neck. Then he wears woolen shawl like rough cloth (Kambal). Here it is significant that among Pardhans, the bridegroom has to put on female ornaments. Why so? Pardhans belong to aborigines of India, who worship the God Shiva. Shiva is famous for his appearance of Ardha-nari-nateshwar! This indicates that the bridegroom and the bride are now become one self-no separate identity is there! In this way this ceremony is very important.

After adoption of female appearance, i.e. of the "Parvati's Roop";

the first bath takes place, which is known as "Nahanorang" in the Pardhans. On this occasion the following song is sung:

*Nahanorang*

Aati Kakana Siri Basenga!
Koika Rajaka Beta Angoriko Baithe Wo!
(Dhekya) Rajaka Beta Angoriko Baithe Wo//
Dai-Dadan Siri Basenga!

*Meaning:* This poor fellow has led his life under the guidance of his uncle, aunt and brothers. Now his own day has dawned. Lo! He is that Prince, who has come forth to have a bath with a majestic ceremony. Don't you know, he is (so and so) Prince, taking here bath.

**Munda**

On the 1st day of the marriage ceremony the Pardhans erect "Munda" i.e. Pandals in the courtyards of the bride and bridegroom. This pandal is adored with the green branches of the Jamun, Pippal and Moha trees. While erecting these Pandals, they sing the following song:

*Mandav*

Hono Ka Kono, Bhai Re Meva, Mandava To Uthayo!
Charoji Bhai Re Mera, Mandava To Uthayo!
Saleka Deri Re Deri, Jamun Ka Saya//
Chandi Ka Adava, Soneki Aduli//
Bhale to Bhale Bhai Re Mera, Mandava To Uthayo//
(Adava=Small earthern Pot; Aduli=Small Basket)

**2nd Day of Marriage Ceremony**

The Kharcha-Saman, sent by the bridegroom to the kinsmen of the bride on the Ist day, is already kept in the house of the bride. On the Second day, it is brought in the marriage pandal with a grand procession! On this occasion, the ladies sing the following song:

Kumbharin Bai Wo Kumbhar Kuthe Gela//
Haati, Kudari Dharala Bai, Maati Khandala Gela//
Maati Khandata-Khandata Bai, Paya Modun Gela//
Kumbharin Bai Wo Kumbhar Kuthe Gela//
Haati Sota Dharala Bai, Gadhe Rakhale Gela//
Gadhe Rakhata-Rakhata Bai, Haat Modun Gela//
Kumbharin Bai Wo Kumbhar Kuthe Gela//

And the "Kharcha-Saman" is taken away from the house of the kinsmen of the bride, and the procession begins to leave for the Pandal. On this occasion the following song is sung:

Hei Kharcha Jaate Hei Kharcha Jaate//
Nawardeo Chya Mandavi, Nawardeo Chya Mandavi//
Hei Kharcha Jaate; Hei Kharcha Jaate//
Konachya Mandavi, Konachya Mandavi/
Aagashi Mandavi, Aagashi Mandavi,
Dharteri Bowola, Dharteri Bowola//

(Dharteri Bowola = The eath itself is a pious seat of marriage).
(Aagashi Mandavi = The sky is pandal).

They wash the feet of the kinsmen near the pandal, salutation takes place, a branch of Salai-tree is enplated, "Dirmatan" is established and then the Second bath takes place. This ceremony is also called Nahanorang.

The process of this second bath is very interesting and amusing, too.

In the open ground two carpets are spread upon two sides, on on side, couples from the equal number Deo-section take their places, while on the other the couples from the unequal number of Deo-section take their places. In between the both, the bride or bridegroom is to be seated.

First of all, a renowed couple gets up and gives bath to the bride or the groom. They first touch their heads to the head of the bride or the groom and then pour a glassful water on the head of the bride or the groom. Then every couple follows the same custom. On this collective bath, the following folk-lore is sung:

Jaati Ro Baati Riyyona Samiyapati Lata De!

Hei Ladi! Samipati Lata De!
(Dhekya) Riyyona Ladi Samiya Hulale Wayeni De!
Samiya Patan Nati Lada, Navor Babo Ranganoor!
Hei Lada Navor Babo Ranganoor!
Nivor Babo Rangan Neti, Joda Ghading Watika De!
Hei Ladi Samiya Halale Wayeni De!
Samiya Hulale Wayan Neti Nava Awati Rangal Ro!
Hei Dulera! Nava Awal Rangal Ro!
Neeva Awal Rangan Neti, Ghodagading Tattika De!
Hei Ladi Samiya Patti Lata De!
Hei Ladi Samiya Hulale Wala De!
Orite Udan Neti Dulera Navor Tammu Ranganoor!
Nivor Tammu Rangan Neti Koda Singru Tattika De!
Hei Ladi Pichi Sokale Wala De!
Pichi Sokan Neti Dulera ~~Nava~~ Tange Rangal De!
Niva Tange Rangan Neti Sari Khagora Sikan De!
Hei Ladi Yere Torile Wala De!
Yer Toran Neti Dulera Nava Selal Rangal Ro!
Selal Rangan Neti Chose Dikali Tattika De!
Hei Ladi Dhoti Siyale Wala De!
Karyale Noote Pandhari Noole Ladi!
Agene Riyyona Rahuti De!
Hei Ladi Rahuti Hulale Wayeni De!
Rahuti Hulan Neti Dulera Inhakya Dhekya Hulanoor Ro!
Inhakya Dhekya Hulan Neti Gona Gamding Watika De!
Hei Ladi Samiya Patti Lata De!

*Meaning:* Whose lamp of youth is burning, it is so and so's! Oh dear lady, would you come to see the lamp? But darling, my father would abuse me with wrath! Oh lady, I would spread carpets on the path of your father on that day and would welcome him. But do come to see the lamp of youth.

But darling, if my mother would be off with wrath, how could I come? Oh, do not you wory darling, I would send horses and coaches for her to come, but do not miss to come! But dear if I would try to come and if my brother would abuse you do not mind, I would send a horse for my brother and would make him happy. But do come to adore holy turmeric. If my sister-in-law would see me while coming to you and if she would abuse you, I would offer her ornaments (Sari and Khogora) and would make her happy. But dear, do come to pour holy water. And if my sister would object your coming there and would abuse you, I would offer her rich clothings-Choli and Saree-, but do come to offer Dhoti, that is woven with black and white threads.

Oh Darling! come to my place!
But, Oh dear Bridegroom! the vagabonds of the
village would blame me, while coming to you.

Darling! do not care, I would offer them carpets (Gona Ghangdi) and would honour them too thus, I would win the hearts of your people.

Darling! the lamp of youth is burning, do come to me?

This beautiful folk-lore is sung by the Pardhans at the 2nd day of the matrimonials. Men and women, boys and girls, young and old all are lured by the melody of this lore and pass the whole night singing and dancing. Every lore has got its own merits and specific identity. The drum-beats, on the musical notes make the people so much sensitive that they do not know when the night passes on.

**3rd Day of Marriage Ceremony**

*Advice to the Bride and the Bridegroom*

Now begins the third day of the function, a day full of sentimental memories and future dreams! Early in the morning, after having their bath, the bride and groom are offered sweets. Women sit around them and sing songs concerning the memories of their past. Childhood has now gone with the past – a life full of joy and happiness, a life with sweet memories of innocent play-things! So touchy are these folk-lores that the bride and the groom burst into tears. Not only these lores tell of the bygone childhood, but also make them aware of the responsibility fallen upon them newly. So these lores are called 'Bondhekimal' i.e. songs of advice, regarding customs and culture of the society. On this occasion the following song is sung:

(a) *Some Folk-lores advising the bridegroom*
Jaati Wo Baati Miyani Yaya! Jaati Wo (Dheke) Miyani Yaya!

Awo Niwate Selomi Wchawo! Balo Weha Burote Weha!
Wattal Katyatoon Hale Dhadami! Pahana Katyatoon
Hale Sedami//
Niwa Sedomi Wehaur! Bhalo Te Weha Burote Weha
Batinik Sedomi Wehkars Kuwara?
Sedomi Muchchuke Jalma Wo Yaya?//
Jayate Wanjer Khand Nawe Yayani
Agas Andoor Baba Ro Kuwara//
Paloke Tallate Yetaka Wo Yaya! Niwa Sedomi Wehava
Dharatori Ande Aawal Ro!
Dharatari Zele Kitaro Kuwara! Niwa Sedomi Kenja Ro//

*Meaning:* Oh! mother, tell me of the class you are coming from. Let me know by what sort of milk I have been brought up! Tell me this way or that, about your class!

Tell me how the log of wood has been dried up without keeping in the sun! What has marketh the wood green, without having an inner spring of water! How could I come to this world? Oh! mother, unless and until you would explain the originality of my blood, how could I believe that I have come from so and so family! Oh mother, why are you keeping mum over my question. This makes me uneasy and puts me to an utter shame! Your silence irritates me and Oh dear mother if you would not speak a word, I would cut off your tongue. Tell me this way or that, but let me know about my ownself!

My dear lad, what can I say? Dear son, the father of all this universe is the sky, which is also your father! and have you seen this earth? It is the mother of all creatures in the world, so it is your mother. This earth has caught you in her womb. This is the secret of your birth, class and family!

(b) Re Re Na Re Re Na Babo Re, Hore Ka Bore Bi Babo Re/
Re Re Na Re Re Na Babo Re, Hore Ka Bore Bi Babo Re/

Niwete Korate Kunwarana Babo Re/
Remite Niltona/Jawanite Watona/
Keyate Miwore Patalin Babo Re/
Dadana Udikane Kutude/
Patali Udaneer Bilate/
Bhidire Chawdinge Taranur Patali/

Tayi Ana Babola Pundika/
Satike Man Daunge Ramgade/
Penuke Mandamunge Jamgade/
Jango Lingo Hirajyoti Sedoni/
Jai Ime Kuwarana Pundiki/

Re Re Na Re Re Na Babo Re, Hore Ka Dhekebi Babo Re/

*Meaning:* Singing the Alap "Re Re Na" the song says: "Who is my father? My father belongs to an illustrious family. Oh father, I am your beloved child. Oh father dreamer of my happiness, you give me an account of the origin of your line. I have grown as a youth under your care and love. I am at the prime of my youth. Are you not aware of this? Call your priest. I take my seat in front of him. Your priest will then refer to the religious books and tell me the origin of our family and I shall get enlightened.

The priest instructs "Oh Soh, Seven *Satis* are concentrated on Ramgad. Your family-Deities are at Jamgad. Jango, Lingo, Hirajyoti are the presiding deities of your family. This is the secret of the source of your family. Your family has a high status. Are you satisfied?

*Folk Lores imparting instructions to the bride*

"Re Re Na, Re Re Na, Nave Don
Bore Andur Nave Badnor Don
Siri To Bhyayawane Nave Kurarioner Don.
Dharteri Awale Nave Kuwarina Don.
Bore To Andure Nave Bainore Pepi
Raja Ka Karunale Bainore Pepi.
Injikune Sara Kare Don Neve Sone Ka Babola
Ana Handakate Rapo Re Sukare Ka Habola
Rande Diyana Ana Phanena Babola.
Dusarona Rota Re Singare Ana Babola
Rone Ka Hakare Sindi Re Babola
Rachadale Hokare Sindane Babola.
Re Na Re Nave Babola!

*Meaning:* Who is the father of my darling child? God himself is the father of this darling child. The mother-earth is her mother. Who is her uncle? The king Karna is her uncle. You are a fortunate child belonging to a high family.

The daughter to the father : Is it because I am so-called fortunate that there is famine at our home? Is it that there will be prosperity at home after I leave this house for my father-in-law's? Oh father, are you fed up with me so early? I am a short-staying guest at your home. My birth entails me to be the property of others (Since I am a girl). When I was staying with you in your home you often called me and I responded at each call from you. Whom will you call after I leave home?

Thus, folk-lores concerning the bride and bridegroom in the Pardhan community are many. These songs are sung the whole day and night. These songs are of great significance in the life of Pardhans.

**4th Day of Marriage Ceremony**

The number '4' has a great significance in Pardhan community.

The number '5' has achieved significance and sacredness from the compound words such as - "Five Gods Five Principles" Five leaves, etc. from the heroic tale of the great Pandavas. In the same way the number '4' has got prominence and holiness in the community by virtue of its four original deities- Jango, Lingo, Hirajyoti and Manko.

On the 4th day: The whole community assembles in the marriage pandal and all the four rituals of the ceremony are celebrated with great fanfare. In this way this 4th day is significant.

From early in the morning the women of the community invite both bride and the groom for bath and feast. Both of them are forbidden to see the marriage pandal till the time of the marriage. There is also a custom to kidnap and conceal the bride and the bridegroom on this 4th day. Hence a vigilant watch is kept on both on this day.

*The Rite of Angmal*

In the evening when the bridegroom reaches the marriage pandal after his bath there is a programme of his shaving. His sisters collect some of the shaved hair in their Sarees and sing the following song:

"Dadi Angale Wale Bai Behona Li"
Niva Dadika Angika Bada
Bati Dayago Si Ki Ro
Mula Dayejo Sika Nave Behona
Elmi Dayejo Sika Ho
Dadi Anjile Wala Bai Behona
Dhroki Miyale Indanuke Dada
Mhaski Miyale Indaruke Ro
Dadi Angile Wayone Dada
Bati Dayeji Siki Ro
Matya Khoaagora Sika Bai Behona
Dadi Anjile Wale Ho
Gund Ghara Sikabai Behona
Dadi Angile Wala Ho
Sonar Miyale Indaumhe Dada
Kasar Miyale Dauwhe So
Dadi Anjile Wayone Dada
Bati Dayeji Sikrin Ro
Niva Rone Vedabai Bechone
Niva Sagure Weha Ka Ho
Sarg Hatta Kereta Hans
Tane Legata Khaprel Ro
Had Niva Behonana Rone
Nake Akhidange Sikin Ro

*Meaning:* (Bridegroom) come on, oh sister to collect my shaved hair. (Sister) "Dear Brother what will you give me as dowry for the same? (Bridegroom) "I shall give you a cow, a buffalo-but do come? Do not forget. (Sister) oh brother, if you give me a cow, people will call me the daughter of a cowherd. If you give me a buffalo, people will call me the daughter of a buffalo-keeper. So I do not want that gift from you. (Bridegroom): oh sister, I shall then give you golden ornaments of the hand. I shall give you copper ornaments. (Sister): But oh brother, people will call me a daughter of the goldsmith or a coppersmith. I do not want this gift also. What will you give me then, oh, brother. (Bridegroom): Oh sister, tell me the address of your home so that I shall come to your house to invite you. (Sister) There is a grove of tall plantation trees near my house and it has a roof of tiles.

You will come for invitation there. You give me this gift only that you will cherish my memory in your heart for ever".

After this "Angmal" rite, there is a function called "Nahanorang"- The following song is sung on this occasion:

"Tumhare Deso Me Ladi Haldika Dukar
Hamare Deso Me Ladi Haldika Sukar
Tumhare Deso Me Dulera Kukuka Dukar
Hamare Deso Me Dulera Kukuka Sukar".

*The Rite of Munda*

After this "Nahanorang" function, in the midnight the relatives bring the procession of branch of "Moha" tree with great fanfare. This procession consists of men only. The Moha tree is worshipped very cautiously and with all the pooja rites. This is very cautiously done, because some of the technicians of the opposite party may, with the help of their magical Mantras, turn the tree upside down when the man is on the tree. This is a superstition in the community. The purpose of this Moha tree worship is that the deities of the Pardhans are supposed to dwell on the Moha tree. These deities are to be invited for the marriage.

When the Munda reaches the marriage pandal after overcoming all the difficulties on way, there is a programme of folk dance and folk-lores and a game of sticks. the ladies sing aloud the following song:

"Jatiro Bati Riyyone Munda Waya Lata
Mahore Nalenja Mahota, Tahore Malenja Tahota
Riyyona Ladi De, Munda Waya Lata.
Dadana Jodito Riyyor Akhada Dehki Latore
Shindare Man Tuladore Riyyor Akhada Dehki Latore
Marka Foding Kanaknor Riyyor Akhada Dehki Latore
Shetiman Kavalnor Riyyor Akhada Dehki Latore
Gada Chakum Chatitor Riyyor Akhada Dehki Latore
Gada Dhurang Kalkaanore Riyyor Akhada Dehki Latore
Adanmda Dehke For Shindoral De
Adamunda Dehke Shindorel."

*Meaning:* Who are these deities coming in a grand procession?

There are the deities of the bridegroom. The sungod and moongod together have escorted these detieis of the bridegroom.

Who is this brave youth with my brother, who is doing gymnastic feats? The brave youth has a big head hook ears, that young man has eyes as large as a stick of a Manko. His arms are like a beam, his ears like a winnowing fan. He has a chest as big as the wheel of a cart. He is doing the gymnastic. This young man with muscular body is doing the gymnastic feats and who is this mad fellow jumping in between? oh he is that foolish Dhendu.

The Munda branch is tied to the post in the pandal. It is again worshipped with all the techniques and the marriage feast is held after the midnight. After midnight on the '4'th day when the marriage feast is over, both the bride and the groom are dressed and adorned with marriage attire and ornaments. This attiring of the bride, the bridegroom is known as "Chorok". The bride stands attired with the auspicious rice in her hand on a raised platform. The assembled people come one by one and apply tilak on her forehead. The following songs are sung on the occasion:

"Kaheka Chowk Likhayo Babola?
Gulyada Chowk Likhayo Kaniya
Kamkata Chowk Likhayo Kaniya
Chowk Udale Wala Ho Kaniya.

*Meaning:* What is this attire you have woven oh daughter, I am adorned with this "chowk" of turmeric. You come for this attire.

| *Song* | *Meaning* |
|---|---|
| Gylyada Chowk Udone Babola | I do not attire with this coloured powder called Gulal. |
| Gylyale Gulyale Disika Re | I shall look red smeared with gulal only. |
| Kamkata Chowke Udone Babola | I shall also not attire with turmeric powder. |
| Kamkange Kamkange Disika Re | Oh I shall look smeared with turmeric powder. |
| Pairdita Chowk Likhayo Kumari | Oh daughter, I am adorned with flour. |

| | |
|---|---|
| Pichita Chowk Likhayoka Ho | The turmeric paste is ready. |
| Chowk Udale Walabeti Kumari | "Dear, come for adornment. |
| Piudita chowk udore babola | I do not want to be adorned with this turmeric paste. |
| Pidinge Pidinge Disikare | Because I shall look all yellow. |
| Pichita Chowk Udore Babola | I do not adorn myself with flour also. |
| Piching Pichinge Disika Re | I shall appear all flour. |
| Gagmotic Chowk Likhayo Sukhon | oh dear, I have prepared a gaj-mot chowk. |
| Mungamoti Chowk Likhayo Ho | I have prepared a mungamoti chowk. |
| Chowke Udale Wala Beti Sakhon | You, therefore, get ready for adornment. |
| Gajmoti Chowke Udone Ka Doh | Oh father, I do not want this adornment. |
| Gajmyale Gajmyale Disika Re | Oh Aunt! I shall look like Gaj-moti only. |
| Mungamoti Chowke Udone Bawa | I shall not adorn with mun-gamoti also. |
| Mungaje Mungage Disika Re | Because I shall look like Mun-gamudh only. |
| Kukuta Chowke Uda Beti Sukhon | Oh Daughter, please get adorned with 'Kumkum'. |
| Kukunge Kungunge Disika Re | I shall appear like 'Kumkum' only. |
| Julwi Julwa Kasoneka Dou | I do not want these ornaments also. |
| Khagora Sakari Bi Karone Ka Re | I do not put on this 'Khagora' chain also. |
| Bade Chowke Udore Ka Dou | I do not want any adornment. |
| Ana Chowk Udore Re | Oh father I never want any at-tire. |

Like the bride, the bridegroom is also adorned. The following song is sung at that time:

> "Parwarini Bai Wo Pariwarinki Samiya
> Wo Hamara Dulera Chowk Baithe Wo.
> Begi Dhoti Bijawo Send."

"Chamanin Bai Wo, Chamrinki Samiya
Wo Hamara Dulera Chowk Baithe Wo
Begi Surpuk Bigawo
(Begi-soon) (Sarpik = Shoes)
Barito Bai Bario Bariyanki Samiya
Wo Hamra Dulera Chowk Baithe Wo
Begi Kakna Lugawo (Send the Bangles)
Ninkarin Bai Wo Jinkaranki Samiya
Wo Hamara Dulera Chowk Baithe Wo
Begi Basenga Bigawa.
Yebuldin Bai Wo Buldenki Samiya
Wo Hamra Dulera Chowk Baithe Wo
Begi Aduli Bijawa (Aduli Small Basket)
Kaladin Bai Wo Kaladanki Samiya
Wo Hamara Dulera Chowk Bathe Wo
Begi Dary To Bijawa.

After the bridegroom is thus attired with marriage dress people come one by one and apply *Tilak* on his forehead. This function is known as 'Mithusmal' The following song is sung at the time.

| *Song* | *Meaning* |
|---|---|
| There To Bore Amanure Dou More | What is the relation of this young man with Dada. |
| Hore to ayanure dou nore | He seems to be some near relative of him |
| Hore to ayanure tado ye | He is perhaps his grand father. |
| Hore to bore atarame dada be | What is the relation of him with Atram? |
| Nore to amanure tammure ye | He seems to be his real brother. |
| Hore to bore mamrame dadale | What is the relation of Masram with the boy? |
| Hore to ayamure yenale | He is the Boy's cousin." |
| Hore to bore gedam dadale | Who is that Gedam? |
| Hore to ayanure sagbale | He is the husband of his wife's sister. |

In this way, this song is sung, with the names of all such relatives.

Everytime the bridegroom is introduced to the respective relation.

**The Function of "Shig Yetmal"**

Following song is sung at the ritual "Shig Yetmal":

| *Song* | *Meaning* |
|---|---|
| Shigo To Lobhi Bheyale Bainor | Poor Chap, What an avarice of your brother? |
| Save Chakita Shigo Bheyana | Your brother 's share is of one and a quarter of a measure. |
| Shigo Khali Arata | But alas the surplus has spilt down. |
| Bai To Chale, Yenat Mivashigo | This woman has left without accepting your surplus. |
| Shige To Yenwala Hale | Who is that? He is her brother. |
| Thore Ka Bore Ataram Dadale.<br>Hore Ka Ayanure Yenale<br>Shinge To Woyale Indit Dada. | Masrambhau What is his relation to the girl?<br>He is the girl's cousin. He said that she would take her share. |
| Pargana Woyal Indit Re<br>Rone Ka Woyala Indit Re<br>Yenat Miva Rone Ka Dow<br>Yenat Miva Rachaka Re<br>Hulat Miva Pargna Dau<br>Wange To Woyawale Hale. | She would take her land, her house-Oh father, have this, your house, your court-yard-Your land. This daughter of yours would not take anything from you. |

In Pardhan Community, the bride and her party goes to the place of bridegroom for celebrating the marriage. The marriage ceremony is performed in the pandal of the bridegroom. In ancient times the marriage function of the Pardhans was celebrated on the place known as Gothan. Later on it began to be celebrated under a tree. After that it began to be celebrated in the marriage pandal of the bridegroom. It is a custom to perform the ceremony with music on the 5th day. Hence the marriage procession of the bride must reach the marriage place on the mid-night of the 4th day, so that procession must start at night on the 4th day. The following song is sung in the bride's procession.

| *Song* | *Meaning* |
|---|---|
| Nava Yayale Palakhite Ne<br>Nava Don Ye, Honda Te Ne<br>Nava Yavane Almani Simate<br>Shejarin Bai Pajarin Wo<br>Mai Sukhon Chale Koi Parades<br>Elunge Ukak Dohtor Wo Babola Mera<br>Elunge Ukak Ungtaye Wo<br>Nave Awal Mera.<br>"Ajane Dori Alala<br>Aajine Afu Charala<br>Maidharmachi Dudh Pajali<br>Bap Kashtane Udar Bharila<br>Slunge Mattana Samatite Dindal<br>Slunge Pekinnor Waho Dindal<br>Nava Nasibe Dohtor Dindal<br>Mai Sukhon Chale Koi Does<br>Nawa Yowon Alimati Simate<br>Wo Bai Shegarin<br>Nawa Babon Alimati Simate<br>Wo Bai Pajarin | My mother is in the palanquin. My father is seated under a royal canopy. Don't let my mother weep. Oh my neighbour to what unknown land have I setforth?<br><br>My father has prepared for me seven swing. My mother swings me in these seven swings.<br>There is a certain Dindoha who lives in a pass in the Seven hills. he has seven children. I am doomed to live with him. To what strange land, therefore. I have started. Don's let my mother weep. Don't let my father weep. |

**5th Day of the Marriage Ceremony**

On the 5th day of the marriage, early in the morning the marriage procession of the bride reaches the outskirts of the village of the bridegroom. The bride orders a palanquin.

| *Song* | *Meaning* |
|---|---|
| Gasoba Palakhi Roha Ro<br>Cla Ri Hajur<br>Nava Yayal Waya Lata<br>Palakhi Tang Daudange<br>Urng Tage Ladi<br>Ye Nave Begun Sukhon De<br>Niwa Awane Since Wadene Ro<br>Gulami Hajur | Who is present there -Yado or Madho. Tell them to send a palanquin. Our princess is coming, but the rods of the palanquin are broken. On Begumsahebal! Sukhon Rani-tell them to mortgage the Bridegroom's mother to |

Dandange Sudhare Kume Ro
Yadoha Palakhi Roha Ro
Gulami Hajur
Nava Yayal Wine Lata
Palakhi Tonge Nalahe
Namatange Lade
Ye nave begun Sukhon de
Nava selane some khatine
Ro
Gulami Hajur
Nalake Sudhara Kimero
Yadoba Palakhi Roha Ro
Gulami Hajur
Vitate Bheyale Baina
Sakhari Turata.
Vitarbai Vitor Haina
Jodwi Turta
Baina Chale Matona
Bheyare
Bheya Baina Adune Chale
Matona

carpenter, order that slave
to repair these palanquin rods.
Tell someone Yado or Madho
to bring the palanquin-
I am a royal princess coming
here. Oh Begum saheba yet
another part of the palanquin
is broken.
Oh! my Begum Sukhon! Tell
them to mortgage his sister
to an ironsmith. Send a
message to the slave to repair
the broken parts of the
palanquin
Tell some Yado or Madho to
bring the palanquin. Oh Dada!
run up, that woman has lost
her chain. Oh friends run up,
the woman has lost her
bangles. Oh brother, this sister
has left all alone.

This 5th day of the marriage is full of mirth and joy. Today is the auspicious moment of the marriage. The quests from both the camps (of the bride and bridegroom) start coming to the marriage pandal. The day has the appearance of a fair of the Pardhan community.

The procession from the outskirts of the village reaches near the pandal. The bridegroom's relatives wash the bride's feet in a dish. All the guests from the bride's side are cordially received. On this occasion the ladies of the both camps sing satirical songs against each other. These songs are somewhat interesting, romantic and at times obscene also.

*Song*

Valdi Pasiya Bhabhi
Jaldi Pasiya De
Ana Varonage Bawaryana
Watona De De

*Meaning*

Oh sister, you come out of the
house forthwith.
I who am mad after you have
dome

Mani Makma Bhabhi Mani
Makma De
Ana Choudharyal Sotaari
Watona Do
Mani Warima Bhabhi Mani
Sodima De
Ana Mivore Migwane
Watona De
Jaldi Pasiya Bhabhi Jaldi
Pasiya De
Dhodang Mattang Wati Ho
Pale Kamang Titti Ho

Boha Pohrata Yer Utti
Dare Bhabhi Dare
Yer Sehore Mata De

Niwa Patwan Jawane
Watona Ho
Nake Bichhona Wata
Dare Bhabhi Dare
Kal Mihichi Simdhare
Bhabhi Dare Kal Sehore Mata Ro
Thathoro Bungalowo
Bona Ro
He Bapuro, He Raja Ro
Bangta Hulshi Ramtona
De
He Rani He, He Laḍi De
Banglat Paro Nava Haugla

De
Hid Haugala Bahadur Hona
Miyan Ige Bor Borwasi
Ro Leltula
Miyan Ige Hutuml Wasi
Ro Leltula
Miyan Ige Dhokume Wasi

Oh sister, you don't try to hide yourself.
I have come with a special rod.

Oh sister, do not be afraid, do not run away.

I am your husband,
You come out of the house immediately.

You have come from the mountains and rivers. You have eaten the buds of the salai tree.
You have drunk water from some body's pot.
Oh sister, that water has intoxicated you.
I, your lover, have come.
Prepare a bed for me.
Give me a glass of wine.
I am intoxicated with
this wine (of love).

"Whose is this mansion full of romance? Oh Raja, Oh babu attracted by this romantic.
Mansion I have come over here- oh dear, oh my queen, let me step in this mansion of yours–what a romantic mansoon is this!
I have taken possession of this mansion.
Oh! boy, who had come to your mother?
Had a camel come to your Mother?
Had a fox come to your

| | |
|---|---|
| Ro Palatula | mother? |
| Miyan Ige Mhasolal Wasi | Had a buffalo come to your |
| Ro Palatula | mother? |
| Miyan Ige Gadhalyale | Had an ass come to your |
| Wasi Ro Palatula. | mother before your birth? |
| Miyan Ige Borbor Wasi | Who had come to your mother |
| Ro Palatula | before your birth? |
| | Who had cast his shadow on |
| | you? |

Various such songs are sung in this way. These are accompanied by drum-beating and flute. Ladies too standing in a circle perform many kinds of folk dances such as – Sehla, Ghera, Dhemsa and Fagunsar. In the end shouting aloud, "Plli sata, was wata, dhan-gyanna ron re Jamosa"

*Meaning:* "The rat died, the foul smell was spread, all should leave for their scheduled place".

**Sama Kimal**

The marriage preparations are going on in the pandal and the ladies are singing their folk-songs:

| *Song* | *Meaning* |
|---|---|
| Yaya Wo Yaya Indanur | Who is this young man |
| Dadale | |
| Badetariyayane Mutanur | Shouting mother mother |
| Dadale | |
| Bachoda Samon Niwa Ata | To whom is he lodging his |
| Yayawo? | complaints? Oh mother, What |
| Sawwa Khandita Saman Niva | worth is your marriage |
| Ataro Beta | preparation? |
| Navo Kuwarani Ro? | Oh son, it is worth one and |
| Dawaoka Jodyana Miyani | quarter Khandi. My dear son |
| Yoyawo | do not be afraid- Oh mother |
| Ime Damo Jode Kite Yaya Wo | Your are the daughter of |
| Nikun Kolyal Tatti Ku Wo | money worshipper-hence you |
| Daw Do Re Dawdo Beta | saved money and made |

Warat Dekho Re
Warat Kya Dekhun Wo Ma
Faoujfata Wo
Ate To Anedeo Beta, Mai
Denewali Khadi
Nawav Duleha Re Mai
Denewali Khadi
Dewdo Re Beta, Dewdo Re Hat
Pakalo Re
Birane Ki Beti O Ma, Kaise
Pakadu Wo
Hato Ka To Dam Dija Hat
Padado Re
Pawo Ka To Dam Dija,
Par Kudo Re

preparation for the marriage.
You have thus brought
into house your favourite
dang.

Such songs go on, the bride eats in the pandal. The bridegroom has to open the fist of bride with one hand. Then he puts an iron ring into the finger of the bride. He also ties a Garsory of black beeds round the bride's neck. The bridegroom has to face many tests from the bride. It is a special feature of the Pardhan Community. These tests of the bridegroom are at the behest of the bride. If the custom is age old, and from then we can infer that they have then method of "Choice of the husband by the girl herself" from ancient times.

**Tarhar Kanyadan**

The rite of the offer of the daughter in marriage.

All the people assemble in the marriage hall. In the centre, the marriage performing priest occupies his seat and declares' the marriage to have been performed. The men and women in the assembly throw the auspicious grains (The grains of Jawar mixed with turmeric and Kumkum) over the bride and bridegroom. At this time ladies sing the following chorus. This folk lore is the peculiar marriage song of five verses in the Pardhan Community.

The Five verses are following of great significance and of importance in the Pardhan community.

**The Peculiar Marriage Song**

| *Song* | *Meaning* |
|---|---|
| i. Ma Dou Waudur Ladi<br>Savati Udanul De<br>Tarhar Kanyadan | "When my father used to come to used to sit in the shade-Let this marriage be auspicious" |
| ii. Mi Don Wandur Ladi<br>Dhadmitine Under De<br>Ganja Ghote Kundur De.<br>Tarhar Kanyadan | "Oh dear when your father used to come here he used to sit in the sun and prepare his gania (A kind of intoxicant like opium) Let this marriage be auspicious". |
| iii. Mi Douna Nali De Ladi<br>Ullina Gangi De Ma<br>Douna Malide Ladi<br>Sonotange Kamdi<br>Tarhar Kanyadan. | "Oh dear, there is a rosary of onions tied to the waist of your father. Whereas my father tied round his waist a golden chain. Let this marriage be auspicious. |
| iv. Mi Dou Paisa Lobhi<br>Nikun Hare Matur De<br>Niwood Neli Udmur De<br>Tarhar Kanyadan | "Your father is greedy for money He has lost you, your father is a heavy indulger in Gania smoking and has sat under a Hiwra tree. Let this marriage be auspicious. |
| v. Suno Narmada Suno Re Ganga<br>Suno Nagari Ke Lok De<br>Niwa Kaya Nava Kayade<br>Tarhare Kanyadan. | "Oh Narmada, Oh Ganga, you hear and you gentlemen, be witness and hear. Your hands are in mine, let this marriage be auspicious. |

**Gargare Uma Dada Awala**

As soon as the bridegroom holds the hands of the bride, there is clapping from the assembled guests. The priest is ahead, his small finger held by bridegroom. Bridegroom's finger is held by the bride, bride's finger is held by the leading woman. At the rear are two ladies carrying two earthen lamps on their heads. This procession moves round the altar. All these members of the marriage procession move round many posts of the pandal with the accompaniment of drums and flute music. If anyone frees his finger then the procession stops moving.

Gargare Uma Dada Awala song comes after the peculiar five verses of marriage ceremony song of the Pardhan.

| *Song* | *Meaning* |
|---|---|
| Sai Gor Gor Uma Dada<br>Awala<br>Sum Gargar Uma Ga<br>Walle Chudur Inma Dada<br>Awala<br>Walle Fala Inma Ga Fala Zap Wata<br>Dada Awala Nail Lacheke Kita Ga<br>Navshika Manda Dada Awala<br>Bijad Bajad Auta Ga<br>Kure Kalhe Manda Dada<br>Wala.<br>Mal Muhre Munda Ga<br>Pitte Mendul Manda Awala<br>Poni Leg Manda Ga | "Oh dada, move your sister quickly round the altar. Do not suppose her to be too young or too old. Oh brother, take longer steps. Look her waist is bending. She is a novice and seems to be confused. She has deer like swift legs. Her face is like that of a peacock. Her body is like a sparrow. Her voice, however, is very low-pitched like a cotton wick". |

**Balang Ahir**

The gifts and presents, received by the bride and bridegroom from the guests and relatives are known as "Tikang". Some of the cloth received by them is distributed amongst the Chief relatives of both of them on that very day. The following song is sung at this time.

| *Song* | *Meaning* |
|---|---|
| Kaika Kakaji Wale Re<br>Mani Ine Anmane Mamabeta<br>Rajannor Marini<br>Nivor Babo Water Ro<br>Dulehe<br>Belong Ahir Tattor Ro<br>Biwa Bija Jode Kitor Ro<br>Rajanor Marini<br>Mani Ine Anmane Manea Beta. | "Oh, you belong to a large royal family. Do not be shy. "Oh Prince, your father has come. What is the present he has brought for your sake? He has produced you and shown you this world. Oh prince, do not be shy. Your grandfather too has come. |

| | |
|---|---|
| Niwaor Todo Water Beta<br>Belong Ahir Tattor Ro<br>Hadeng Ugwe Kitor Ro<br>Rajanor Marini.<br>Mani Ine Anmane Beta. | What gift has be brought for<br>You; He has created your<br>bones. Oh Prince donot be<br>sky. |

**Chudure Usaro Pitte** (The poor sparrow)

The most pathetic scene in the Pardhan Marriage is the one of taking leave of the bride by her relatives. After the ceremony with all its entertainments are over, the bride, bridegroom are made to sit on the lap and are blessed. The Pardhans celebrate the occasion namely Chudure Usaro Pitte in a unique way. This rite is known as "Korate Upusmal" so tragic is the occasion that the bride, and the bridegroom and their relatives shed continuous tears. The tunes of the flute become full of pathos. The ladies sing the following pathetic song:

| *Song* | *Meaning* |
|---|---|
| Paro Inga Sahote Miwa<br>Teri Doure<br>Khalwo Sahote Bhailola<br>Doure<br>Neva Teri Niwa Korate<br>Doure<br>Natite Bhailola Korate Re | Oh father, parents, love is in-<br>comparable. People's love is<br>very showy. To-day I enjoy<br>your company for the last<br>time but from tomorrow I<br>shall bend under the burden of<br>the strangers. |
| Chudare Usaripitte Douna<br>Korate<br>Douna Koratal Partiale<br>Usaripitte<br>Zado Zadi Alal | This beautiful poor sparrow<br>bride is to-day under the<br>origin love of her father. But<br>she will soon fly away and<br>weep through forests".<br>To-day this sparrow is happy<br>in the lap of her mother. |
| Chudure Usaripitte<br>yayana Korate<br>Yayana Koratal Piritale<br>Usaripittee<br>Zado Zadi Alal | But she will soon fly away and<br>weep through forests.<br><br>This sparrow is in the sweet<br>company of her brother, but<br>she will now fly away, and |

| | |
|---|---|
| Chudure Usaripitte<br>Dadana Korate<br>Dadana Koratal Piritale<br>Usaripittee<br>Zado Zadi Alal | weep through forests. |

This young bride is very much like this poor sparrow. Sitting on the lap of her relatives, she weeps very much. She feels the impending separation with her near and dear ones. The relatives too are full of sorrow. The bride takes leave of her relatives one by one. The relatives give her a rupee or two for sweets. In the end she comes and sits on the father's laps. After that she goes and sits on the lap of her father-in-law. In this way this leaving-taking function comes to an end.

**Bhetuni**

After taking the bride with him, the bridegroom bows to his father-in-law and mother-in-law. He then bows to all the elderly guests and relatives present there and takes their leave. This occasion is called "Bhetuni"-or the leave taking ceremony. The song sung at the time of leave taking occasion is as follows:

| *Song* | *Meaning* |
|---|---|
| Hore To Ayanure Mulyale<br>Gape Kalke Karana<br>Hore To Ayanure Tainulyale<br>Gape Kalke Karana<br>Hade To Ayale Porale<br>Gope Kalke Karana<br>Hade To Ayale Tangorale<br>Lake Kalke Karana | "He is your father-in-law,<br>bow to him. He is your<br>elder brother-in-law, bow<br>to him. She is your mother-<br>in-law, bow to her. She is<br>your arrogant mother-in-law,<br>bow to her from a safe<br>distance." |

The bride's procession turns back after taking leave and leaving the bride with her new relatives. The ladies of the bridegroom's side sing the following song:

| *Song* | *Meaning* |
|---|---|
| Warke masi sarke mayalata<br>Late De Bhabhi Dare<br>Bakara Khaun Takkar Marun<br>Jate<br>Jate De Bhabhi Dare<br>Maske Masi Dhaska Jiya<br>Lata<br>Lata De Bhabhi Dare<br>Gitke Kisi Milka Jiya<br>Lata<br>Lata De Bhabhi Dare<br>Atake Masi Satke Maya<br>Lata<br>Lata De Bhabhi Dare<br>Warke Masi Sarke Mayalata<br>Lata De Bhabhi Dare | "The newly wedded bride knows us and yet tries to be away from us. She is moving away from us. She has eaten meat and wants to dash, she has become angry and she wants to knock. She has eaten (Meat) with great taste. She has joined us and wants to flee away. She knows us all and yet she wants to hide from us. |

After celebrating the whole marriage ceremony of five days with great fanfare, on the 6th Day the turmeric paste applied to the ladies, of the newly wed, is wiped off, and they are let free. This function is called "Pichi Usamal". This function is held in the pandal of the bridegroom. This function is attended solely by the near relatives of the bridegroom.

| *Song* | *Meaning* |
|---|---|
| Teda Bhabhi De<br>Kor Kusta, Fal Walita<br>Teda Bhabhi De(Refrain)<br>Teda Riyor Wo<br>Kait Paro Kal Waltor<br>Teda Siyor Wo<br>Teda Siyor Wo<br>Kad Paro Kal Waltor<br>Teda Siyor Wo<br>Teda Bhabhi De | "Oh sister-in-in, law, get up the cock crows the day dawns. Get up soon (Refrain)<br>Oh! but my husband does not allow me to get up. He has placed his hand on mine.<br>He has placed his legs on mine He does not allow to me to get up. Oh! sister-in-law get up soon. |

**Deva-Devi**

After turmeric paste-removal ceremony the family deities of the bride and bridegroom, are worshipped at their hands. During this worship the newly-wed couple is introduced to the other members of the family. Ancestral history is told and the family tradition is let known. This ritual of family worship is called "Deva-Devi". They offer sweets to the Gods and Goddess and then distribute it. With this the marriage function ends.

During the course of data collection the respondents and other informants of the area under this work, told the author that the traditional pattern of performing the marriage for continuous five days is gradually disappearing and the attitude of completing it at the most within two days is a new trend that has been adopted as a new pattern by the Pardhans of Vidarbha.

# 5

# The Family Structure

Though family is the basic unit of social organization, the term itself remains one of the most loosely defined in the vocabulary. E.W. Burgess and H.J. Locke in their book *The Family* (1953) attempted a definition of the family in the following words:

> "The family is a group of persons united by the ties of marriage, blood, or adoption; constituting a single household, interacting and inter communicating with each other in their respective social role of husband and wife, mother and father, brother and sister; creating a common culture".

The family is the basic and universal social institution. It fulfils needs and performs functions which are indispensable for the continuity, integration and change in social system. In one sense the whole social system begins with the family because the society is a living entity that must continually be replenished. In societies of all types the family is fundamental multipurpose organisation for many of the principal life functions of the individual and of society.

The nature and composition are important aspects of family in every society but more important in context of the tribal community. Family has been the very foundation from the tribal social structure. It plays a very decisive role in all aspects of their collective and co-operative living. The family is a "multi-functional" unit in the tribal societies. All the important functions, namely socialization of children, status assignment, economically productive unit, division of labour based mostly on sex and age, political, religious and educational functions are centered round this fundamental unit of tribal social structure. Therefore, any study pertaining to Tribal community cannot afford to leave out of consideration this most nearly universal human group, namely, the family. Historically, the joint family has been considered characteristic of Indian life. The large joint families have always existed in India. The nature and composition of family are generally embedded in the character of relationship and the nature of economic activities being pursued by a community. Tribal societies being simple in way of life with collective and co-operative economic activities, the large and joint family in its ideal form could exist.

**Traditional Joint Family in India**

In order to understand the nature and composition of the family structure in the tribe under study, it is necessary first to sketch the traditional attributes of joint family in Indian society. Sociologists and anthropologists have made a closed study of the characteristics of the joint family in India. They have noted the basic structural, psycho-social and functional features of the type of family in India. In order to do this we shall adopt here Iravati Karve's definition of the Joint family which is one of the most precise and comprehensive. "A Jointfamily is a group of people who generally live under one roof, who eat food cooked at one hearth, who hold property in common and who participate in common family worship and are related to each other as same particular type of Kindred "[1] I P Desai adds, common income as well as properties, and also stresses mutual rights and obligations.[2] On the basis of the above definition of the Joint family an outline of the attributes of Joint family will be as follows:

1. The members of the Joint family generally live under one roof. The traditional family household was composed of a number of separate family units living under one roof. The whole family used to share the common roof for all the living activities.
2. A common kitchen was another important characteristic feature of a joint family. Cooking was considered to be a common activity of the family. The whole family used to share the food cooked at the common hearth.
3. The traditional joint family was both producing and consuming unit. The production and consumption were familistic. There was also a common purse into which all members put their earnings. The senior male member of the traditional joint family usually manages the family's finances. Sometimes the eldest son, who takes over the management of the

properties on the father's death, will be assisted by his mother. The property of the joint family passed down in a strictly prescribed way from father to son.

4. Participation of members in common family worship is one of the striking features of the Indian Joint family. Each family has its own Gods, which help to bind that perticular family. All important family events and festivals are deeply steeped in religious rituals and ceremonies and daily family worship has always been a part of family routine. Religious and other ceremonies have for their object the security and prosperity of the family. Even the relationship between the Gods and Goddesses are familistic, they being related to one another as father, mother, brother, sister etc. In the traditional joint family religious and ceremonial rites are performed, when all the members of the family gather together and the eldest the 'Karta' has the controlling voice in the affairs of the family.
5. The joint family is far more homogeneous, stable, integrated and organically functioning group. The ties binding the members of the family, for instance, the husband and the wife, parents and children are stronger and last longer.
6. Joint families being homogeneous, compact unit, strengthen emotions of solidarity and co-operation among the family members. They develop more collectivistic family consciousness and less individualistic emotions. There is greater interdependence among the members of the family.

Therefore, ideally speaking, traditional family is a corporate group whose members act together to meet their common purposes. Typically they live in the same house and eat food prepared in the same kitchen, they work together, put their income, expenditure and property and perform religious rituals as a family.

The large joint family is characterized by intimacy, mutuality of interest, strong, primary group controls mutual assistance in times of need. It is a system which strongly limits social mobility and social change because it binds the individuals to others on the basis of birth, and forces him to contribute to the support of a large group independently of their ability. In the joint family, affection as well as dependence are diffused among so many relatives. Each family and kin position is a complex of detailed duties and rights, attitudes, sentiments and expectations which must be carefully balanced if the whole unit is to function effectively.

The large family is eminently suited to a stable society in which life is relatively simple and there has as yet been no need to develop separate institutions to care for the needs of the group. It means the large joint families were best suited to such societies where the economic activities were collective and co-operative endeavours. As stated earlier the nature and composition of family are deeply embedded in the character of economic and social organization of the community, author will see how the large family norm was adequately suited to the tribe under study.

**Traditional Family Among the Pardhans**

In the light of the nature of traditional joint family in the Indian society; a description of the traditional family among the Pardhans with its similarities and differences from the Indian joint family will not be out of context. Since the Pardhans traditionally lived as priests, Pujaris and musicians and consequently had nomadic way of life, joint families are very common among them. The large and joint families seemed to have worked effectively in the past owing to typical way of living and their traditional order.

The traditional economic activities of the tribe were based on solidarity among the members of the family as well as the tribe and it also involved risk. Therefore, joint families have become more or less common feature among the Pardhans.

The typical Pardhans joint family consists of a man and his wife, his sons and their wives and children, his daughters until they are married. The Pardhans are patrilineal and patrilocal in residence. The general practice among the Pardhans is that the sons after their marriage continue to live in the family of their parents with their wives and children. After the death of the father, the property can be divided, if they so desire, equally among the sons. Some of the respondents, during field investigations, have remarked that so long as the father (the head of the family) is alive, sons have no right to be separated, it is only after the death of the head of the family, the sons can think of separating themselves, if they so desire. A similar thing is also observed in the study of the Tikopian family by Raymond Firth. "The household in Tikopia usually includes more than one nuclear family. Sometimes two brothers with their wives and children live together each taking a section floor. More often the man will have his unmarried brothers and sisters or his father and mother, living with him. On the other hand more than two nuclear families live together since the rule is that brothers divide their property, if any, at the death of their father, specially if all are married."[3] Women among the Pardhans families do not inherit the property rights. As long as the family remains undivided it is regarded as joint in food, worship and estate. Family is an economic unit. All the members of the family including the aged and children participate in some kind of traditional economic activity and contribute to the maintenance of the family. Economically the entire family functions through the common pooling of resources and their utilization according to demands of all its members. As a result of this, each member has a share in the property and the expenditure. The father is the head of the family. He is the owner of the property. The traditional joint family among the Pardhans approximates to a great extent the ideal model of traditional Hindu Joint Family. There are striking similarities in terms of the attributes of joint family as mentioned by renowned sociologists. The attributes such as common property and common participation in the economic activities are predominantly noticed among the Pardhans. All the members of the family eat food cooked at the common health. They have common cooking activity in which all the members (sometimes the male members) are seen engaged in it. All the members of the family, though separated for particular period of time for doing their economic activities, do participate in the rituals and ceremonies performed by the members of the family. During interview with some of the respondents it was remarked that the members of the family were expected as a matter of tradition to participate in the functions, social and religious of the family. Non-participation would mean that he had been separated from the parental family. This shows that common participation of members of rituals and ceremonies is one of the striking features of the Pardhans joint family. The Pardhans joint family appears to be a very diffused family in terms of intimacies among the members and mutual obligation of the members towards family. There is one striking difference between an ideal pattern of a joint family and the joint family among the Pardhans. Historically speaking, there was no concept of common roof as these people were in nomadic phase and had no houses of their own. They used to have a small tent which was being used for storing their belongings and all other activities centering around the family used to be performed in the open in front of those tents. It was more of a collective and community living. There was no clear-cut division of labour among the members of the family and it was basically an economic unit. The family activities were performed jointly or collectively. There seemed to be very little separation of family activities. It was only after the father became feeble and incapable of managing the family affairs, that the eldest son takes over the family affairs. Thus, the joint family affairs among the Pardhans represent an ideal model of the Hindu Joint family in terms of the common residence, common kitchen and common participation in the rituals. The joint family among the Pardhans is far more homogeneous, stable, integrated and organically functioning. The tribes in India still remain a cluster of joint families, though being influenced through the impact of industrial-urban growth. The family structure among those people is composed not only of the members of the family but also frequently includes distant relations.

It has been stated that the traditional joint family structure of the Pardhans tribe is being subjected to the domination of developing urban economy of Vidarbha area being thrown into such unfamiliar situations that consequently there has been modifications in their social and cultural values. The traditional family structure of the Pardhans seems to be under transformation giving rise to new adaptive structures of adjustment. It is not therefore, surprising that the urban way of life is slowly but steadily pushing its way into the social pattern of life of the Pardhans of Vidarbha, replacing some of their characteristics of traditional family.

Prof. K.M. Kapadia has also shown that in modern times the circumstances are changing. This itself can be called a new factor to reckon with. He deals with the impact of urbanization on the Indian family. Urbanization in his view is an important factor in all social change. Adjustments have to be made quickly and there is the possibility that more concessions will be made to the circumstances than under the situation of slow change. New circumstances bring with them a new cultural element inimical to the traditional element. This new element is referred to by various names such as the Philosophy of individualism, nationalism etc.[4] The author task is to find out how far the situation in the institutions of the family can be described as the adjustment of traditional culture element to the new circumstances.

## A Few Studies on the Changing Family Structure

Anthropological and sociological analyses usually regard the structural components of societies as being so closely interrelated that the change in any part of the system would have repercussions in all other parts. Hoselitz and Moore have stated that, "If a model of extreme functional interdependence is adopted, the characteristics of any component of the system would determine the characteristics of all others".[5]

Sociologists might review a few major trends of structural changes in the family in India. The transition from extend family based society to nuclear family based society in essence is an example of structural family change. This involves systematic changes in the role structures through processes of differentiation. Compared to an extended family the combinations of the role structures in nuclear family are fewer. The net works of kinship relations are also different. A nuclear family is itself an example of structural differentiation from the more composite social structure of an extended family. Changes are now taking place in the traditional family forms. This bears significant relationship with the direction of social change and modernization in India. Wherever the economy expands through industrialization, family patterns change, extended kinship ties weaken, lineage patterns dissolve, and a trend towards some form of conjugal system generally begins to appear. Then the nuclear family becomes a more independent kinship unit. Modern commentators have reported this process from many parts of the world.[6]

The studies concerning the distribution of family types (structurally) in India show results which considerably fluctuate on the basis of criteria employed for the classification of jointness. The jointness among the members of the family has been defined in terms of residence, property and mutual obligation among the kin. It has also been explained with reference to the nature and quality of social interaction which involves in it sentimental bonds, ritual and economic obligations to other family units. The families may be functionally joint in obligational ties. Family jointness still continues to be a major sociological phenomenon in the Indian Social Structure. Greater degree of jointness was observed co-existing with agriculture as well as business and other occupations and it was found that the "longer urban stay did not dissolve jointness". The findings of K.M. Kapadia support the conclusions of I.P. Desai[7]

K.M. Kapadia found that the joint family pattern was not only predominant, but stronger in the towns. Kapadia concludes that "not only the total complement of the joint family is higher in the town but even its size is larger there than in the rural areas. In M.S. Gore's study among the Agarwals in Delhi, three fourths preferred the joint family but only 54 per cent believed that brothers should continue to live together after the death of the parents. It has been observed by I.P. Desai and other sociologists that nuclear family in India is merely a stage in the joint family cycle. S.C. Dube makes the following observations on this point,

> Simple families grow into extended families and then break up into simple families again. A simple family emerging out of this process may retain some adhesions from the former extended family. The changes from simple to extended and extended to simple are fairly frequent. Nevertheless, Indian values and attitudes are still generally in favour of the joint family and that a number of important structural changes in the joint family are occurring.[8]

A wider picture of the changes in the family structure in India can be obtained only by comparative regional studies. Kolenda analyses, "the factors which could possibly be associated with the predominance of joint family in one region or in one group and that of the nuclear in another. She concludes that neither economic explanation nor classical Hindu Law, nor caste identity nor ownership of land, nor the dominant or subservient status of castes has a universal association with preponderance of joint family types".[9] The basis for structural limitations as clearly recognised by Murdock and other Anthropologists who have made comparative studies of social structure, lies in the existential situations or the material and economic resources which could be commanded by social units with in and outside the family structure.

The changes have also been observed in the internal structure of families in India which A.D. Ross describes as the sub-structure of rights and duties, of power and authority and of sentiment and work. In her study of the upper and middle class urban families in Bangalore, Ross finds that with the increasing strain of new types of activities in urban context many traditional forms of family role expectations are changing. Children now often tend to be more independent on certain issues; traditional division of labour between man and wife breaks down in an urban nuclear family as the husband has to share some work which was traditionally the duty of the wife. From the point of view of authority, the family still continues to be the most important institution for enforcement of discipline and its authority remains strong. Transition from joint to nuclear families also alters the nature of affection and sentiments in the interpersonal relationships of family members, altering the very structure of traditional joint family sentiments. But changes in this sphere of the family are rather slow.[10]

> Changes in the structure of families have also been reported in the matrilineal Tarvada families of Kerala, where accumulation of private property, growth of business connections or higher education prompt a person of the younger generation to establish a separate home for himself, his wife and children, away from the traditional Tarvada from the joint family.[11]

In the light of the above mentioned studies, it was hypothesized that during the period of economic development "The multifunctional family structure changes into several more specialized structures" (Separation, differentiation and more specific role structures emerge). As the family is stripped of its economic functions, there emerges a setting for institutionalization of relatively autonomous economic systems that exhibit a greater emphasis on values like universalism, functional specificity and rationality.

The joint family seems to give way to nuclear family but even that is not suitable to their way of living. But in the present context author may say that the husband, wife, and children type of family structure is emerging in terms of residential and compositional pattern. Thus, the structural transformation of large joint families of the Pardhans may be attributed to economic reasons as the members of the family are pursuing new economic activities in the area of occupations. It shows mere separation in terms of residence of large families into small units; but this does not imply that the jointness is declining. The separation may be due to occupational and economic exigencies.

To substantiate the above arrangement the views of I.P. Desai may be given here, "The phenomenon of structural changes in the joint family on the basis of incidence of structural differentiation from joint to nuclear families is rather vague. What matters more is not the composition of the residential family group but the nature and the quality of social interaction emanating from the supposedly nuclear family which interlinks it in sentimental bonds, rituals and economic obligations to other family units in the same place".[12] Therefore the trends of nuclearity among the Pardhans may be attributed to the reasons of occupational necessity. However, it was observed that the members of the constituents households consider themselves duty bond to meet on occasions such as the celebrations of Dussehra, Diwali and especially Holi festivals and marriage ceremonies.

Such occasions keep feelings for joint family activities. But it has been observed during field work that the occasions for such family obligations are decreasing in the changed context and joint family sentiments will be weakened in consequence.

In the light of the above, two probable conclusions are, that the majority as a whole still largely conforms to the pattern of joint family living in behaviour and attitudes. The second is, within this overall pattern of conformity, separation in residence and new occupations, do seem to introduce a slight trend towards small family from among the Pardhans of Vidarbha. The direction of this trend is indicated more clearly in the study on the position of the family structure. It also indicates the affirmation of traditional patterns of behaviours in the acceptance of family obligations, the continuance of the pattern ot collective living on ritualistic occasions and in terms of mutual obligations and property.

**Inter-personal Relations within the Family**

Family relations are changing as a result of overall transformation in the structure of family. As described earlier that the Pardhans have large joint families having at least three generation depth, the family being basically the unity of interaction personalities, the observations were focussed on certain set of relationships. The family in the context of tribal society is a multi-dimensional functional unit. It is a functional unit in the sense that all the significant functions are centred round the basic and fundamental institution. Conversations with a few respondents revealed that the people of the tribe are proud of large joint families because large families have been associated with more economic gains and domination over the members of the tribe. However, the structure of family is in the process of transformation as a result of the interaction of the Pardhans with other tribals and also non-tribals of the area under study in particular and with Vidarbha in General.

### Husband-Wife Relationship

Husband-wife relationship shows variations according to the economic activities pursued by the family. However, the husband is generally the head and the master of the household. He enjoys the highest status in the family and he has by virtue of his position the major say in the affairs of the family. This is only due to the fact that the nature of the family among the Pardhans is patriarchal and patrilocal. The wife is expected to be submissive and to pay respect to the husband in the usual manner. Wives are expected to be faithful to their husbands. The husband is of course in a superior position. It should not be assumed that women are looked down upon but do enjoy a status in the family.

There appears to be no clear cut division of responsibilities between the husband and wife. The husband is responsible for the maintenance of family. Household duties are exclusively done by the wife and very little assistance is given in such duties by the husband. It is noteworthy here, that even though household duties are managed by wife, when the wife is outside for economic activities such as begging or any other petty economic activities, the cooking is managed by the husband or the young children under supervision and guidance of the husband or some male member in the family. Sometimes he prepares it independently when the wife is away on economic activities. This appears to be an internal adjustment among the members of the family, particularly the husband-wife relationship, as the women also contribute economically. Though the care of the children is primarily the responsibility of the wife, the husband must sometimes take a hand. There appears to be an adjustment on the part of the husband in connection with the household responsibilities of the wife. The relationship between the husband and wife appears to be quite informal and less reservations are observed in their personal and family relations. The wife has a sense of freedom in her relationship to her husband. However, wife takes the permission of husband in all important matters of the family including the economic activities being pursued by them. The power of the husband over the wife was clear in several cases when the husbands were seen abusing and even beating their wives in the locality. However, it should not be inferred that women have no authority in family affairs. They are observed being consulted on matters of family concern, wives are in a way an economic asset to the entire family even though the wives contribute to the income of the family. It has been observed that all the funds and expenses are controlled by the husband to a large extent. Drinking liquor is very common among the Pardhans, wives also join their husbands in drinking country liquor. There seem no restrictions regarding drinking in this tribe. If the wife is suspected of having illicit relationship with an outsider, or other than the husband, she is severely punished. It means adultery is considered to be a severe offence in this tribe. It is due to the fear of punishment or harsh treatment by the husband, that the women are submissive and obedient. The women are not shy; but free and frank with outsiders also. Women are observed gossiping about their contacts with outsiders particularly about the tricks used in befooling them while doing their economic activities.

Even though there have been changes in the structure of family organization of the Pardhans, they seem to have a traditional outlook on the husband-wife relationship. This traditional pattern of relationship between the husband and wife appears to be strong among the Pardhans.

**Parents and Children**

The relationship between the father and son appeared to be more intimate and affectional because he could help and protect the family from the enemies and the outside world. He would also be an economic asset. He not only brings income through his work, but he might eventually become the family's economic support. Field observations revealed that the birth of a son was a matter of happiness for the entire family. The members of the tribe also cherish certain superstition about this. Russell and Hiralal in their book *Tribes and Castes of Central Provinces of India*, Vol. IV mention, "After the birth of a child the mother and another woman stood on opposite sides of the cradle and the former tossed her child to the other commending it to the mercy of Jai Gopal, and waited to receive it back in like manner in the name of Jai Govind. Both Gopal and Govind are names of Krishna".[13] The relationship pattern within the family shows that the children are looked after by the mother. When the parents are out for economic activities, the children within the age group of 4-8 years are mostly left to themselves in the locality for their socialization. Many a time the children are left uncared for and unattended by the parents. The parents seem to have no concept of cleanliness and the young kids in the family are seen without adequate clothes on their bodies. The parents show no concern about this mainly due to their ignorance and typical tribal style of living. The parents appear to be not concerned with the education of their children. The nomadic way of living was an important hurdle in the way of children's education. Another reason as stated by respondents was the nature of their new non-traditional economic activities which required constant help of all the members of the family and consequently the children are not encouraged to go to school. Mostly the children within the age group of 8-14 years accompany their mother for their new economic activities, mostly begging and quarrying etc.

The relationship between parents and children appears to be extremely informal, free and frank. The children do not seem to be scared of the parents. They are also expected to participate in new-non-traditional economic activities. They are also found sharing with parents family matters very frankly without any reservations. Inspite of such informality between the parents and children, the parents are highly respected and obeyed by them. When directed by parents for doing certain household duties, the children are expected to carry out household responsibilities ungrudgingly. Even the married sons consult their parents and refer to them all their problems. Thus parents seem to be chief advisors and counsellors for them. The children have been given freedom to pursue their economic activities independently. The head of the family still yields power in the family structure among the Pardhans.

## REFERENCES

1. Karve, Iravati, *Kinship Organization in India*, Poona, 1953, p. 5.
2. Desai, I.P., *Some Aspects of Family in Mahuwa: A Sociological Study Jointness in a Small Town*, Asia, Bombay, 1965.
3. Fifth, Raymond, *We the Tikopia*, 1957.
4. Kapadia, K.M., *Marriage and Family in India*. Oxford University Press, Bombay, 1966.
5. Hoselitz and Moore, *Industrilization and Society*, 1963, p. 136.

6. Goode, W.J., *The World Revolution and The Family Patterns*. Free Press of Glencoe, New York, 1963, p. 6.
7. Singh, Yogendra, *Modernization of Indian Traditions*, the quotation I.P. Desai, 1973, p. 177.
8. Singh, Yogendra, *Modernization of Indian Traditions*, the quotation I.P. Desaid, 1973, p. 178.
9. Kolenda, P.M., (Ed.) Regional Differences in India Family Structure, Quoted by Yogendra Singh in *Modernization of Indian Traditions*, 1973, p. 179.
10. Ross, A.D., *Hindu Family in its Urban Setting*, Oxford University Press, Bombay, 1961.
11. Singh, Yogendra, *Modernization of Indian Traditions*, 1973.
12. Singh, Yogendra, *Modernization of Indian Traditions*, Quotation by I.P. Desai, 1973, p. 177.
13. Russell R.V. and Hiralal, R.B., *Tribes and Castes of Central Provinces of India*, Vol. IV, 1916, p. 192.

# 6

# Religion and Rituals

This chapter deals with the religious, ritualistic and cultural aspects of the life of Pardhans. In and for the conduct of his daily life man has evolved certain mechanisms. There are his economic organization and technology. There are his responses to himself i.e. to his own biological needs, and bring him into particular contact with his natural environment. His relations to other human beings, necessitated by the need to organize, (without doing which no basic drive can be satisfied) are made possible by language, education and social organizations and are controlled by political organization. Then there is religion, it is the human response to the apprehension of some thing, or power, which is supernatural and suprasensory. It is the expression of the manner and type of adjustment effected by a people with their conception of the supernatural. Religion had been regarded as a product of civilization until E.B. Tylor[1] gave convincing proof that primitive societies have their own versions of religious activity, not very different from that of civilized societies. Ever since Tylor's views were published no ethnographer or anthropologist has reported any primitive society without religious beliefs and practices.

All religions consist of a mental attitude regarding the supernatural. The most widespread manifestation of this attitude is in the shape of beliefs and rituals, the former often wrongly called myths. What we call myths are believed in by the people to whom they belong, and are therefore better designated as religious belief or beliefs. All religions, primitive and modern have this base of belief and ritual. Ritual consists in the observance, according to a prescribed manner, of certain actions designed to establish liaison between the performing individual and the supernatural power or powers. Beliefs are the chapter for the rituals, as also a rationalization of the same.

A text-book knowledge of the religious lore of India, and an acquaintance with her ancient classics and their modern exposition will hardly give one a true picture of the actual religious beliefs, thoughts, feelings and practices of the people living the country. A classification of the beliefs and rituals is not an easy task. Folk-lore and myths, religious teachings of the saint-poets, and contacts with persons having knowledge of scriptures and popular religious books have all influenced the religious ideology, and consequently the religion is a mixture of animism, animatism and polytheism. To these must be added the living faith in spirits, ghosts, demons, witches, and magic. The complex of all these diverse factors constitute the picture of the supernatural world as it is understood by the people, to which they call religion.

The concept of Dharma, which has often been translated by western writers as 'Religion', hardly conveys the original meaning of the word Dharma, which covers all the phases of the human life-cycle and fixes several details of intra and intergroup life. Therefore, it will perhaps be more appropriate to describe the term religion as, "the way of life".

In order to collect the information about the religion from the respondents i.e. the Pardhans of Vidarbha in general and from the areas selected for the book in particular, a question, to which religion you belong? was put to them. The answer received, falls under three categories viz. (a) Hindu (b) Gondi and (c) Tribal.

Since there is no specific mention of the Gondi and tribal religion in any of the text book, knowledge of the religious lore of India, and acquaintance with her ancient classics and their modern expositions, as also in the *Census of India* 1961 Vol. X Maharashtra Part V-A Scheduled Castes and Scheduled Tribes in Maharashtra Tables, one always gets into some kind of a doubt about answers received from the respondents, that, 'their religion is either Gondi or Tribal'. At the same time there is a sufficient ground to believe them when the Pardhans say that they belong to Hindu religion. The Pardhans generally worship their tribal Gods and Goddesses as well as Hindu Gods and Goddesses and observe almost the same rituals and rites and celebrate all the major Hindu festivals though in a different manner and in different atmosphere.

The Pardhans have full and firm faith in the wisdom of their forefathers and therefore they follow the faith founded by them sincerely and scrupulously. They observe tribal traditional rites and rituals inherited by them from their ancestors. They have no scriptures since nothing of the religious rituals, mythology, social laws, tribal traditions, community custom and their tribal history have ever been rendered in writing any time in past. Each and every one of them had been compiled in poetic verses and are committed to memory. They have been handed down by generation to generation from mouth to mouth by oral narration. Yet the Pardhan priests are well conversant with them and these have been retained till now. This is perhaps because of their regular recital and repeated rehearsal at festive functions and ceremonial celebrations.

Since no scriptures (written literature) exist, every information about the religion, mythology, rituals and the cult of the Pardhans can only be had from their priests and elderly persons who have full knowledge thereof. From the information available from such sources one learns, that their cult and religion is a simple and straightforward one, suited to their smooth, straight and strenuous normal life. It has no mystic principles or intricate philosophy. Their faith, traditions, social and religious rites are all founded on their mythology and their mythology is much of a legendary nature. There are many legends and though they differ in details the basic founding facts are almost the same and uniform.

The Pardhans believe that the tribal tutelary deity of their's and that of the Gond Aboriginals is, "Lord Lingo" also known as, "Pahadi Kuper" and he is coupled with Jango Devi. He is the supermost Lord among all their deities and, therefore, called Bada Deo or Phalapen in the Koitur (Gondi) dialect. He is ommiscient and ommipotent and blesses the Koitur tribals by bestowing his grace on them if his favour is invoked by proper worship and offering oblation (Sujara) of beef.

This almighty Bada-Deo created four deity couples and distributed the entire Gond Tribal families amongst them for supervision. Thus every deity couple is the supreme supervisor of the families under its control and it reared and cared them as its own children. These first four couples or pairs are:

1. Kolasur and Kali (having Kings' power)
2. Hira Jyoti and Madako (Philosopher)
3. Sungal and Turapi (Army Chief Commander)
4. Phalore and Mahakali (Angel).

Thus four family groups (Sagas) came to be created. Under the four presiding parently guardians. Each Saga therefore, forms a clan sect of the community and being under a common divine parenthood, the families of the common Saga (group) become brethren.

Twenty-two other divine deity couples were created corrosponding to Nature's powers, of them, eleven each, belonged to heaven and earth. (Swarga and Mrityu Lok). They were also divided and distributed in numbers of four, five, six and seven to every Saga for worship by the families of that particular Saga. The Sagas, (clan sections), therefore, came to be recognised by the number of deities worshipped by them e.g. 4 Deo, 5 Deo, 6 Deo and 7 Deo Saga. The families allotted to a Saga being created as brethren, they are prohibited matrimony amongst themselves. In the ancient long past, it so occurred once that a wedding was arranged between two families who happened to be descendants from a common mother. The fact came to be noticed only after the matrimonial rituals had been finished. The groom belonged to 6 Deo Saga and the bridal family also descended from same Saga mother. Both the wedding parties, therefore, agreed to worship six deities each (i.e. in all 12 deities) of the grooms and known as 12 Deo Saga for the descendants of these two familites, though in reality it is an off shoot of six Deo Saga.

The Pardhans consider that the 4 deities of the first Saga correspond to Soma, Gandharva, Agni and Gana. The 5 deities of the 2nd Saga are the five natural power elements i.e. the earth, water, fire, wind and sky. The six ones of the 3rd Saga are, the six seasons, and the 7 deities of the fourth Saga are the seven planets i.e. the sun, the moon, mars, mercury, jupiter, venus and saturn.

Every Saga has its fixed number of deities for worship and a sacred place of residence, a flag partaining there to and also an animal as the sacred symbol of the deities. They are as follows:-

The Pardhans feel and contend that the deities are beings of divine dignity. They are higher in honour than the human beings and hence they should not be housed in human homes on the same or lower level of their worshipping men and women. They, therefore, instal them in shrines i.e. deities on the trees. Thus the tree whereon deities reside are considered sacred and are also worshipped as the sacred shrines. So is the case with the symbolic animals who are supposed to be vehicles of their deities and therefore sacred signs thereof. Their sight is highly hailed and heralded with respect and reverence. Respective sacred flags are affixed on the trees to adorn the adored abode of the deities.

| Sr. No. | Saga | Deity couples of worship | Divine dynasty | Sacred animal | Sacred tree for divine Shrine | Sacred Flag | No. of Families belonging to Saga |
|---|---|---|---|---|---|---|---|
| 1 | 2 | 3 | 4 | 5 | 6 | 7 | 8 |
| 1. | 4 Deo | 1) Shri.Mal Lal Devi<br>2) Shri.Lal Hira Devi<br>3) Shri.Kal Sona Devi<br>4) Shri.Pal Rupa Devi | Devi-leer Pedi-gree | Tor-toise | Sag tree | Red Flag | 105 families. |
| 2. | 5 Deo | 1) Aherahood Shipa Moti<br>2) Maherahood Bala Moti<br>3) Reka Rahood Kalare Moti<br>4) Shri.Mal Rahood Dhara Moti<br>5) Dondalya Rahood Agara Moti | Rahood Pedi-gree | Ram-Laks-man Bird i.e. Saras Bird | Salai tree | White Flag | 18 Families. |
| 3. | 6 Deo | 1) Ahe-Udal-Khushal Turupo<br>2) Mahe-Udal-Mashal Turupo<br>3) Apayee Udal-Bayal Turupo<br>4) Tipayee Udal-Mangal Turupo<br>5) Bhande Kusur Udal-Gangal Turupo<br>6) Koidoo Udal-Sungal Turupo | Udal Pedi-gree | Tiger | Moha tree | Green Flag | 29 Families |
| 4. | 7 Deo | 1) Dhanwai-Tuipe Budo<br>2) Dhan Takuar-Suyi Wellal<br>3) Pindake Juga-Malai Koido<br>4) Rai Muda-Dhunai Koido<br>5) Chikat Raj-Dhugai Koido<br>6) Bhande-Sur-Waghai Koido<br>7) Bhui-Gota-Chidai Koido | Pen Pedi-yor | Sarai tree | Bel Flag | Yellow Families | 36 |

| | | | | | | |
|---|---|---|---|---|---|---|
| 5. | 12 Deo 1) Reve-Gangalia 2) Rande-Kasal 3) Indali-Jagal 4) Indali-Lingal 5) Tata Muri-Tataral 6) Isumi-Dhad Mullal 7) Tadaki-Sural 8) Tadaki-Mural 9) Reve-Jungal 10) Reve-Sukal 11) Kosaven-Rayatal 12) Paren-Kispenal | Jang-leer Pedi-gree | Parrot and Goat | Bel tree | Yellow Flag | 7 Families |

Hymns are chanted in praise of the deities to invoke and invite them at the shrine for worship. During the Puja, birds and beasts are sacrified and their flesh and liquor are invariably and necessarily offered as oblation to the deities. The flesh and the liquor is then distributed as *Prasad* (sacred offering) to the presentees and fellow-men. In the worship of the "Phala Pen Puja" beef is preferred as oblation of prime importance.

A few particular days are fixed and are marked during the year for such annual traditional worship of different deities. Puja and praise prayers are also offered on social ceremonies and celebrations to gain the grace and fond favour of the deities to make them rule smoothly and sucessfully. Folklore and folk dance follow the function as a favourite feature thereof.

**I: Ritual of Life Cycle**

The basic pattern of ceremonies of the Pardhans connected with the major crises of life are the same as that of the Hindus; but in minor details of ritual there is a little difference in the performance of the ceremonies. Religious rites or the ritual of the life-cycle of the Pardhans are but few and they are as follows:

Conception.
Birth or Delivery.
Naming the New-Born.
Puberty Rites.
Wedding-Marriage.
Death.

*Conception*

On the first conception, the lady is offered new saree and garments and green coloured glass bangles. *Kumkum* (Red powder) is applied on her forehead and a coconut is placed on the portion of her new saree near the womb.

*Birth (Delivery)*

A girl goes for her first delivery to her father's house. She takes her normal diet during pregnancy. Delivery is generally done at home, with the help of experienced woman (of the Pardhan tribe who knows the midwifery) who, attends as midwife. On the birth the mother, as well as other members of the family are considered as ritually impure. The navel link of the child is cut with a bamboo chip or a sickle and buried in a pit dug near the cot of the mother. The mother and the child are bathed on the pit and clothes are also washed there. On the fifty day, the midwife worships the pit and the mother and the childs are given bath on it. On this day (Fifth day i.e. Pachavi) til and gur are distributed among those present. The pit is filled with earth in the evening and five to ten tribemen are served with meals. From the sixth day the child and the mother are bathed outside. The woman (mother) is deemed to be impure for twelve days after, delivery. On the twelfth day the mother takes bath and is given cows urine. It is also sprinkled in the house which is washed and cleaned with cowdung and earth. The mother is then allowed to mix and mingle with members of the family. A worship to deity is offered on the third day of the delivery.

### *Naming the New-Born*

After consulting the elderly persons of the family the Pardhans fix up the day for naming the new born. In some cases they refer to the *Panchanga* (almanac) for the time of naming. It is not a practice in general. But the Pardhans living in towns have borrowed it imitating the other castes. The child's head is sheared and hair collected in a new cloth are buried. The child is then baptised (named) with a suitable name. It has been noticed that most of the Pardhan families have selected Hindu names for their children. The few names come across in the villages under study are Lakshman, Dharma, Maruti, Saraswati, Kusum etc.

### *Puberty Rites*

The problem of the puberty rites of the girls is very interesting and one of the most important thing in Indian life and also among aboriginals. The mutual attraction of the sexes, the importance attached to virginity, the initation into the secrets of sex life and the physiological, surgical and spiritual accessories traditionally utilized during the operation of rites, are some of the vital points of study that are directly based on these customs.

Puberty rites are very common. They take place either (a) at the advent of the first menstruation whether or not the girl is married, (b) at the first menstruation before marriage (c) at the first menstruation after marriage.

Among the tribal communities sex relationship between girls and boys starts much before the marriage and many a time even before the puberty. In certain areas of the aboriginal territory where the dormatory system prevails, on the advent of the puberty girls get an entrance into the dormatory. No elaborate ceremonies take place at this rite. The girl has to observe the mestrual seclusion for four days in a special hut or room or place.

Among the Pardhans, the girl after first menstruation is attended with the ceremony. She is secluded for four days, she is not allowed entrance into the kitchen, family favourite shrine, etc. When a girl attains puberty, her *Oti* (Lap) is filled with haldi (curcuma longa) rice and coconut. At the end of the menstruation period i.e. of four days she is given bath and dressed with new clothes.

### *Wedding*

Matrimony is mostly a matter of much concern for the Pardhans. It poses a problem for them because of the tribal tradition particularly peculiar to them. Search of a suitable groom is quite trying, taking and vexing too. Though Pardhans belong to the Gond group of tribals, marriage amongst the various sub-sections of the Gond Tribe (viz. Zadapi, Gatoli, Dholi, Khaloli, Jam gadi, Koitur, Pardhan etc.) is not permissible. The field for choice of a groom is limited. This limit is lessened further; by the Saga System, the beeja class system and the milk class system. Wedding within the same Saga i.e. between the families belonging to the same Saga is not permitted. It is prohibited by the religious tradition. Similarly marriage of a groom with bride belonging to his beeja, gotra or class is also prohibited. The Pardhans are divided in two groups of beeja (a) Families having even number of deities (Deo) of worship form one group, known as 'Enda beeja class'. (b) Families having odd number of deities (Deo) of worship form the other group known as 'Unda beeja class'. The Enda class groom cannot wed with Enda class bride. 'Enda' beeja should marry the 'Unda' only, since the girl from the same beeja gotra is considered as sisterly related. Again a boy can-not marry a girl who belongs to the same Saga to which his mother belongs. This mother class tradition is called 'Milk class tradition'. Bride of the milk class is considered to be maternal aunt in relation. To ascertain the class, clan, caste and place of the groom he is questioned by brides' party. Three questions are asked, (1) How many deities do you worship? (2) Whose son are you? (3) Whose milk you are fed on? The first determines his beeja gotra, the second his clan and caste and the third his mother's class and clan. Now-a-days this 'Milk' tradition is abolishing and a maternal uncle's or maternal aunt's daughter is permissible for marriage. People are also seriously thinking of doing away with the "Saga System" too. These ancient customs prove a great hinderance in getting a matching mate for the modernised and educated youth suiting his status and standard.

An ancient social custom further hurts a hurdle to hinder smooth settlement of marriage. The groom designate has to stay with the father of the bride and had to prove his ability to earn his livelihood and gain love of the bridal girl. On his proving so satisfactorily the selection was stamped for settlement of the wedding. This custom called as 'Lanijade' selected the groom conditionally and he could be discarded if found incapable by the bride and her father. This custom has also been abolished now.

(a) *Settlement*

When 'Bhirdi' i.e. groom is fixed a meeting of the bride and groom's parties is called by the tribal chief or leader. The groom has to pay Rs. 12 and the bride pays Re 1 towards the expenses of the meeting. In the said meeting the groom's party fixes the amount of dowry they would offer to the bride for her ornaments, clothes and foodgrains. When settlement is finalized the groom adorns the bride by Kumkum mark on her forehead as a token of his acceptance. (In Vidarbha it amounts to silver ornaments, five sarees and about 50 kilo grain). On settlement of the dowry donation, the groom has to keep it ready and deliver it to the bride five days before the marriage date without fall.

(b) *Wedding Date*

Like other tribals the Pardhans do not approach the priest for fixing the wedding date. It is almost an unwritten rule amongst the Pardhans that marriages are performed during spring, in the months of Phalgoon, Chaitra and Vaishakh (corresponding to March, April and May) and that too on the 5th or 9th day after Amavasya (No moon day) of the month (i.e. the marriage date is fixed on the 5th or 9th day of the bright fortnight of the month of Phalgoon, Chaitra or Vaishakha only).

(c) *Marriage*

Marriage among the Pardhans are always arranged by the parents. Pardhans wedding is usually performed in the bridgegroom's village at a particular place, known as, *Gothan* (Gothan is a place where animals assemble for rest during noon time). The customary bride-price is Rs. 12 but it varies in different localities and places.

The Pardhans celebrate marriage on any week day excepting Monday, Tuesday and Saturday, which are considered as unauspicious days. They do not perform marriage on eclipse day, Amavasya (Dark night) and in the month of Paush (December-January). They consult a Brahmin priest or an almanac for an auspicious day for marriage. Marriages are generally celebrated at Gopal Muhurta (the time at the break of the day) on auspicious day between the fifth dav following Shimga and at the end of Vaisakha.

The marriage ceremony is celebrated for full five days with traditional rites on each day. They are accompanied by folk-dances and folk-lore, containing humour, advice to bride and bridegroom in respect of religious rites, rituals, social customs and culture, thus acquianting the newly married couple with the way of life they would have to live in future.

For the details of marriage rituals refer Chapter-4.

*Death*

Among the Pardhans a person is not allowed to breath his last on a cot. If a person dies on the cot immediately he is lifted off the cot and put on the ground which must be freshly cowdunged. The house wherein death occurs is seculded and segregated till the dead body is removed for cremation. The dead body is given bath before it is taken for cremetion. If the deceased is a *Suvasini* (Married woman) the dead body is dressed in a new sari and Kumkum is applied to her forehead. After that the body is laid on a bier and carried to the cemetery by four persons. The chief mourner, who is a son of the deceased or if there is no son, any other male relative carries a new earthen pot without fire at the front. While the corpse is carried, its head is towards the house. Relatives and tribes men, including women accompany. The bier is lowered at the *Visava* (resting place) and the articles lying with the shroud are kept on the ground. The persons carrying the bier change places and the body is carried to the cemetery and kept at the side of the grave. If a man dies leaving his wife, she accompanies the corpse, her bangles and garsali are broken and the Kumkum wiped off. The body is then undressed (in case of the women, the garment or Sari is only loosened) and it is laid in the grave with face downwards in case of a male and face upwards if it is a female, with its head towards the south. The deceased is generally buried. Palas leaves are placed on the eyes, mouth, genitals, navel, and all other parts of the body which have openings. The chief mourner first throws earth in a grave and others follow him. Then the grave is filled up by ber branches and thorns are pressed into the earth. Then the chief mourner takes up the earthen pot and accompanied by others, goes round the grave. The pot is broken at the head of the grave. Afterwards the accompanying people if possible bathe in the nearest river and return home. When they reach the house of the deceased, a woman brings a pot water putting a live charcoal in it from the house. She sprinkles water on the right palm of every body, who sprinkles this water on his own feet.

Then, they again take bath either at the house of the deceased or at their own houses. In the meanwhile the place where the person breathed his last is cleaned with cowdung. The chief mourner worships the spot, lights incense sticks and camphor and breaks a coconut. Then the tea is offered at the place in the name of the deceased and shirni (bits of coconut) is distributed. Then, they (people) return their homes. The Pardhans generally bury the dead but now a days, as it has been noticed, that those who are well-to-do burn their dead. Pregnant women, children, persons who died by accident are buried. Those who died in epidemics are cremated.

Ritual i.e. Sutak is observed for three days. On the third day of the death worship is offered to a 'Moha Tree' and a hen is sacrificed in oblation thereto. Before performing this worship the members clean their feet by chewing Moha branch stick. Puja and prayer is also offered to God Shiva (Parshan Pen) and welfare and prosperity of the deceased is prayed for. Liquor processed from Moha is consumed by the members of the deceased. This function is called, "Kormara". People then approach the widow of the deceased and then console her and the family members. They advise her to lead a pious widowed life and not to remarry. Her livelihood and protection is promised. She has to abandon all ornaments of a married woman, and crescent Kumkum mark of the forehead. Thereafter, a 'Karana' function, wherein the community people, friends and relatives are fed with rice and liquor is performed. It is called *Kadu Bhat* or bitter dinner. It is done on the third day and unless it is performed no marriage ceremony or other auspicious celebrations can take place in the concerned family. On the fourth day, the mourners bathe, wash their clothes, clean the house with cowdung and are deemed to be pure. In case of priest this ceremony is known as "Madi Chadhavine" (raising higher). All these rituals have to be performed strictly and scrupulously. Those who avoid or neglect it are fined by the community jury. Refusal or denial of the fine invites even expulsion from the community. On the following Pritumoksha Amavasya day (the new moon day of the month of Bhadrapad) there is ceremony of recalling the deceased in the family and offering him honour and food. If it is not done the Pardhans feel, there is fear of the deceased reappearing in a wandering ghost form and haunt the family.

It will be clear from the above, that though divorce with husbands many a time during his life time is permissible and practised by the Pardhan yet widow's wedding after the death of the husband is not desirable and it is discouraged and discarded.

Similarly the Pardhans believe in the existence and operation of the ghosts and evil spirits and also black magic, witchcraft and sorcery an effectively remedy against their evil troubles. They assign causes of calamities, malady, ailments and unexpected occurrences to the haunting of and possession by such spirits. They approach priests and persons possessing divine powers to remove and remedy them, by magical miracles, and invoking divine grace of their deities. They also offer oblation to these spirits to please them and ease the person possessed by them for any offence and displeasure he might have done to them knowingly or ignorantly. Pardhans like other tribals are aware and acquainted with medicinal herbs and roots and they at times are seen selling them to earn their livelihood. Yet they are seen to tend to take recourse to mystic magic methods for cure of their ailments.

REFERENCE

1. Majumdar, D.N. and Madan, T.N., *An Introduction to Social Anthropology* Asia Publishing House, Bombay, 1957, p. 151.

# 7

# Festivals and Culture

The Pardhans observe following major religious ceremonies and festivals during the year. These are worships of Bada-Deo (Maha Deo) Narayan Deo, Bhiman Deo, Phalapen, Parsapen, Chaitri, (New Year day) or Gudhi Padva, Akshaya Tritiya, Nag Panchami, Rakhi Purnima, Ganesh Chaturthi, Dussehra, Diwali (Deepavali) Makar Sankrant (Til Sankranti), Holi, (Shimaga Fag.). They also observe fast on Ram Navami. Ashadi and Kartiki Ekadashi, Maha Shivratri, Gokul or Krishna Ashtami, Ganesh Chaturthi.

**Chaitri**

New year day. It is an important festival. It is observed on the first day of the Hindu month of Chaitra. (March-April).

**Ram Navami**

This festival is celebrated on the ninenth day of the Hindu month of Chaitra (Birth day of Shri Ram). (March-April).

**Ashadi Ekadashi**

The Pardhans observe fast on the eleventh day of Ashadi (June-July) in honour of God Vishnu.

**Rakhi Purnima**

The Pardhans observe this festival on the full moon day in the month of Shravana (July-August).

**Krishna Ashtami**

The Pardhans observe on the eighth day of the dark fortnight of

Shravana (July-August) (Birth day of Lord Krishna) the festival of Krishna Ashtami.

**Chauti**

Chauti is observed on the fourth day in the month of Bhadrapada (August-September). This festival is observed in honour of Ganesha, the son of God Shiva.

**Dussehra (Dasera)**

This festival is observed by the Pardhans on the tenth day of the Ashvina (September-October). In the afternoon they worship of bunch of Shami leaves and the ancestral weapons is performed. As a general rule elders and persons with a recognized superior status are respected by giving leaves of Shami by the Juniors, and Juniors bend down to touch the feet of the elders to show their (Juniors) respect towards the elders. On this day people are expected to forget their quarrels of the last year, and to meet each other in a spirit of friendship.

**Diwali (Depavali)**

The Pardhans observe Diwali festival for four days. viz. Narka Chaturdasi or Bhogi; Laxmi Pujan; Padva (Bill Pratipada) and Bhaubij. This festival is celebrated on the fourteenth and fifteenth day of the dark forthnight of the month of Ashvina (September-October) and first and second day, i.e. full moon fortnight day of Kartika (September-October).

**Kartiki Ekadashi**

Kartiki Ekadashi and Kartiki Purnima, these festivals are observed in the month of Kartika (October-November)

**Makar Sankrant (Til Sankranti)**

Makar Sankranti is celebrated on 14th January. On this day women worship (earthen pots) and til and gur (Sesame mixed with gur) is distributed.

## Holi or Shimga Fag

The Pardhans consider this festival as a major festival of the year. It is observed on the full moon day of Phalgoon (February-March). Shimaga has a principal and prime position in the life of the Pardhan.

It is the crest of all their ceremonies. It is more than a marriage for them. They put their heart and soul solely in its celebration. The Pardhans go mostly mad to make it magnificent and mirthful. Planning and preparation of all the paraphernelia thereof start long before the actual event. Funds are collected, fuel is procured, cutting wood from the woods, meat and sweet eatables, roots and fruits are acquired, liquor is stored, ganja and tobacco are accumulated and musical instruments are repaired and new ones are prepared. Recital of songs and hymns on their rhyme and rhythem are practised during recess from routine work and at night after dinner. Dances are rehearsed. New songs and poetry is composed and the old ones are compiled. The whole energy and enthusiasm is deviated, diverted and directed devotedly to the preparation of Holi even a month before its day of celebration. They are anxious till the day of celebration. They are not happy until it happens to their satisfaction. Then, youths and youngsters are however, more bound but they do work under the able matured persons guidance and supervision of the elders. Thus, therefore, the differences and disputes, excesses and extremeties, quarrels and clashes are almost avoided and/or amicably settled within the locality and the community. Exceptions however, are always there to any rigid rule or regulation and they are but natural with any society. When the preparation of all the paraphernelia of the festival and the material necessities need for the performance are ready, they eagerly and vigorously await the actual augment thereof. The festival falls on the fifteenth day of Phalgoon month of the Indian ancient calendar month. It is to be celebrated for two days but the buoyancy of the people drags it further also for few days.

On the augment day, the Pardhan people gather together on an open outside ground nearby their locality. They clean and clear the ground and then erect an elevated neat pedestial platform. Thereon their divine deity the Goddess, 'Tondyal Manko' in whose honour and memory the festival is celebrated is installed and enshrined (some say that the festival is in the memory of tribal tutelary deity

Lingo or Pahadi Kuper, the faith-founder of the gond culture–as stated by Mr. R. V. Russell in his book *Caste and Tribes of C.P. & Berar*). She is worshipped in the tribal traditional manner and there, fuel is piled up before her shrine in a huge and high hill like heap. A branch of the 'Moha' tree or a tree known as 'Pheteri Mela' is erected in the centre thereof. It is set on fire in the evening by the chief of the ceremony. The priest worships the deity and sets the Holi heap fire and offers oblations to them. The assembled gathering, goes round the deity and the holi fire is lighted in a clockwise way i.e. in praise and honour of the deity for her gay and graceful glory and beg for clemency of her bliss, and blessings on them. The sacred offering is then distributed to the assembled people and they return home.

After dinner, wherein meat is the main menu, they drink liquor and smoke ganja. They, then again assemble around the holi fire at night. Gathering is divided into groups and they sit on either side of the holi. Rival songsters are seated on opposite sides. The musical instruments are set on one side and the dancing parties on the other. (The orchestra constitutes of the drummers, (small and large) trumpets, Kingre, Surnaya, Pilampoya, Ronga, Tahrang, Tiparee, Gomti, Gonghar, Ghungroo and Katolee etc. Recently they have been using harmonium and table too). When all are set, the drummer beats the drums with striking stick and suggests the sounds are started. The trumpet is blown and Kingree is bowed on. The Singers on either side then adjust their tone and to the tune thereof by uttering "Rena, Reniya Re Re Na" or "Retan Retan SS", Reretan. Retan SS" (Legend singers however use the utterence of "Tar Har De S De SS NA SS Re"). When some songster tunes his tone to top tip, raising it in a rising rhythm and slowing it to the basic tune, he is applauded by the aroused assembly and set the songster to start his songs. The programme proceeds on. Performance is given by parties on either side, swinging the singing of songs alternately. At times it is in the nature of queries and responding requisite replies thereto. Simultaneously, sonner starts the traditions tribal dance, by males and females and mixed one too. The whole night is spent in singing, dancing, drinking and smoking and cracking jokes, frivolities also follow, filling the hollow gaps in between.

Variety of songs, on very many matters, and in varying manners are presented during the performance. They include tribal mythology, historic happenings, patriotic and brave deeds of heroes and martyrs, nature's beauty romance devotion to deities, social evils and social vices, social and cultural reforms love and affection anxiety ambition and appreciation of the poverty stricken Pardhans, and even fun and frivolities (Formerly serene and sublime subjects had the supreme sway on the occasion but now a days, new poems and songs depicting personal censure and abusive language are presented which, at times create tension, invite insulting incidents and rude rowdyism resulting in freely assaulting and attacking rival group with sticks and bricks). Dances too shed similar shades, of serene and sublimes rousing romance and appreciable attracting art of the aboriginal tradition. Thus in the energetic enthusiastic and encouraging environment, every and all enjoy the whole Holi night merrily in melody, singing, drinking and dancing.

The next morning the whole party of the songsters and dancers goes-round to locality from house to house, starting first from the Priest's giving performance and collecting funds for the fusture function. They throw mud, sprinkle colour and shout slogans at the houses they visit. The inmates of the house also co-operate and join them in their enjoyment and rejoicing and merry making. In the latter half of the day eating, drinking and merry and continues. Thus the Pardhans forget every thing in their ecstasy of enjoyment.

The enchanting environment of Simaga starts much earlier before the actual date continues even for few days further. During these days their heart and mind is possessed, so to say by the Holi Goddess and the Simaga Songs and music seems to seize them. They like to linger on their lips longer still.

Many a legend in connection with this festival is told but the one common amongst the Pardhans runs thus.

Long Long ago a tribal king had a Minister (Pradhan) named Sundi Bhurang who was popular with the king and subjects. He had all property and pleasures yet dejected for having no issue. He, therefore, devotedly worshipped Goddess Tondyal Manako (Mahakali with protruding tongue). To invoke her bliss and boon he vowed to offer his first son to her in oblation. In course of time the Goddess blessed him with a son whom he named after her as 'Manago'. He then begged for her further favour and begot seven daughters. Yet he did not offer her, his son and kept on avoiding for a long time. It resulted in her wrath on him. His daughters on attaining puberty did not get grooms nor the son got a suitable bride. Not being married for long the young maiden daughters sought resort in a 'Pheteri Mala' tree situated on the outskirts of the village. Disgusted and disappointed for matrimony, they treated the tree as their mate and started worshiping and embracing it daily. One day their brother noticed them doing so and when they returned home he steadily went to the tree and cut it down. The following day when the sisters knew it, they felt sorry and mourned for it. In sheer agony, they collected all the parts and branches of the tree cut off from it and piled them in pyre and set fire to it. They then, circumambulated the pyre and they all jumped into the fire simultaneously. The brother Manago, who was witnessing it in hiding behind the bush readily ran to rescue them but the seven sisters kicked him out of the flame, in consequence, the sisters were burnt to ashes in fire and the brother Manago got bitterly burnt and died as a separate heap at a near distance from them. Sundi Bhurangi lost his heart and kept on weeping for the loss of all of his issues.

Later the village had a heavy drought and famine. Drinking water was not available. The king ordered digging a tank but it yielded no water. While the village populace was in distress; the Goddess appeared in the King's dream and demanded him to offer a human sacrifice to her on the tank ground to beget water therein. But the condition was that the person should be a one who will imprint his footmarks on the tank ground while going to its centre, as one does on marshy land. The king searched for such a person but could not get any. He, therefore asked the Minister Sundi Bhurangi to make such a one available. Knowing the wrath of Goddess the minister told the secret to the king and advised him to place the ashes of Manago into the tank pit. The king did it and lo! The pond was filled with water. No person needed to be sacrificed. The whole village got overjoyed, the people thronged at the tank and shouted in chorus 'Si-Manago' (In Gondi dialect it means 'Manago a boon'). They worshipped the Goddess Tondyal Manako and celebrated the event ceremoniously in her honour and in the memory of Manago who proved a boon donated to them. It is since then that this occurrence is similarly observed with the same solemnity by the tribals in their memory.

Though the Pardhans from all the villages did not mention or refer to God Narsimha, (an incarnation of Lord Vişhnu in a half-lion and half-human form) whose festival is observed and celebrated by the Hindus on the fourteenth day of the month of Vaishakha (April-May), the Pardhans of a village viz. Anjee-Nrusimha (a village in Kelapur tehsil of Ghatanji Block, told the author that they did not observe and perform the festival of God Narsimha as one of the festivals of theirs, still they participated in it with the same belief, faith and enthusiasm, as they participated in their tribal festivals, and also the other festivals of Hindus like Rama Navami, Krishna Ashtami etc. The Pardhans of the said village also told that it is their daily practice (Daily routine) to visit God Narsimha temple for *Darsan* without which they do not go to sleep.

**Superstitions**

The Pardhans way of life is very much influenced by the thoughts and customs of Hindus and Gond. They believe in omens. A cat crossing the path, a woman with an empty pot, a man sneezing, three persons starting for one and the same work at a time, an owl sitting on a horse, are considered bad omens. On the other hand, a dead serpant, a woman carrying a pot full of water, a cow with a calf, a blue bird, a black bird and a fox crossing the road from left to right are good omens.

The Pardhans attend the marriage and pujas of the Gonds and other groups, and also of the other castes of Hindus on their invitation. It has been reported by some Pardhans of Bori and Mukutban that they have attended the Satyanarayan Pujas at the houses of the Hindus.

Though the Pradhans have cordial relations with the other Hindus, they usually have a separate well assigned to them from which they draw water. They accept food from the Gonds and the Kolams, but both Gonds and Kolams treat Pradhans as untouchables, and do not return the compliment. The Pardhans regard Mahars, Mangs, Chambhars and Thoti Gonds (A tribal group) as inferior to them and in the past were not used to take food and water from them. At present it is not followed very strictly and they accept food and water from Mangs, Mahars and Chambhars. However, even today the Pardhans do not take food and water from Thoti. In many villages of Yavatmal District, particularly in Kelapur and Wani tehsils, the Pardhans found as village Kamdar (village Kotwal, these posts are generally held by Mahars). A good number of Pardhans have taken to agriculture as their principal occupation for their livelihood.

## Dancing and Singing

The Pardhans perform dances practically during all the festivals but dances performed during Holi and marriage have their own religious socio-cultural value and importance in tribal community. The dance performed after the actual marriage ceremony is over, is called a Dhemsa or Zulve. In all they perform 16 (sixteen) Dhemsas. Only males take part in this dance. They dance round the Bohala (Altar) with the accompanient of Dholak (small Drum) Dhol (Big Drum) cymbals and small bells tied round their ankles throughout the night of the marriage.

Though some of the festivals of the Pardhans are purely religious and some are socio-religious, the devotional and dedicational worship of the deity, presiding function is done in all festivals. The Pardhans celebrate them ceremoniously and mostly collectively. Every individual co-operates with the other with cordial co-ordination to make the festival a success. Eating meat, drinking liquor, smoking intoxicating Ganja, reciting folk lyrics, love to the tune of lyre-like Kingree, and dance to the tune of trumpet and beat of humming drum are but favourite features of all the functions. The Pardhans are scrupulously sincere in their performance of these festivals.

Long old livery and lovely traditional tribal life, lurk in the minds of the majority of the Pardhans. Superstitions, traditional beliefs and ancient tribal customs have still a strong hold on them. They prefer their tribal attires on festive functions and ceremonial celebrations, they necessarily wear their traditional tribal constumes. They are fond of flesh and they have a special flavour and favour for the flesh of animals they hunt. They have liking, nay lust for liquor and they long for it at all times but more so on community celebrations. They always maintain a mood for music, and melody is mostly a malady inherent in them. They play on very many musical instruments, trumpets, drums, hollow horns etc. yet a string instrument, known as Kingree is their fond favourite. It is in fact the emblem of the Pardhans. Kingree and Pardhans are always associated with one another. They merrily play on it as and when they find free time during their daily routine. When the Pardhans sing in ecstasy their traditional tribal ballads, mythological holy hymns, ancestral historic achievements and felicious festival song, the Kingree is the main instrument which keeps up the time and tone, rhyme and rohythm and mood and melody. The Pardhan is known for his Kingree and by his Kingree. Though the Pardhans are known for their Kingree and by his Kingree still the Pardhans of Vidarbha, are seen to have given up their traditional profession of playing on Kingree and have accepted other occupation like cultivation, agricultural labour and other jobs etc.

They have a devotion to dance too. Males and females, young and old join together and mix freely in the traditional dance which they may perform on almost all social, religious or matrimonial ceremonies. In fact, flesh, liquor, music and dance are the favourite features of all functions. Animal sacrifice and offering of oblation of flesh and liquor are necessary needs, many are must, at the worship of their divine deities.

Pardhans, males or females have a taste and tendency towards tattooing the body. Especially women consider it auspicious and young girls take to it necessarily as need before and after wedding. Males also tattoo their favourite Kingree, the number of their deities, on their hands and arms. Females tattoo variedly in various fashion, their hands and arms, breasts, foreheads and even the full thigh and leg, some do it on the entire body.

Females take part in festive functions, with equal enthusiasm as do the males. They mingle and mix with male folk, dance and enjoy in ecstasy the charm and warmth of the happiness and rejoice of the function. They are not supposed to be of sub-status or sub-standard to the males.

In brief, the Pardhans in general love and long for light kind of a life of eat, drink and be merry kind. They enjoy their social life, with delight and rejoicing fully fed with flesh and lost in liquor, when they take to their traditional tribal dance in dedication to their devoted deities.

They sing merrily in ecstacy and forget themselves and the world around them in their rejoicing rhythm.

It will be of interest to know the details of their Shimaga Fag and the folk songs literature associated with it.

## SHIMAGA-FAG

The Holi Festival is being celebrated since the vedic days. Much information can be collected about it from ancient literature and scriptures viz. Puranas and other books. But its ceremonial form, resembles and coincides with that of the Adivasis. Liquor drinking, mud-hurling and slogan shouting are a speciality with the Adivasis festivals.

This 'Shimaga Festival' originally belonged to non-Aryans and later adopted by the Aryans. It is evident that while Diwali festival exhibits higher culture, the 'Shimaga-Holi' festival presents a lower one.

The Adivasis are in reality Nature Worshippers. Earth, Wind, Fire, Rain, and Space etc., are their deities of worship. In the Holi festival they worship Fire-God. Every tribe has various ideas, stories and legends about this festival.

Among the Aboriginals, the culture of the Gond tribals is considered to be superior and greater. Some say that Gonds observe this 'Shimaga Festival' in the memory of their faith-founder 'Lingo'. Mr. R.V. Russell has given in his book *Castes and Tribes in Central Provinces* Vol. IV the Legend about Lingo. But the history of this festival and the story related thereto as narrated by the Pardhans is noteworthy.

In fact Gonds and Pardhans have not different culture, their traditions, customs, beliefs, dialects are very similar. The following Pardhans song denotes it.

**Song**

Phala Pen Patalee Ata Ye
Selomee Gondeeta Keeta Ye
Undee Natoo dore Koyatore Palale
Bhilee Palee Sara Undeeye
Penkala Ichhchode Paree Soyarana
Reetibhatee Sara Undeeye
Gondawana Awale Ataye. (1)
Saga Pade Pade Noore Noore Paleene
Tustore Bhate Kholyane
Janako Phala Pene Manako Parsapene
Paree Nee Tammoo Talane
Kirya Bhilee Ghawaleete Dohataye (2)
Yeddeete Allale Rapokola Rame
Takeete Mawa Phalapene
Mawamuchchuke Tane Machcho Ye
Pirtite Paro Kikom Tane
Tanamawan Roopa Undee Ataye. (3)

*Meaning:* One great God has become a Bard poet. He has researched into the original source of the gond tribals. Koytoors (Gonds) and Pardhans belong to same blood. Their family names and history of the descendency is one and the same. Their deity worship and matrimony system are all one and same. Social customs, traditions and dialect are also one and the same only.

The Mother source of origin of both these tribes is the main stream of the Gond Community.

In ten-twelve family groups the great God bard poet, has created family names in hundreds. And allotted them equally to both the Janako, Phala Pen, Manko Parsa Pen etc. deities, to witness, to superwise and to frame matrimonial and family laws, and integrated the community by bonds of oath and affidavits. Allah of the Muslims and Ram of the Hindu are captivated in the open Sun and temples. But our great God is enclosed in our heart. Nothing is dearer and nearer to him than we people. We dance with dedication to him lifting his banner and raising high our God and we coincide concurrently.

This song depicts the devotion of Pardhan to their great god Phala Pen and then affinity towards the Gonds.

Russell quotes Tawane's statement in his book as "Nothing is there in the ceremonies or religion of the Pardhans to distinguish these from the Gonds". In the very volume Russell says "As the Priest of the Gonds the Pardhans are employed to conduct the ceremonial worship of their great God Bura Deo". This denotes the social status of the Pardhans and their relative connections with the Gonds. But to-day there are differences, disparity and disputes between them to a great extent. As the brahman has a superior status amongst all the castes of the Hindus, the Pardhans had the same and similar solemn status amongst the various Gond tribal sects.

As the Koytoor people introduce themselves to others as 'Gond' similarly the *Palal* people acquaint themselves to others as 'Pardhan'. Pardhan is an incorrect colloquial form of the proper word "Pardhan" due to lack of proper pronunciation. It is like a villager pronouncing his name incorrectly as 'Ishinath' for the correct name 'Vishwanath'. The Government also has recorded this incorrect form 'Pardhan' for these people in the list of Scheduled Tribes.

## Shimaga–the Holi Festival of Pardhans

The Pardhans celebrate ceremonially their Shimaga Festival with extreme energy, worship Narayan Pen, Bhimana, Karnas, Phala Pen and Parsa Pen. Though they celebrate many other festivals, yet Shimaga Fag holds a very important and special place in their life. The Shimaga is the very life stream or the live nerve of the Pardhans. They incur so much debt for this festival that they may not be able to repay it during the whole year.

A legend in vogue, amongst the Pardhans gives rise to a doubt that this Shimaga Festival might have original source in this society only. Pardhans trace the origin of the Shimaga (Holi) in various legends viz. 'Hasha Kuwari' story 'Sohel Batan-Mohana Ram' story and an independently important legendry of the Jangal'. But the one about 'Shimago', much current among the society, seems to coincide with it well.

Since then the festival is performed every year. The legend in detail is already referred to previously in this very Chapter.

Pardhans perform 'Shimaga' in a peculiar way than it is done by others. 'Shimaga Fag' does not denote the sense of festival but it connotes the songs and dances to be performed on the occasion. The word 'Fag' or 'Phag' means Pato and Yendmal'.

## Musical Instrument and Preparation for Phag

The Pardhans set themselves for the preparation of Phag about a month or so before the actual date of the festival. On occasions of the celebration of other ceremonials such as 'Malmiyev' (Matrimonial) settlement, 'Penakala' (Deity worship) 'Yayana Ganyan' (Worship and Sacrifice to the Goddess) etc. they do have their folk dance and folk-lore on the beat of drums and blowing of trumpets and also playing on wooden musical pipes. Performing small or big festivals throughout the year, they enjoy a festive life. The musical instruments, therefore, have a great importance in their life. Such instruments are repaired and new ones are prepared for Shimaga. Fresh leather is tanned for small and large drums. Other instruments of music viz. Surnaya, Pilampoye and Ronga are also repaired and set ready. We get reference to these instruments in the Pardhan folk songs of Phag.

**Song**

Yendanawe Minda Ho
Nilayand Tanona Bandona Phunda
Nilayano Yendale Dhol Malokitona
Dholkyana Talate Yenda Nawe Minda Ho (1)
Nisathee Yendale Timakee Beekitona
Chalangyana Talate Yenda Nawe Minda Ho (2)
Neelayano Yendale Jantoor Bee Kitona
Jantoorta Soorate Yenda Nawe Minda Ho (3)
Neelayano Yendale Pilampoyatatona
Basareeta Sooraté Yenda Nawe Nawe Minda Ho (4)

*Meaning*: The instruments mentioned in the above song-Drum, Chalanga, Jantoor and Pilampoya are prepared by the Pardhans themselves. Besides these, Taharang, Tiparee, Gomti, Ronga, Katolee, Ghongar and Ghungaroo are other musical instruments which they play on in festival dance and songs. Now-a-days, they use, harmonium and tabla also. Having made repairs to the instrument and other prior arrangement for the Shimaga festival, they hold practice meetings daily till the date of the festival. Every night after dinner, they meet together to hold rehearsal so as to set themselves for proper performance on the due occasion. Even during the day time, while doing their daily duties, i.e. chopping the wood, and toiling in the fields, the Phag song and music is on their lips. While sitting or strolling, the priase-hymns of mother Holi and Goddess Girija they continously chant. All anxiously await the augment of Shimaga. Where to arrange the Holi meet?

At last the Holi has augmented Goddess Girija has arrived. How to stage her? Where to place a seat for her. Hurry and worry all over to carry out the programme. In one of their Phag song this staging of the Goddess Girija has been well described. The song is as follows:

**Song**

Kahan Rachaoon Niwe Holee Ho Girijamaya
Bege Rachaoon Niwe Holee
Baharo Rachaoon Niwe Holee Ho Girijamaya
Maidan Raghaoon Niwe Holee

*Meaning:* Oh Goddess Girija where to stage thee. At which place tc arrange Holi. Oh Goddess! outside the village Holi I arrange. On the vast open ground the Holi I arrange.

In the further stanzas the material for the Holi they use is mentioned.

**Song**

Holee ke wasate re kyakya bula-yo
Holee ke wasate re Gedanga bula-yo
Holee ke wasate re kyaykya bula-yo
Holee ke wasate re Daroo bula-yo
Kahan chadhaoon Niwe Daroo Ho Girijamaya
Holee ke wastate kyakya bula-yo
Holee ke waste mala bula-yo
Kahan chadhaoon Niwa Mala Ho Girijamaya.

*Meaning:* What to bring for Holi? Wood be brought for Holi. What to bring for Holi? Wine be brought for Holi. Oh Goddess where to offer this wine. What else to bring for Holi. A garland be brought for Holi. Oh Girija where to hold this garland.

On arranging the Holi and with the above material at hand Ghatya or Bhumka (The Gond-Priest) performs the worship and thereafter other people offer worship and oblation to it. What were the articles or worship in the former ancient days, is not traceable to-day but we get some idea thereof from the Gondi Bhajan as cited below:-

**Song (Bhajan)**

Akee Pungare Ro
Bele Patareeta
Poonja Niwa Ayala
Rale Kapoore Ro
Homa Udabattee te
Poonja Neewa Ayala.

On finishing the worship they have a good dinner, which includes flash of a hen, goat, sweets etc. according to one's ability or simple food. But liquor is a must.

*Phag*

The Phag folk songs are to be recited around the Holi fire throughout the night. The Pardhans meet together around the Holi fire after dinner, equipped with their musical instruments. The drummer sits in the middle. On his right, sit the Timki and Chalanga players and on his left, are seated the pipers and pilampoya blowers. In front of the drummer the chief Phag song singer sits and around him are the artists of other instruments. Public surrounding them chant praise, slogans of the Goddes Holi.

It may be mentioned here, that the present practice of shouting slogans in lewd language, does not seem to be in vogue with the Pardhan people. Now-a-days some Pardhans do so imitating other communities. But it is not their real system. Pardhans consider Holi as Goddess Girija-Paravati. They call her Tondyal-Mandako also (Mahakali). Obscenity is not permissible in presence of that sacred deity.

When assemblage is full, the drummer beats the drum with the drum stick to invite the attention of the folk-singer. Timki and Chalanga beaters follow him in response. Pipers and Pilampoya blowers tune their instruments suitably and the singer adjusts his tone to the tune of the instruments when all are set in harmony the audience becomes attentive. Meanwhile some songster tips his tone to a top-tune wave and lowers it slowly and steadliy to the basic one. The assembly greets him with praise and pleasure.

Before the start of the song, the songster adjusts his voice by tuning notes. In Chandrapur region, they do it by uttering such letters as "Re na Re na Re Re na Rena" while in Wardha and Amravati Districts it is achieved by muttering "Rena Rena Re Re Na". The legend singers however, set their voice to the tune by sounding notes "Tar Har De De Na Re".

When voice is tuned to musical harmony, they sing the opening auspicious praise song of Phag, as cited below:

**Songs**

Jhula Rahe Bapa....,
Bhowatala Dewaraya Jhula Rahe
Badakonya dewawara Ghouranga dole,
Phalalpena Dewawara chouranga dole.

Bhowatala Dewaraya Jhula Rahe (1)
Konya Konya dewawara Chouranga Dole
Hanumana Dewawara Chouranga Dole
Bhowatala Dewawara Chouranga Dole
Bhowatala Dewaraya Jhula Rahe. (2)
Konya Konya Dewawara Ghouranga Dole
Janaako Manakowara Chouranga Dole
Bhowatala Dewaraya Jhula Rahe. (3)

*Meaning*

Deities assembled around are rocking
What god is fanned with Chouri
The great god is fanned with Chouri
Deities surrounding are moving Chouri.
On which god moves the Chouri.
On Hanuman the Chouri is moved
Dieties surrounding are moving Chouri
On what god moves the Chouri
On Janako and Manako Chouri is moved.
Dieties surrounding, are moving the Chouri.

Thus the song continues mentioning many other deities. Pardhan people do not seem to be acquainted with Lord Ganapati. Since no reference appears to be recorded thereto in their folk-lore. Nor any legend is traced in respect of him. But legendary about Mahadeo and Bheem is abundant. Many songs pertain to Bheem. Therein Arjun is mentioned as his father and Garjun (Thunder) has been cited as his grand father. Bheem is considered to be the God of rains.

*Evil Trend in Phag*

The Phag songs and the folklore are the very valuable stores of the aborigins. They contain in them social and cultural values of the Adivasi tribals. They have some shortcomings but they are ignorable. But some Pardhans feel that "all that is old has become out-of-date and is hence abandonable". As such Pardhan folk singers are attempting to compose and compile new Phag songs for recitation at Phag festival. They desired change in the ceremonial form of the festival. Good new items may however help to be beneficial. Instead, if evil lewd and ill-ominous are adulterated it may add curruption to community culture. Formerly, at the end of every line of the Phag song they used to add *Kenja Nawe Daoo* meaning Oh my brother. This helped maintenance and continuance of affection and affinity amongst the community. Even the rival singer would be treated as a friend, at such an additional vocative. In olden days the Phag celebration would begin with recitation of religious rituals followed by the social and historical ballads, and ending with Phag songs. Recently they are being deformed to Kawwala type to some extent. Two rival Phag parties attack each other with query and counter query songs, resulting in abusing and assaulting one another. Old songs were also competitive but their nature was, of inquisitive enquiry into the descent and dynasty by one and descriptive response by the other. Attempt of abuse on the rival was absent. Following is an illustration of the new sort of Phag song.

**Song**

Wala Rande Punee Ho
Siya Neeka Sotata Dhoonee
Come ye forward oh!
Wretched widow Punee
I will cense thee with a stick

The rival songster recites in response an equating song.

**Song**

Kuchchee Niharo Heeda
Heeda Kharjilyal Nayadune
Kuchchee Niharo.

With such abusive start the whole song is set to slander or to censure than to praise and consequently free use of the sticks hidden under the carpet, would be made on one another. Such is the new way of change. But that would not minimise the importance of Phag tradition. On the contrary, study and research into the Phag Folklore, alone, can present traditional way of life of the Pardhans wholly and properly.

**Social Life of Pardhans as depicted in Phag songs**

To know fully the inner and outer social community life of the Pardhans, Phag folk-lore will have to be studied well. They can be a subject for an independant treatise.

The Pardhans arc originally an aboriginal tribe dwelling in jungle. They are therefore, wedded to nature. They rock in the cradle of nature and their early life is spent in the vicinity of creepers and wild folliage of trees.

**Song**

Mattata Tongee Tata Chhawa Bane Kita
Jo Bapu Jo Jhoka Siya Lata
Re Re Na Re Pata Waree Lata
Karela Weleeta Ukale Dohata
Tana Paro Aiwatala Gamalee Bee Tarata
Jo Bapoo Jo Jhoka Ungee Lata
Re Re Na Re Pata Waree Lata
Parsa Weleeta Ukale Dohata,
Tanaparo Aiwatala Dikalee Unde Tarata;
Jo Bapoo Jo Jhoka Ungee Lata
Jataye Weleeta Ukale Dohata,
Tanaparo Alwatala Gindobonda Tarata
Re Re Na Re Pata Waree Lata
Bande Rehameeta Tena Sheiowana Ata,
Aivatala Jeewata To Lee Kiya Lata,
Re Re Na Pata Waree Lata.

The above Phag song illustrates a befitting lullaby of the Pardhans. It is very much popular with the Pardhan people. Even the ordinary person feels joy and pleasure in hearing it. A month or so before the Holi and ten to twelve days thereafter the Phag songs are ceaselessly recited. Soon after the Holi ceremonials, colour sprinkling and mud throwing add pleasure to the programme. Shimaga is an unique performance of the Pardhans.

**Dhuli Vandan**

While celeberating the 'dust ceremony' the next day the Pardhan people forget every thing in its ecstasy. Accompanied by the colour throwing team, the party, singing Phag during the entire night, proceeds to the priests' house and holds their first sitting there only. Tea and liquor is served to them there. Then during the entire day the whole team with all their paraphernalia move from house to house singing Phag, playing colours and collecting Phag donations. Dancing party also follows and adds pleasure to programme. Colour spray-play is considered to be in respect to the memory of Radha-Krishna.

**Song**

Koun Koun Khele Gulabheekee Chhidya
Hanuman Khele Shendudaka Pudiya
Radha Krishnkee Jaya Holee
Koun Koun Khele Abira Kee Pudiya
Radha Krishan Kee Jaya Holee
Koun Koun Khele Gulabee Kee Chhidiya
Bheemaraj Khele Malakhamba Badhiya
Radha-Krishankee Jaya Holee
Koun Koun Khele Naturnga Holee
Radha-Krishankee Jaya Holee.

*Meaning:* Who plays the colour and red powder (Gulal)? Hanuman sprinkles Shendoor (red lead oxide). Hail to Holi! in memory of Radha Krishan. Who plays colours and Gulal powder? Rahman throws the Abir dust (Black scented powder, Hail to Holi in the name of Radha Krishna. Who plays with colour and red Gulal dust. Bheem plays Malkhamb (Pole feats) Hail to Holi in the name of Radha Krishna. Who plays with colour and gulal powder? Mankobai (Mahakali) sprinkles blood for colour, Hail to Holi in memory of Radha-Krishna.

This song describes who plays and what? The Muslim God Rahman who has no connection with Holi colours, has also been included by Pardhan as throwing Abir (Black scented powder) Pardhans have specifically made it clear here that their Holi festival is in the honour and memory of Radha-Krishan. Hindus also carry the same belief.

Which god is great? The Pardhans narrate the greatness of their god as depicted in the verses below.

**Song**

Sub dewatnse Koun Dev Bada?
Sub Dewatanse Phalapen Bada,
Doorsene Naliyal Phodobe Lala
Mathura ye Nagar Suwano Be Lal
Sub Dewatanse Koun Dev Bada
Sub Dewatanse Parsapeńa Bada
Doorsene Nattoorko Chhodo Be Lala
Mathura Ye Nagar Suwano Be Lal
Sub Dewatanse Janakoyala Bada?
Sub Dewatanse Bheemaraj Bada,
Doorsene Paddeepeela Chhodo Be Lala
Mathura Ye Nagar Suwano Be Lal
Sub Dewatanse Rawadeva Bada
Doorsene Piyala Chhodo be Lala
Mathura Ye Nagar Suwano Be Lal.

| *Meaning:* | Nattor | : | Blood. |
|---|---|---|---|
| | Nankoyal | : | Janko Mata mother Goddess Janko. |
| | Nesa Pila | : | An egg and the chicken of a hen. |
| | Paddeepeela | : | A young one of a pig. |
| | Piyala | : | A Glass of wine or a pipe of Ganja. |

Eggs, mutton, chicken, liquor and ganja etc. anything and every thing can be accepted as oblation to the deities of the Pardhan people. Yet nothing is acceptable from a lala. A lala means a person from foreign community other than the Pardhans. If a 'Lala' he or she desires to oblate anything to the Pardhans deity he has to do so from a distance (i.e. without touching it or coming within the sacred limit). They say the Pardhans formerly did not accept food or eatables from foreign persons other than Pardhan. i.e. Non-Pardhan. An inference can, therefore, be clearly drawn that Pardhan of the olden days treated Non-Pardhans as untouchables.

**History Through Phag Songs**

Formerly Phag songs contained some historical descriptions too.

Here is an illustrative evidence thereof:

**Song**

Mogal Senata Gondawanata,
Rogadya Ata Ladhase,
Rantene Khuba Lade Mata Heeda Rani Durgawatee
Manyana Bhesa Yechee Wata Heeda Rani Durgawatee
Rantene Khuba Lade Mata Heedarani Duragawatee
Kodatene Bahanmiachee late Heeda Rani
Rantene Khuba Lade Mata Heeda Rani Durgawatee
Jhara Jhara Teera Jiyala Heedarani Durgawatee
Rantene Khuba Lade Mata Heedarani Durgawatee
Mogal Senata Gondawanata Ro Gadya
Ata Ladadee, Rantene Khuba Lade Mata.

*Meaning:* Fierce fight took place between the Mogul forces and the Gond troops. In the field the queen appeared on the battlefield in the male army attire and she gave a tough brave fight. On the steed-back she moved briskly and gave a firm fiery fight. The queen Durgavati was throwing arrows from her bow very rapidly and repeatedly. Durgavati really fought the field fearlessly and forcefully. Between the Mogul forces and the Gondwana oh friend a fierce fight ensued. She fought the battle forcefully.

**Romance and Attire**

Principal subject matter of Phag songs pertain to romance, union of a lover and a beloved, play and athletics, charm and beauty etc. Pardhans are by nature delightful and mirthloving. Their Phag songs are therefore, enchanting. Many a youth male and female, lose their balance at these enchanting recitation of Phag song and behave out of way in moral manners. Hence recently woman folk is forbidden to take part in Phag celebration.

**Song**

Jhummana Le, Balkuwaree Tana
Jhummana Le;
Sariyana Le, Balkuwaree-Tana

Sariyana Le;

Oh! Beloved, you are still a maiden, Come to dance Jumuna, Have this neck ring, oh! maiden accept the neck ring.

Here is another song of the same sort.

**Song**

Heeda Mohan-Mala Jatantene Ira Ho,
Heeda Mohan-Mala Jatantene Ira,
Daho Da Tulee Dikaleena Sathana,
Dikalee-Mikalee Ponda Tulee, Yendee Lene Wala Ho.

Oh! ye friend, keep this necklace with care. Carefully keep this necklace. Come! come ye maiden to the saree market. Adorned with the attire and ornaments come to dance. Oh enchanting one!

Pardhan people offer many ornaments to beloved girl. Besides, they invoke and please her with ornamental words and ideas. The song following, illustrates it. Words used are rythmetic but unmeaningful.

**Song**

Daho Da Tulee Khagora Yetakata
Khagora Karnake
Unnur Ka Jhunnurka
Appana Jhappana
Aliwanda Paliwanda
Balakuwaree Ho!
Ajaka Diyo Karelan
More Gatoyon Men.

Come oh darling! We shall purchase Khagora. But what after putting on the Khagora. Well then have these Unnurha Jhunnurka etc. as addition. Oh maiden girl, dear darling! I shall ever remember this day in my life.

It is customary with the Pardhans to enter the inlaws and make jokes about them. In the song cited below the husband tells his wife to hand over all her ornaments to him, since her relations-his-in-laws are all thieves and they may deprive her of their ornaments. The song narrates various ornaments of the Pardhan People.

**Song**

Nadee Kinara Baithe Sonara
Tara Niwa Chhika Challa Jholate Wataka,
Jholanabee Le Bayoe Parbateewale
Nadee Kinara Baithe Sonara (1)
Tara Niwa Natbesara Jholate Wataka?
Jhola Bee Katliya Parbatiwale (2)
Tara Niwa Baresuree Jholate Wataka
Jhola Bee Chhupa Liyo Parbateewale (3)
Tara Niwa Angurads Jholate Wataka
Jholate Dabaliyo Parbateewale (4)
Faraniwa Golutyange Jholate Wataka
Jholate Udadiyo Parbatee wale. (5)
Taraniwa Khagora Khisate Wataka
Khisa Katekitoor Parbateewale. (6)

*Meaning:* The Goldsmiths are sitting on the bank of the river. Hand over your rings (Chika and Chhalla) we shall keep them in the bag. People from Parvati have stolen the bag. Goldsmiths are on the river bank fetch your nose ornaments (Nath and Besar) we shall put these in bag. People belonging to Parvati have cut the bag. Bring me oh darling! your necklace (Gold Galsutri) to keep in a bag. But these people of Parvati have hidden the bag itself. Give me your Angurdana for keeping it in the bag. That bag has been taken away by those people of Parvati. Let me have your 'Golati' to be kept in the bag, but where is the bag? Those Parvati people have usurped it give me your Khagora, I will keep it in my pocket. But these persons from Parvati side have cut my pocket. They are perfect thieves.

The Pardhan females have a great hobby and liking for ornaments. Even after putting on ornaments all over the body they feel wanting. Even nature falls short to adorn and ornament them. Even after adorning themselves with all the seasonal leaves and flowers of nature, they will not leave even a straw if they avail of it, such a straw adds a valuable ornament for them to adorn themselves.

A Pardhan youth adorns his mate as very lovely and beautiful in whatever form and state she may be. They behold beauty even in simple meagre article and get enchanted in its admiration. Like young girls the young boys also have liking for enjoyment and delight. The following song describes how a youth by placing a bunch of leaves in his head will feels happy and delighted as if a monarch himself.

**Song**

Ye Gondee Raja Banadiyore
Jamunaka Turra Laga Diyore Raja Kewada
Gondeen Ka Sadee Pata Diyore
Jamuna Ka Turra Laga Diyore Raja Kewada
Jarmmal Ka Paniyana Jaware?
Paneeke Bichome Kewada
Uparase Turra Laga Diyore Raja Kewada
Shero Ke Dudhiyana Jaware,
Dudhiyake Bichome Kewada,
Parodale Turra Basa Diyore Raja Kewada.

*Meaning:* By fixing the bunch of leaves in his head-wear this Pardhan youth feels himself like a king. Though not in reality, the very idea gives him royal pleasure. Pardhans are mentally rich in their ideas and emotions.

In this way the Shimaga Fag festival songs depict the lovely and romantic life of the Pardhans.

## DHEMSA (DANCE)

Dhemsa is a dance accompanied with the music to the tune of drum beat in different ceremonial rites performed while celebrating the wedding of the Pardhans. In all, there are Sixteen (16) Dhemsas, which the Pardhans perform along with singing and dancing. Only male folk take part in Dhemsa. Generally, the female part is performed by the male by wearing female dress.

**The Sixteen Dhemsas are as follows:**

| | Dhemsa-(Dance) (Dance, Song and Music) | Ritual performed |
|---|---|---|
| 1 | Kam-Kavelu-Sival | carrying the auspicious turmeric powder from the bride's place to the groom's residence. |

| | | |
|---|---|---|
| 2. Yerdoswal-Navar Devana | -- | Giving auspicious bath to the bride and/or groom at their respective places. |
| 3. Munda-Tarval | -- | Bringing the pole of salie tree to the Pandal in ceremonial procession. |
| 4. Dareng-Tarval | -- | Bringing small branches and leaves of Jamun (Black Beri) and Umbar (Fig-tree) for covering the pandal. |
| 5. Vleeng-Java | -- | Ceremonial meeting of the bride's and groom's father on the out-skirts of the village. |
| 6. Janosa-ron-Sonval | -- | Going to the place allotted to the groom's party for the residence. |
| 7. Kuma-Kumalir | -- | The maternal uncle of the bride and the groom go to the outskrit of the village for offering traditional worship to their deities. |
| 8. Lagin-Tayarin-Kimt | -- | The traditional music and dance is offered while the preparation for actual marriage. |
| 9. Nevar-Deva-Tedant | -- | On this occasion the music sounded at the time of taking out the groom out of his residence for the marriage. |
| 10. Navar-Devan-Gotante Owiwal. Navrin-Tarval | - | Songs, music (dance) sung while taking the groom to outskirts of the village for marriage. |
| 11. Dhemsa-Vaja-Chalu Aata | -- | Beginning of the music and dance of the wedding party. |
| 12. Akashat-Toosat | -- | To distribute auspicious coloured grains to be used in marriage. |
| 13. Porana } Kalnurat Porina } | -- | Music offered while the groom washes the feet of the bride, and the *vice versa*. |
| 14. Akashta-Vatat | -- | Song, music and dance played at the time when the assembled |

| | | |
|---|---|---|
| | | people throw auspicious coloured grains (Akashata) on the heads of the wedding couple, in token of blessings. |
| 15. Khoda-Kukadee | -- | Offering a hen to the sister-in-law of the bride in token of her honour. |
| 16. Navari-Navaral-Sarkiwal | -- | The final music and dance (Dhemsa or Zulva) offered in token of completion of marriage rite. |

# 8

# Economic Institutions

## ECONOMIC STRUCTURE OF THE PARDHANS

### Phase-I

In this age of modern science and speed, economic conditions are of a great importance with reference to the nation, as well as the individual citizen. The progress and the prosperity of a country are mostly judged in terms of the economic conditions of her people. The economic condition and progress are two interdependent and interrelated things, hence the economic conditions have prime importance in a study of this nature. This chapter proposes to describe, economic structure of the Pardhan community. In order to understand the changing economic frontiers of the Pardhan tribe, the author has taken into account the traditional as also the new economic activities engaged in by the people. The members of this tribe have taken to new economic activities as an adaptive response to new emerging occupations after their permanent settlement in area. It was reported by respondents that in the past the Pardhans were gainfully employed as Princely Ministers, Priests, Pujaris, Bards in the Gond community and were known for their qualities, like administrative ability, lofty learning, poetic performance, piety and penance, dedication to deity and meditation. Therefore, the Pardhans were held in high esteem and commanded commendable confidence and respect and were placed in prime prominance and pious position, like the Brahmins among the Hindus, in the tribal community in general and among the Raj Gonds in particular.

The Pardhans in the past depended largely on the hereditary, traditional profession, as their way of earning a living. But as stated in introductory Chapter, after the downfall of the Gond rulers, the various Gond tribal groups spread over the adjacent regions for maintenance and livelihood. The Pardhans got detached from the Gonds and started wandering from the place to place in search of their livelihood. Russell and Hiralal in their book, *The Tribes and Castes of the Central Provinces of India*, throw some light on the traditional economic structure of the Pardhans[1] ; and this may have been the original occupations of the tribe though the bulk of them now seem to be living as cultivators, agricultural labour and other non-agricultural labour jobs, such as begging, quarrying, tending livestock, forestry etc.

Economic structure as it obtains among Pardhans as of today will be of immense value in understanding the adaptive changes that have taken place in their traditional economy. The following pages contain the account of the economic structure.

The Pardhans having come to permanently settle down in Vidarbha area in general and in Kelapur and Wani tehsil of Yavatmal district in particular, have adopted and are in the process of adopting the new professions based on the new needs faced by them and of the local village economy.

The traditional economic activities of the Pardhans typically include the following sources of livelihood.

(i) The Administrative chief or Ministership of the Raj Gonds i.e. Ruler,
(ii) Hereditary Priesthood, Pujaris of the Gond tribe, and
(iii) Musicians, Advisors and Bards and craftsmen of the Gond community.

A brief description of the traditional economic activities, their nature, participation and the relationship of the Pardhan with the other tribal groups and the outside world, which the author has already described in Chapter 2 under the caption, "The Pardhans : Their Origin" has not been reproduced here in order to avoid the duplication of content.

It was reported by the respondents that in the past the Pardhans were completely dependent on the above mentioned economic activities for their livelihood mostly on the Gond tribe, especially on the Raj Gonds.

Since the main concern of this chapter is to take into account the traditional economic activities and the changing economic frontiers of the tribe, it is imperative here to explain the occupational shifts of the Pardhan who were required to adapt in the process of adjustment with the changing environmental circumstances and with the other groups and castes. The occupational shifts will show and also help us to understand the transitional, occupational and economic structure to the present trends in respect of the changes taking place in the traditional economic structure of the Pardhans.

**Phase-II**

*The Changing Economic Frontier of the Pardhans*

So far the author has discussed the traditional economic phase in the economic activities of the Pardhan, the pages that follow will be devoted chiefly to describe the present economic structure of the tribe. The traditional economic activities of the Pardhans have been to a great extent modified to accommodate themselves to the demands and needs of the present day situation. The main concern of the author here, is to explain the changes that have taken place in the traditional economic activities of the Pardhans as a result of their permanent settlement in the Vidarbha area of Nagpur Division and in various villages of Yavatmal District, mainly in Kelapur and Wani Tehsils, and of the interaction with the pattern of adjustment to the sphere of occupational structure and emergence of a new economic structure as the pattern of adjustment to the occupational structure of the tribe.

TABLE : 8.1 **Table Showing Pardhans Main Occupations and Nature thereof**

| Traditional Occupations | Non-Traditional Occupations |
|---|---|
| i. Administrative Chief i.e. Prime Minister | i. Cultivators |
| ii. Hereditary Priests, Pujaris | ii. Agriculture Labourers |
| iii. Musicians, Advisors and Bards | iii. Liquor Business |
| | iv. Money Lenders |
| | v. Other occupations (a) Begging quarrying etc. (b) Non-Agricultural wage earners and and others |

As the Pardhan is known for his Kingree and by his Kingree, the Pardhans of Vidarbha have given up their traditional profession of playing on Kingree and have accepted other occupations like cultivation, agricultural labour, and other jobs. Many are reported to be pursuing the traditional occupation as Bards. The other tribe of the area viz. *Totis* (Thotis) are found reciting the stories by singing songs of the origin of the tribal communities of their deities, heroes and heroines in their honour accompanied by playing on Kingree and wandering from village to village for their livelihood, as the Pardhans were following the profession as a bard in the past. The Thotis following the traditional occupation mostly wander in the neighbouring villages and nearby localities for their economic pursuits either alone or with their family members.

*Non-traditional Occupations*

Non-traditional occupations signify the new economic activities accepted by the members of the tribe owing to their permanent settlement in the Vidarbha area and to their interactions with the other groups, classes and castes. In the traditional economy of the tribe, the Pardhans were hardly required to do any cultivation or physical labour because of the higher position as Priests, Pujaris, Advisors and preservers of the tribal mythology, traditions and culture.

These days most of the Pardhans are found engaged in non-traditional occupations and only a few are pursuing traditional profession as musicians. The new occupations shown in Table 8.1 reflect upon the changes in the occupational structure of the Pardhans and also the changes in the inter-action patterns of the tribe. The non-traditional economic activities include such activities as, cultivation, agriculture labourers, wages earners, i.e. labourers not directly or indirectly engaged in agriculture, liquor business, money lending business, begging etc.

In the pages that follow, the author has given the nature of the non-traditional economic activities, the respondents have taken to, as a mode of adjustment to demands of living.

The non-traditional economic activities are considered by the respondents to be very profitable for them and they preferred them because of the cumulative earning associated with it. Most of the respondents following non-traditional professions reported that they have taken to these professions, firstly, because of down-fall of the Gond kingdoms and secondly, because of the multifarious economic advantages, especially the free and unrestrained life. Some wander in neighbouring villages and adjoining towns such as Pandharkawada, Kelapur, Wani, Maregaon, Pusad, Ghatanji tehsil places and Parva,

Metikheda, Hivari, Both, Mangurda, Zatala etc. villages of the tehsil in Yavatmal district.

The table 8.1 further shows that the non-traditional economic activities are the main source of the livelihood of the Pardhans of Vidarbha. These people are not considered as good agriculturists. Initially, the reasons may be that they don't have sufficient land and secondly, because of their poor financial condition.

*Non-Traditional Economic Activities*

(i) *Cultivation*
(ii) *Agriculture labourers*

How the Pardhans have changed over from traditional to non-traditional economic activities; (which reflects in the transitional phase in the economic structure of the tribe)? the reason stated is that when the Pardhans were in the phase of nomadism they might not have had any attachment with the land. But it was only after their permanent settlement in the area that these people have taken to agriculture as an occupation as their economic activities. It was reported that earlier these people were faced with the problem of getting labour work, because they were reluctant to work on meagre wages and on the land owned by the other people. But in course of time they were subdued as comparatively more wages were paid to them. It was through this way, this difficulty was overcome by the Pardhans. There was also some kind of resistance from the villagers, but it was with the passage of time, over through the contacts of the villagers with the tribals. Another adjustment made by the villagers with the labour-force was that the other agriculturists started paying the wages after the completion of days' work and not on weekly basis. This proved to be a sufficient motivation to the tribal workers and they slowly started attending to the agricultural operations on daily cash payments. Agriculture is completely a new economic activity for the tribe which has brought them into interaction with neighbouring villages. This non-traditional occupation seemed to have brought about changes in the interaction patterns with the villagers.

It is seen in the table that there are some cultivators among the Pardhans. The land they hold, is either their own land i.e. they are the owners of the land or they have taken land on lease.

Following is the description of the 4 Pardhan households, two of cultivators and two of agriculture labourers from Kelapur and Wani tehsils.

The household of Shri Y.M. Soyam of Matharjan (Wani tehsil) has 7 members including himself, his wife, three sons, two daughters and one daughter-in-law. They had 30 acres of land taken on lease. The household gets Rs. 400 a year from cultivation of the land and Rs. 1000 as wages of the three sons. The annual expenditure of Rs. 1300 does not include expenditure incurred on cultivation of land possessed by the household.

The household of Shri W.B. Meshram of Bori (Kelapur tehsil) consisted of 8 members including himself, his wife, three daughters and three sons. The household owned 21 acres of land in village Bori. He earns Rs. 250 a year from cultivation and Rs. 700 as wages earned by his daughters and sons.

The principal occupation of Shri Naitam's and Shri Uike's household (from Pendhari and Isapur villages of Kelapur and Wani tehsils respectively) is agricultural labour. These two households have 5 and 10 members respectively. Shri Naitam and his wife work as agricultural labourers on daily wages from which they earn Rs. 600 annually. They do not get work throughout the year and consume wild roots and fruits when food stocks run low. The couple has one son and two daughters. Uike's is a high household of 10 members. The head and the wife and three sons are the agricultural tenants. But the annual income falls short of the total annual expenditure of the household.

The cultivation practices (procedure) and the crops grown by the Pardhans are the same as followed in general by the other people or cultivators of the area is as follows:

In the Kharif season, they grow Kharif, Jowar and Cotton (the main crops) and tur, mug, urad, and other pulses (the minor crops). The main rabi crop is wheat, gram and linseed are minor crops. The preparation of the soil begins in February. On a piece of land, where Jowar and Cotton are grown as main crops, horrowing is done first and the remnants of the old crops are removed from the field. Then small bushes and grass in the field are dug out with a Kudal. Horrowing is done three times. Cotton-sowing is done by dusa or tisa with the help of a Sarata ( sowing implement ) in the second or third week of June after receiving sufficient rains. Two pairs of bullocks are yoked for pulling the dusa and three pairs are used in the case of tisa. A man or a woman sows the Cotton seeds through the Sarata. Jowar is sown either in the last week of June or in the first week of July after Cotton sowing has been completed. A Tifan is used for sowing Jowar. Tifan is pulled by two pairs of bullocks. Weeding to cotton and Jowar is generally done for four to five times. Cotton harvesting starts in October. Jowar is harvested from November. Cotton is plucked by women in a week or in a fortnight. Thus six to eight pluckings of cotton are done in the season. When Jowar is ready for harvest, the plants are cut and kept in the fields for a week or so, for getting completely dry. Then the corns of Jowar are taken to the Threshing ground. Threshing is done with the help of bullocks or in some cases the grains of Jowar are taken out by labourers by beating the corns with sticks. After winnowing the produce is taken home.

The Rabi season starts in October. The few who hold good land sow wheat, gram and rabi Jowar. Rotation of crop is done by some cultivators, cotton in one year is followed by Jowar in the next.

The cultivators both the Pardhans and others- use the following agricultural implements for their cultivation and agricultural operations. They are :- Vakhar (wooden plough) (harrow), dawara, dundi (weeding), tifan (sowing harrow), Sarata (made of hollow bamboo pipe for sowing cotton), Kudal (to dig up the earth) fawada (to collect the earth) sickle for cutting the plants and grass, Kurpi (small sickle for weeding) and nangar (wooden plough) for ploughing.

The Pardhans purchase these implements from local carpenters, blacksmiths and from local markets. Use of fertilizer or green mannure is not general. Recently they have started using cattle manure for their fields. The Pardhans generally do not mortagage standing crops but sometimes they mortagage cattle, ornaments and their household utensils in times of financial difficulties with the money lenders on personal security.

It may be noted that those engaged in agriculture as the main economic activity, occupy a significant position in the tribe.

### (iii) *Liquor Business*

The Pardhans are generally addicted to drinking. Liquor, (country liquor) Ganja, Meat, Music and Dance are the favourite features of all their festive functions. Animal sacrifice and offering of oblation of flesh and liquor are necessary needs at the worship of their divine deities. They offer meat and liquor to their deities in oblation on religious and social functions and distribute it (liquor and meat) as *Prasad* (sacred offering).

The Liquor business is the main source of livelihood for some of them. It is not the Pardhans in particular but most of the tribal communities were and are found addicted to drinking. Now a days the habit of drinking liquor and addiction to various intoxication in rural areas is increasing by leaps and bounds. The switch over from traditional occupational activities to the new liquor business of non-traditional economic activity marks the occupational shift in the changing economic structure of the tribe. Though there is no corresponding relation between the traditional economic activities and non-traditional activities of the tribe in respect of liquor business but as stated earlier the importance of liquor in the socio-religious life of the Pardhans, it can be said that the respondents might have accepted this new occupation as a main source of their livelihood; firstly, from the point of view of fulfilling the needs and requirements of liquor of the tribe in particular and of the villagers in general. The respondents actually started regular liquor shop in the village against the Government restrictions on the open sale of liquor. In course of time they got the licence and entered into a regular business establishing contacts and contracts with the main supplier of liquor in the tehsils. But the Pardhans and the other people of the villages being financially poor they preferred country liquor to high quality of liquor, which is comparatively cheap in price. This provided the respondents impetus to illegal production of the country-liquor business. It was noticed during the investigation that the Pardhans and other persons of the village and of the neighbouring villages used to visit frequently to shops run by the respondents. These respondents earned a good amount through this business. They have constructed permanent houses, purchased cultivable lands in the villages. Though the number of actual respondents who are engaged in this liquor business is very less still they are developing a new image as the leaders of the tribe who exercise influence over the members of the tribe.

Thus it can be said that the aspect of the importance of the liquor in the socio-religious i.e. traditional life of the Pardhans and the congenial circumstances like increasing habit of drinking and demand of liquor in the villages must have worked as an impetus for the selection of this new non-traditional economic activity by the respondents.

(iv) *Money Lenders*

It is known that there are only a few respondents, one each from Bori and Matharjun, Kelapur and Wani tehsils respectively, whose main economic activity is money-lending. They are known as *Sawkars* in the community. These respondents took to money-lending as their main economic activity after being permanently settled in the villages. They further reported that money-lending activity, in the beginning was confined to the members of the tribe exclusively for socio-religious functions like Marriage, Holi, Diwali etc. It was observed and was reported by the respondents that persons of the tribe and other villagers too approach these money-lenders for borrowing money. This shows that the persons to whom these money lenders lend money are mostly such persons who have capacity to refund it; and some time to the labourers of the tribe and also people of the village. It helped the respondents on one side to have adaptive interactions with the villages and on the other side must have worked well in accepting them (respondents) as persons having a high status and importance in the village, and therefore they enjoy high status in the tribe and are found to be exercising control over the affairs of the tribe.

It was reported by the respondents that the things received in criminal pursuits by the people other than the Pardhans; were deposited with or sold to them. Such things were bought at a very cheap rate and then sold to the needy, on a price which gave good profit to these *Sawkars*. As such these, 'Sawkars' played significant role in providing economic security for the Pardhans who in the beginning were denied financial help of any kind to them by other money lenders due to the stigma of untouchability attached to the Pardhans.

Thus this, non-traditional economic activity of money-lending business appears to be facilitating and helping activity to the poor and needy Pardhans and changing traditional economic pattern of the tribe.

(v) *Other Occupations*

(a) Begging, Quarrying etc.
(b) Non-Agricultural wage earners and other.

(a) It is known that some respondents have stated begging and quarrying as their main source of economic activity. These people earn their living ostensibly by begging. Since these people had no legitimate means of earning, they relied mostly on begging as their main source of subsistence. Mostly the women, the aged, and children are found to be engaged in begging. Begging seemed to have served many functions for the tribe. In addition to earning the means of subsistence, the people could invoke the sympathetic attitude of villagers and outsiders towards them. Through begging the members could locate the houses where they could successfully carry on minor thefts. Some of the respondents in the course of interview stated frankly that they are compelled to do such activities as and when they do not get even the minimum for their subsistence by begging. These respondents are seen begging either in their village or in the adjoining villages. They move out for begging or for soliciting alms in the morning and return to their places either in the evening or even after a couple of days. It has been noted that the entire family members are seen engaged in this begging business.

(b) It is known that some respondents are engaged in begging. But in actuality the number is more than has been reported because most of the respondents whose main source of livelihood is agriculture labour, do not get work throughout the year. Therefore, along with the seasonal agriculture labour work, they (respondents) earn their livelihood by other means. This includes, the work of road construction, services, like talatis; village level workers, teacher in Ashram school, primary school, peons in Panchayat Samiti office etc.

From the data it appears that economic structure of the Pardhans is more of heterogeneous nature. Such heterogeneity in occupations can be easily explained in terms of its relationship with the others as the Pardhans to some extent depend on them for their livelihood.

## Participation in the Economic Activities by the members of the Respondents Family

The respondents were asked to mention the economic activities of the other members of the family. This was done with the intention to know the participation of those members in economic activities in the respondent's family. The institution of family being an economic unit among the tribals in general and in particular among the

Pardhans has its own importance in the study of social organization of the Pardhans. Economic activities are mostly cooperative and collective affairs in the tribal communities and the Pardhans are no exception to that. In the past when the Pardhans were leading a nomadic life, there was no clear cut division of labour among the members of the family as every one was required to participate in the pursuits of economic activities as a matter of necessity. But in the light of changing economic structure of the tribe, there is observed some kind of division of labour of economic responsibilities. It was with the intention to see in what way the women, the aged and the children as the members of the family supplement the family income. The respondents were asked to point out the participation of these family members in economic activities. The women folk from the majority of the respondent's families are reported to be engaged primarily in agricultural labour activity, begging and any kind of daily wages labour as the major non-traditional economic activity of the tribe. These women work on the fields (either of their own, or as labourer) along with men, and also move about in the village for begging.

Some respondents very casually remarked that in these days of economic hardship there had been no other alternative than to stick up to this non-traditional method of earning livelihood such as begging. It seems that economic hardships and non-availability of minimum food stuffs have been responsible for the Pardhans to adopt this activity of begging. It may be stated that the women folk of the Pardhans immensely contribute to family income through begging.

It was also revealed through the interviews with the respondents that the aged members and children of their family contribute to the family income through begging and wages by remaining outside the family for a few days mostly in the adjoining village areas.

## Economic Relations of the Pardhans with outside world

It is obvious that the Pardhans have established considerable economic ties with the outside world. It seems that they have established economic relationships with outside world at three levels due to their traditional and modern i.e. non-traditional economic activities. These three levels of interaction of the tribe include -

(i) Village Community

(ii) Neighbouring villages, and
(iii) Towns, tehsil places within the District of Yavatmal

The Pardhans are linked with neighbouring village communities through their traditional and non-traditional economic activities such as musicians, labourers, business like liquor and money lending etc. which has strengthened their economic ties with them. The importance and consumption of liquor in the socio-religious life of the Pardhans has given impetus to them for the liquor business which can be viewed as an extension of economic frontier of the tribe to the neighbouring village communities.

This has reference to F.G. Bailey's, *Caste and the Economic Frontier*. "It is obvious that the Gajam distillers have considerable ties with the world outside the village. Although they are resident in the village and count themselves as members of that community rather than of any other village, yet in a sense they are more citizens of the region or the state than are men of other caste in the village".[2]

It was reported that in the beginning villagers used to visit the liquor shop of the respondents on weekly market days but gradually, they started visiting the shop frequently as and when they feet it necessary. It is also interesting to note the linkage of the business of money-lending.

The third and the important link of the tribe with outside world can be seen in the migratory trend of the young generation towards towns and cities in the pursuits of new means of livelihood and attraction for city life.

The nature of the economic activities of the Pardhans is such that these people, are required to face number of difficulties, which makes their life miserable. They spend lavishly on drinking and in celebration of festive functions like marriage and the Holi (Shimaga Fag).

REFERENCES

1. Russell, R.V. and Hiralal, R.B., *The Tribes and Castes of the Central Provinces of India*, 1916, p. 357.
2. Bailey, F.G., *Caste and the Economic Frontier*, Manchester University Press, 1957, p. 206.

# 9

# The Pardhans in Transition

## Traditions in Transition

This Chapter aims at understanding the process of change in the traditional social system of the Pardhans of Vidarbha, who are mainly concentrated in Kelapur and Wani tehsils of Yavatmal District of Nagpur Division of Maharashtra State. In a general way, this ethnographic study of the Pardhans who are in the process of acculturation and modernization purports to bring to light the changes taking place in the Pardhan society.

Change is the inevitable law of nature as well as of life. It may be rapid or slow, good or bad and complete or partial. Change is not a specific phenomenon with specific cause. Change may thus be defined, as, "the process in which is discernible significant alteration in the structure and functioning of a particular social system. The term change, itself is wholly neutral. It only implies that there is some difference through time in the object under study. When we speak of social change we simply assert that there is some change in social behaviour, social structure and social and cultural values".[1]

Culture itself is never static. Since culture is dynamic, the life of a person or community or society (may be primitive or modern) cannot be static.

Towards the end of the 19th century and at the beginning of the 20th century, Sociologists and Anthropologists were preoccupied with the problem of how societies evolved from their original primitive state. A number of eminent sociologists have contributed to the understanding of the process of acculturation and modernization. Prominent among them being A.L. Kroeber; Talcott Parsons, N.J. Smelser and S.N. Eisenstadt.

Acculturation has a reference to the process whereby an individual or a group acquires the cultural characteristics of another through direct contact and interaction. From an individual's point of view this is a process of 'social learning' similar to that of adult socialization in which linguistic communication plays an essential role. From a social point of view, acculturation implies the diffusion of particular values, techniques and institutions and their modification under different conditions. It may give rise to culture conflict.[2]

Modernization implies some typical forms of change in the social structure of societies. According to N. J. Smelser, the concept of modernization, "evinces two closely connected but distinctive aspects. The first is the development of a social structure with great variety of structural differentiation and diversification of continually changing structural forms, activities and of system transformation. And secondly, the crucial problem that modernization creates in its wake is that of the ability of the emerging social structure to deal with such continual changes i.e. the ability of developing an institutional structure capable of absorbing continually changing problems and demands".[3] It is this which constitutes the central problem and challenge of modernization. S.N. Eisenstadt fundamentally views the process of modernization, "as of structural change or system transformation and the ability of a society to develop an institutional structure capable of adjusting to continually changing problem and demands".[4]

Thus he focusses ones' attention on two aspects of modernization: Structural characteristics and adaptiveness of socio-cultural systems.

The process of modernization has assumed greater significance in the countries where economic development is a viable national goal. Developing countries are faced with the promise and challenges of modernization. Although the process of modernization will show certain general properties, it is likely to evince some distinctive patterns as the social structure of traditional societies varies from one another. This outlook is evident in various studies of modernization in Indian society. Prof. Yogendra Singh views modernization, as, "a process of adaptive changes". According to him, "the process of modernization in India is mainly carried forward through adaptive changes in the traditional structures rather than structural dissociation or break down".[5] T.S. Epstein, in her book on "*Economic Development and Social Change in South India*" has distinctly shown, "certain fundamental relation between economic development and the different aspects of structural and cultural change in the light of the changes which occurred in Dalena and Wangala during the past 25 years".[6]

This is the broad conceptual frame-work in which an attempt has been made to show how the Pardhans of Vidarbha have changed in respect of their socio-economic, and religious structure which they have adopted for themselves while living in the district of Yavatmal. Thus, the study reveals the modifications in the traditional substructure of the tribe and the emergence of new pattern of adjustment. Theoretically, it discusses the interactions of the Pardhans with that of the other people (tribe) and castes and changes supposedly brought about by this interaction.

The following aspects of the social system of the Pardhans have been analysed in preceding chapters. They are clan, marriage, family, economy and religion.

It is already shown, how the Pardhans have permanently settled down in the area of concentration i.e. Yavatmal District. Traditionally the Pardhans are nomadic people, always on the move from one place to another. However, the downfall of Gond Kingdom offered them new opportunities for earning their livelihood. This encouraged the emergence of permanent habitation in Vidarbha area. They appear to have depended more on outsiders rather than on their tribals for their permanent settlement in the area.

## Some Social Institutions and the Changes

### *Clan Organization*

The existence and the importance of clan as a social organization has been accepted in the life of all the tribes of India especially, in the tribal communities of central zone, by all the eminent Anthropologists and writers like Verrier Elwin; A.A. Goldenweiser; G.S. Ghurye; R. Lowie; Risley; Furer-Haimendorf; M.P. Buradkar; Shamrao Hivale. In his book, *Totemism in India*, John V. Ferreira has states that "Since the Pardhan economic and religious system depends on the community of clans between the Gonds and Pardhans, the clan organization of the latter closely resembles that of the Gonds and in its main outline is based upon it. In detail, however, and especially in the development of local sub-clans, their is considerable divergence. There is no clear-cut pharatry system or classification of the clans according to the number of Gods worshipped, but groups of class do regard themselves as related.[7]

Hivale has stated that these are five groups of clans among the

Pardhan of Upper Narbada valley. As such in Vidarbha also there are five groups of clans viz. the Four Gods, Five Gods, Six Gods, Seven Gods and Twelve Gods. (For the concept of Saga i.e. God on which the clan system of the Pardhans is based has been given in Chapter 3. But during the investigation it has been noted that though the respondents could tell about the five groups of clans, actually they have been recorded in four groups viz. four, five, six and seven Gods, clan groups.

The clans are numerous and the Pardhans are unable to enumerate all the classes of their respective phratries. Though the main function of the clan was to regulate and keep restrictions on marriage on the basis of Saga, it has retained its vitality in organizing its member round the clan-God for celebrating festivals, rituals and memorial customs.

To-day, however, the clan system is seen in a state of decline and confusion. The members of each clan are expected to marry outside their clan and clan group. There is some confusion among the Pardhans about the matrimonial relations towards members of the other groups. Elderly and middle-aged people are found complaining against the younger generation about the new attitudes and desires regarding the selection of life-partner not only from any clan group of the Pardhans and of the other tribe but even from any castes like Mang or Mahar of the Hindu society.

*Marriage Patterns*

Among the Pardhans marriages do not take place between boys and girls having same number of Gods i.e. Saga. They do not marry with father's sister's daughter, but prefer to marry mother's brother's daughter.

Structural changes do not occur in a vacuum but are often related to the changes in attitude and behaviour. The traditional joint family provided its members with a wide enough group of people to make it a satisfactory recreational unit. But the gradual trend towards the nuclear family among Pardhans encourages its members to seek friendships outside the family circle. These will normally include members of the opposite sex; for the boys and girls, men and women, cannot avoid social contacts in the city. These contacts are fundamental in that they prepare them for the new division of labour and for more freedom of choice in marriage. Though, marriages among the Pardhans are always arranged by the parents and are performed traditionally still the author has recorded some new trends on the basis of the information given by the respondents and other persons of the tribe, and the introduction of a few new modifications in the existing patterns of marriage. The changes were visible in their views regarding the preferred age of marriage both for the boys and girls. As soon as the boy attains puberty he should be married. This slowly growing trend towards consciousness among a few of them that the boy should first help the family economically and then get married. Such a consideration was not present when the Pardhans were leading a cooperative and collective nomadic life. This may be attributed largely to the changes in their economy. Regarding the preferred age at marriage for girls, the majority of them are found in favour of 14-18 years as the preferred age at marriage i.e. as soon as the girls attain puberty.

Regarding the time and place of marriage a remarkable change has been noticed. Customarily and traditionally the marriages of Pardhans were usually performed in the bridegroom's village at a particular place known as 'Gothan', maintained on the outskirts of the village which is the grazing ground for the cattle, and a place for animals assembling for rest during noon time, and used to be solemnized invariably early in the morning at the time of day-break, (known as 'Gopal Muhurta').

The personally attended marriage ceremony of Soyam's son of Matharjun village, was solemnized at 11.30 a.m. at Soyam's residence of Matharjun.

A new trend of celebrating the marriage at bridegroom's place also indicates the changing attitude of the Pardhans regarding the place and the time (Muhurta) of the marriage ceremony. When asked about the change in place and time, the Pardhans were found saying that this is nothing but a convenience and mutual help.

The appreciable participation of the people other than the Pardhans in the marriage ceremony points to the remarkable change in the attitudes of the community towards the Pardhans. This was due to their constant interaction with other tribals and people of the village.

Some new cultural practices have been noticed as introduced in marriage ceremony as a result of their interaction with other communities. The marriage ceremony among the Pardhans has to some extent has become a costly affair. It is due to the inclusion of more pomp and show, such as, printing of invitation cards, hiring loudspeaker, lighting, inviting photographer for snatching photos of the marriage ceremony; pandal liquor etc. One of the significant new pattern these people have taken to is the practice of giving gifts and announcing the nature of the gift and the name of donor on the loudspeaker. This may be attributed to the interaction of the Pardhans with the other community and imitating the patterns of the dominant group in the village.

Though the Pardhans celebrate the marriage ceremony with full faith and devotion of their respective deities and strictly follow the rites and rituals of the marriage ceremony according to their religion the impact of Hindu religion has been observed and noted by the author.

After the actual marriage ceremony of Shri Soyams' son was over, the bride and groom were asked to go inside the room for prayer. There, they chanted a long prayer in praise of, *Santoshi Mata* for blessings. When Shri Soyam was asked about it, he said, 'though Santoshi Mata is not our traditional tribal deity still we pray to her and don't allow the newly wedded couple to take food unless they perform the prayer, and now it has become a part of religious ritual of marriage ceremony.'

The sociological literature shows numerous examples of castes or sub-castes in any one area, having achieved social status, trying to establish itself at a higher level in the caste structure.

M. S. Srinivas first introduced the notion of Sanskritization as an underlying process of social change, in India, in his book, *Religion and Society among the Coorgs*. He calls the process whereby a caste or tribal or other group tries to raise its status in the ritual sphere, 'Sanskritization.' He writes "A low caste was able to raise to higher position in the hierarchy by adopting ritualistic patterns of the dominant group of a society".[8] The similar process is also evident among the Pardhans of Vidarbha. This indicates an assimilation of new patterns rather than the displacement of the old by new patterns of behaviour.

## *Family Pattern*

The majority of the Pardhans still have the joint family structure. However, the major changes in the structure of the family can be attributed to the changes in economic structure, particularly the transition from the traditional economy to the non-traditional i.e. new economy.

There appears to be a slight trend towards nuclear family among the Pardhans. The aspects of family life such as family obligations, the pattern of collective living on ritualistic occasions, mutual obligation seem to be compatible even in changed situations.

It is said that kinship ties tend to be loosened as a result of the impact of industrialization and urbanization. But the family pattern shows that the joint family structure has by and large been retained. K.M. Kapadia also propounds similar views in a comparative study of family patterns in the Navasari town and fifteen villages from the same region with varying degrees of urban impact. According to him, "Joint family pattern was not only generally predominant but, contrary to the popular image, was stronger in the towns in comparison to the villages".[9]

The study further reveals that the separation of members from the parental family is becoming apparent in the community of the Pardhans. Although on the whole the majority of the respondents still continue to live in joint family, it was observed that whenever it was necessary people allowed or connived at some members of the joint family establishing a separate household.

This was largely to enable such members to pursue their new occupations and such other different situations. It was reported that some members of their family were living in same village or nearby village by establishing an independent abode. Such a separation, according to them, became necessary in order to adopt themselves to the conditions of diversified economic pursuits. Although in this way these members lived separately, they continue to fulfil their joint family obligations and participated in joint family functions. They, thus gave ample evidence of the existence of the sentiment of jointness. Diversified economic activities and an opportunity to lead an independent life were the main reasons given by the majority of the Pardhans for the phenomenon of separation. F.C. Bailey in his study on Bisipara, an Oriya village, has made similar observation.[10]

Among the reasons for family separation, separation effected in economic activities seems to be the dominant reason. It suggests that their differing economic gains due to diversified economic interests seemed to be responsible for separating the members of the family.

It was further observed that the majority of the separate family members have maintained economic ties with the parental family.

They continued to render financial help as and when occasions demanded of them. This is symbolic of the sentiment of jointness. I.P. Desai makes similar observations which may be quoted here:

> what matters more is not the residential separation of the family group, but the nature and quality of social interaction which interlinks it in sentimental bonds, ritual and economic obligations to other family units in the place or in other places and thus functionally may be joint in obligational ties.[11]

The ties of jointness among the Pardhans are so strong that even when people are residentially separated from each other, they continue to maintain the sentiment of jointness which may be the mode of adaptation.

*Economic Change*

Data on the economic structure of the Pardhans of Vidarbha show changes in their traditional activities. These changes are visible in the diversification of economic roles and relationship in the patterns of cooperation and mutual aid and help. The changes seem to be largely due to their greater participation in the rural-urban economy, and also the tribal-non-tribal relations of the villagers.

The study reveals that when the Pardhans came to this area with a view to permanently settling down, certain temporary non-traditional economic activities were taken up by the tribe. These occupations were to mention the important ones, cultivation, agriculture, labour, wage labourers, liquor business and money-lending business, begging and other minor economic activities. There does not appear much positive correspondence between the traditional and these non-traditional economic patterns of the tribe except the religious, social importance of liquor in the life of these people and the liquor business. This marks the transition in the occupational activities (liquor business) by a few respondents of the tribe from nomadism to the present occupational structure of the tribe. It appears that the occupational shifts in the initial stages of interactions seem to have produced an opportunity for the Pardhans to adopt themselves to the village rural-urban economy.

Regarding the changes in the traditional economic activities, a few have continued to pursue traditional occupations such as musician as the primary source of their livelihood. Majority of them have taken non-traditional economic activities, as the primary source of livelihood. These new occupations show a relationship with the needs out of an emerging urban development. Thus through their diversified economic activities (both traditional and non-traditional) the Pardhans got an opportunity for closer adjustment into the larger economy of the region. It seems that the major part of the traditional economic structure was incompatible with the economy of the present needs, in the changed economic development, for instance, to act as Pujaris, Priests, Bards or even musicians and their traditional means of subsistance. Because the traditional occupations were not so viable even as to provide with the minimum requirements of the family, the Pardhans in the beginning received stiff opposition from the village dwellers, as the new non-traditional economic activities proved to be a potential source of nuisance to the villagers.

New non-traditional economic activities have to some extent been transferred to women, the aged and the young children of the family in the new set-up. In the past there were not such economic activities as non-traditional, still there was cooperation and helping attitude in the occupational set up of the tribe. Thus, it may be said that the continuation of traditional economic roles by the women, the aged and the children, enabled the men to participate in the new economic activities of the tribe. This, thus sets in the progress of role differentiation in the economic structure of the tribe.

The economic differentiation between men and women is becoming compatible with the participation of the Pardhans in the wider economy of the area. T.S. Epstein her book, *Economic Development and Social Change in South India*, makes similar observations in connection with the differentiation of economic roles. She states, "the economic role of women is unaltered in the new system. They continue to operate in the customary subsistence farming economy. Their continued work on the land is not merely compatible with the new economic system it is in fact essential to sustain it".[12] Therefore, it may be stated that the cooperative and collective character of their economy is slowly changing into different and individualistic basis.

In the past due to the nomadic pattern of life, the Pardhans had no attachment to land. Cultivation and agriculture as new economic activity seems to have provided an opportunity for many members of the tribe to integrate themselves with the neighbouring village areas. Mutual help and participation in economic activities, show that, most of the respondents stated that they required the help of others in their economic activities.

The economic dependence of the tribe on the family members and relatives is becoming more dominant. The economic activities are becoming more family concerned than the tribe concerned. The need of respondents relatives as the source of help obviously stresses the role of the wider kin group in economic relations.

The Pardhans have considerable economic contact with the outside world. The persons pursuing traditional as well as non-traditional economic activities have a link with neighbouring rural areas. The economic ties with the outside world may be attributed to their participation and expansion in the range of economic relations, opportunities the Pardhan getting in new economic set-up.

Thus, as the members of the tribe pursue diversified economic activities, they have increased considerably their economic and social ties with the out-side world.

## Change in Religion-Cultural Aspect

They generally worship their tribal Gods and Goddesses as well as some of the Hindu Gods and Goddesses and celebrate the same rituals and festivals as that of the Hindus. It can be said that though the Pardhans have full faith and devotion in their religion in the celebration of there traditional festivals and ceremonies, the impact of the Hindus is more present on their culture and life than primitive tribal culture.

The majority of them are not clear about which religion they belonged. They often mention 'Gondi' 'Adiwasi' and even Hindu as their religion. In respect of worship and the remembering of the God and Goddesses in daily life and also during the ceremonial festive functions elderly people of the tribe are seen fully devoted to their tribal deities rather than to the Hindu Gods and Goddesses. The younger generation assembles, participates in ceremonies, the festive feasts and recreation. Among both men and women, only the elders seem to talk about the changes of time and the decline in religious attitude and ethical standards of the tribe. In everyday thought and speech of the younger generation there is very little of religion and little conscious effort at seeking any deep religious experience is to be found among them.

Though, R.V. Russell and R.B. Hiralal in the book, *Tribes and Castes of the Central Provinces of India*, Vol. IV mentioned decades back that the Pardhans were employed as, 'Priests' by the Gonds to conduct the ceremonial worship of their great God 'Bura Deo', these days no Pardhan mentioned his occupation as priesthood at any of the Gond family. They are invited by the Gonds to attend religious and social ceremonies not as Priests or Pujaris but as 'invitees' like others.

In the ritualistic structure of the tribe no significant variations have been found except of inclusion of new outlook in the celebration of the rituals.

The reason for change must be sought in a multiplicity of factors. In, *Indian Village* S.C. Dube quotes Raymond Firth,[13] "structural change is a product of social interaction, in which pressures are felt, advantages perceived and responsibilities recognised", which are really responsible in bringing about the changes in the social organization of Pardhans. The factors of utility, convenience and availability have played a more important role in bringing several new elements into the life of the Pardhans of Vidarbha.

The influence of urbanization and modernization has brought about adjustment and modification in socio-cultural life of the tribe.

*Medicines*

The opening of small dispensary in the villages and the availability of good facilities of modern medical treatment in the tehsil places, town and in cities have considerably changed the attitude of the people towards diseases and their treatment. Although the people still believe that smallpox and other incurable diseases are the result of the wrath of Goddesses, the old fear of vaccination and inoculation to some extent has disappeared. Divination, protective magic chants and spells are still employed to ward-off disease and difficulties, but at the same time increasing use is being made of modern medicine. Age-old prescription of indigenous herbs are generally used for fevers and other common ailments. But when the disease takes a serious turn the patient may even be removed to a hospital in the city. The changes in the acquisition of new habits and styles are noticed in dress and ornaments. The old-style tribal dress and ornaments is now giving place to the new styles of clothes cut and stitched in imitation of the urban style.

*Dress*

A traditional dress of a Pardhan male is generally a dhoti, a Bandi and a *feta* (turban). Present elderly Pardhans put on dhoti on all occasions. The feta is gradually yielding place either to cap or no cap. The younger generation is taking to trousers, pyjama and manilas. They do not wear caps.

The dress of Pardhan women consists of a *lugade* (sari) (Nine yard) which reaches right upto the ankles or knees and a *choli* (blouse). The young girls wear five yard saree and blouse. Women of older generation do not wear a bodice but cover the upper part of body with the end of the sari. Women have no special ceremonial dress.

*Ornaments*

There is practically no section of human beings that does not (wear) use one kind of ornament or other. Irrespective of caste, creed, and nationality men and women are everywhere alike in their love of wearing ornaments, and one general statement that may be enunciated is that, love of ornament is practically ingrained in human beings. All do not, however, use the same kind of ornaments everywhere; each section of people has got its own specific types of ornaments and its own mode and place of wearing them. This difference in age, sex and nationality of the wearer, the lapse of time, the march of civilization and culture contact – these also do account for considerable differences. Nowhere does the old order changes yielding place to the new, so quickly and considerably, as in the nature of ornaments. Consequently the real 'Prakriti' could still be discerned in the apparent 'Vikriti' that the world holds out in this field. This abundance of variety in the types of ornaments and the innate craving of human beings to adorn their body, render a rare charm.

Prof. Sir William Ridgeway, Disney, Professor of Archaeology in the University of Cambridge, who was the first to introduce a scientific discipline into this subject and his studies have led to the Ridgeway the theory of ornaments, feels that, "ornaments owe their origin not to Asthetics but to magic".[14]

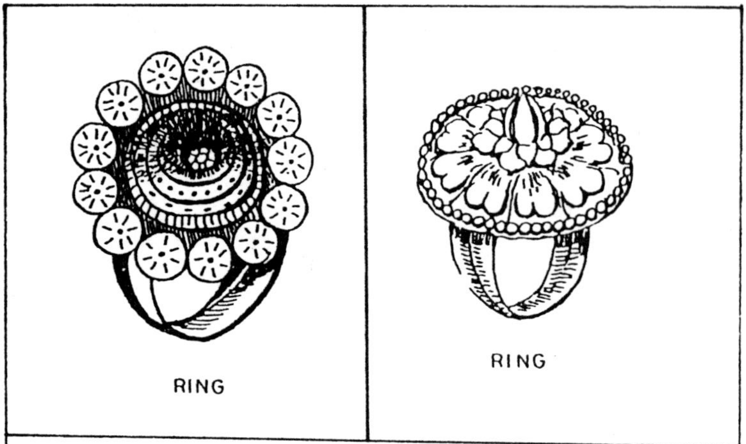


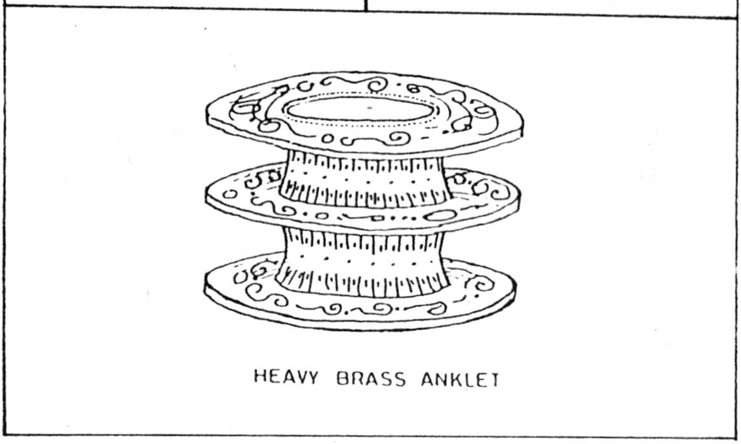


5. i. A Finger Ring of a Pardhan woman.
   ii. A Finger Ring of a Pardhan woman.

6. A Brass Anklet of a Pardhan woman.

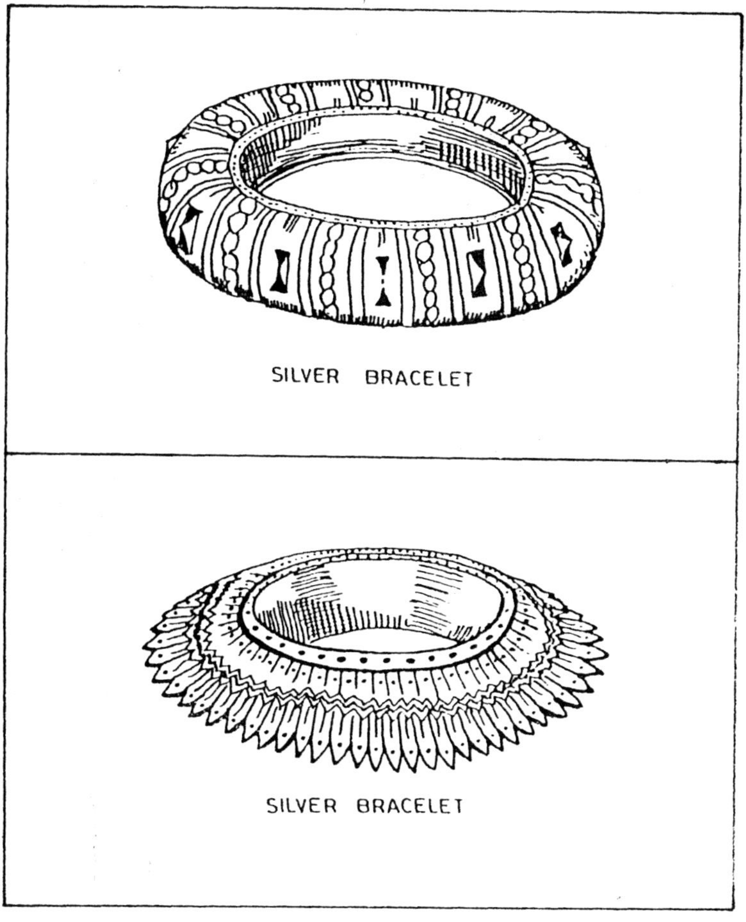


7. i. A Silver Bracelet of a Pardhan woman.
   ii. A Silver Bracelet of a Pardhan woman.

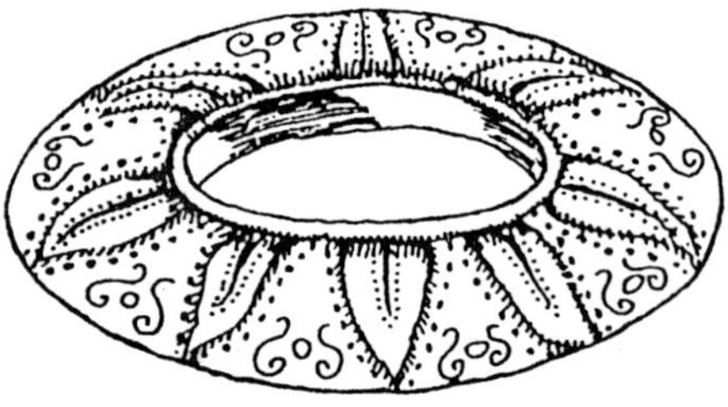


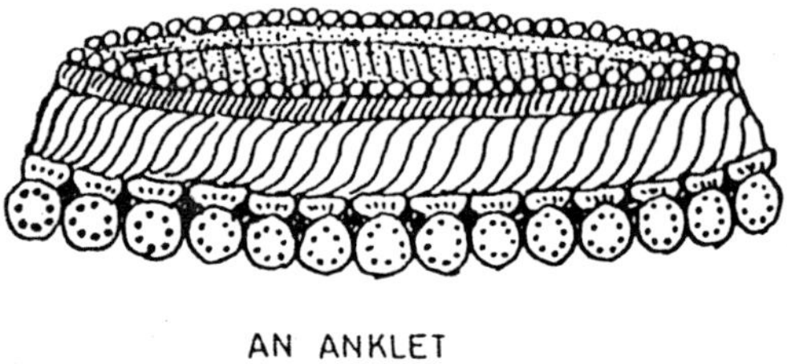


iii. A Silver light

8. An Anklet of a Pardhan woman

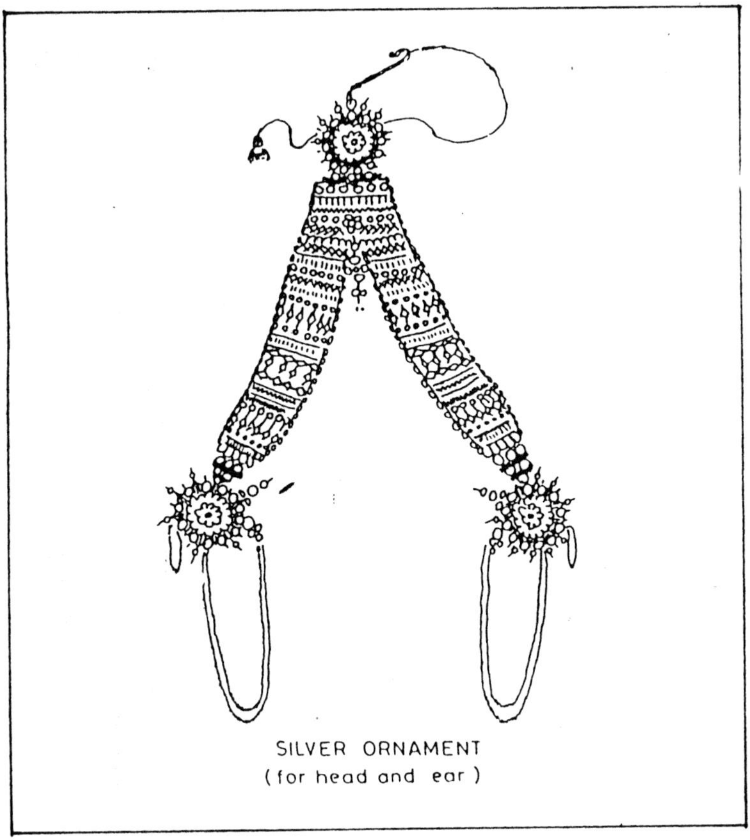


9. Dhar and Sutia elaborate silver ornament for Head and Ears

10. Pardhan busy in thatching the hut

11. Wall decoration in mud relief showing the Tetomic symbolism on a Pardhan's house.

In the light of the above theory the traditional ornaments which the Pardhan males used to wear consist of, (a) *Anguthi* (ring of silver, brass or copper) (b) *Bali* (a pair of ear-rings made of silver or brass used on upper lobes of the ear). (c) silver Kardoda (a chain round the waist).

The traditional ornaments of the Pardhan women consist of (a) A sikk muda (a ring made of silver rupee or half-rupee coin) (b) Silver kada (a hollow bracelet) round the wrist (c) patalyas (a solid bracelet made of silver) round the wrists.

The ring made of silver or brass and very rarely of gold is the only ornament which the present Pardhans wear.

Among women brightly coloured and gaudily printed clothes have become popular. City manufactured trinkets are eagerly brought by them. Bangles which every woman whose husband is alive must wear were formerly made by local manufacturers from indigenous materials. Now factory made glass bangles and other ornaments, silver patalya (bracelets) gold polish ekdani (necklace) or silver chain have taken the place of old ornaments.

Originally, the Pardhans being Gond aboriginals, Gondi is their mother tongue. In the investigated area i.e. villages the Pardhans reported that among themselves and with the family members they speak either Gondi or Telugu but speak Marathi with the people of other castes and with outsiders. Hindi is generally understood by them, but it is not in common use among them.

The Pardhans in the area under study speak Telugu very fluently. About the 'Gonds of Adilabad', Setu Madhorao Pagdi writes "the Pardhans in Adilabad spoke Marathi as their mother-tongue and even in the Telugu part of Laxatipet tehsil they spoke corrupt Marathi among themselves. He adds that no Pardhan had Gondi as his mother tongue and they used Gondi only when they talked to the Gonds.[15]

Adilabad being an adjoining district of Yavatmal of Maharashtra State and being on the opposite banks of the Painganga river there must have been close contacts between the Pardhans of both the regions for centuries and hence Gondi must have been replaced by regional telugu language, which is at present the main language of daily life of the Pardhans used by them among themselves in Vidarbha (Yavatmal District).

**Summing-up**

The region of the origin of the Pardhans, is unknown even to them. From their tribal traditions, clan, creed, folk-culture, mythological anthology and dialect, it may however, be inferred and history confirms it too. The Pardhans consider themselves as belonging to the Gond group of the tribals and designate themselves as "Pardhan Gonds". Their mythology, tribal traditions, creed, culture, religious rites and rituals, social institutions, festive functions and ceremonial celebration closely resemble those of the Gonds. Hence,their claim to the kinship with Gonds, does not seem far from the factual truth.

The Pardhans also claim that in historical times and prehistoric ages, they had been much higher in social position and possessions. They came from priestly class of the Gond clan and many of them were ministers, minstrels, advisors, administrators and religious heads of the Gond rulers. Some of them were royal bards, musicians and compilers of anthology of the ancient ancestral history and mystic mythology. There is no authoritative evidence to prove this claim properly but the social system, tribal tradition, religious rites and rituals, tribal trends towards talented skill and intellectualism, do not allow one to set aside their claim as wholly untrue either.

That the Pardhans are the offshoots of the same tribal trunk as that of Gonds can be affirmed by and large beyond doubt. Their region of origin may have therefore, been the same as that of Gonds. History tells us that the Gonds flourished for a fairly long period in the Central India, especially, the eastern part of the Vindhyas and Satpura ranges and the Narmada Valley. They had their strong progressively flourishing kingdoms in Sagar, Damoh, Mandla, Jabalpur and Chhindwara districts of Madhya Pradesh, during the medieval period till the massive aggression of the Moguls. Especially, the Mandla dynasty was so powerful that even the Rajput rulers of Rajasthan had social, political and matrimonial relations with them. Rani Durgawati of Mandla had created a heroic history by her power and martial acumen in giving a decisive dreadful opposition to Akbar, the aggressing Mogul emperor. There is room to believe that Pardhans belong originally to the same soil of the Gond settlements. They later seem to have moved south of Satpuda, alongwith some Gond groups, in adverse circumstances and calamity, who then established their dominations at Chhindwara, Nagpur and Chandrapur. It is thence that they appear to have migrated further to Painganga plains of Yavatmal district of Vidarbha and Adilabad District of Telengana (Andhra Pradesh).

To-day the Pardhans have a very low social status. The Gonds have largely disowned and outlawed them. The Pardhans plead, that this outlawed position and despisable treatment, by the Gonds in general and Rajgonds (Koiturs) in particular, meted out to them is due to their patriotic proclamation to defy and defend the ancient Aryan aggression on their tribe, against the will of their ruling Gond Chiefs, who wanted to surrender to them and accept their servillience to save their position as rulers and possessions of the region they ruled over. This plea of the Pardhans however, does not stand to reason, in as much as, the Gonds had their flourishing and powerful dominations, even after the ancient Aryan aggression in the remote past, till medieval days and they also had respectable social and political relations with Aryan rulers. The Pardhans had enjoyed responsible and respectable posts under rulers as ministers, administrators and priests till then. Therefore, while the Pardhans claim of patriotic defiance might be true, the time of Aryan aggression appears to be miscalculated and misleading. The plea appears to be an after effect of the wrong conception of the Aryan and non-Aryan division of population, impressed on the Indian people by the Britishers to suit their "divide and rule policy". This was the time of massive aggression by the Mogul rulers on the Gond rulers. It was then, history tells us, that many a Gond rulers accepted conversion to Muslim faith, to save their position and status as rulers under the servitude of Mogul emperor; while the faith-loving and patriotic courtiers and common people fled, to save their lives and faith, to woods and thickets.

When there is mass migration from the native nest to a distant destination, to seek a satisfactory settlement and solace, a change is inevitably a corresponding corollary, as a result of constant contact and impact of the surrounding situation. The Pardhans were no exception to it. The Pardhan populace in Yavatmal district and the adjacent region has undergone such a change in all walks of life, (social, religious, cultural etc.) and in their dialect too. The Hindu impact on their day-to-day-life is so much, that they can hardly be called non-Hindus, even though they may claim to be so due to ethnocentic attitudes. Their Gondi dialect has disappeared in their common routine dealings at home and outside too. They rarely use it only when they have to deal with the Gonds people. They usually speak clear Marathi with people outside the community and talk in Telugu while dealing amongst themselves. A very few only know and can talk in Hindi. They have almost abandoned their tribal tongue and have adopted Telugu as mother-tongue and they are aptly adapted to it.

As a result of Hindu impact and coming in contact with the industrial development in villages, towns and cities a process of acculturation has already set in and started slowly and steadily on their society. Steadily are their tribal traditions and community customs disappearing and they are deviating to those of the surrounding society. They are accepting and acclimatizing to many Hindu ways of life in social and religious forms. Their aboriginal attire is hardly visible any more. Only a very few elderly persons are seen clad in it, on some ceremonial celebrations and that too rarely. The bulk or the masses use the local rural dress in their daily life and even at the festive functions. The semi-educated and somewhat cultured young generation has adopted modern dress. Dhoti and turban have given place to pyjama, shirts and caps, even further to trousers and manila and without any headgear. Female folk also follow in their footprints. Youngsters wear 5 yard sari and blouse while the midagers put on 9 yard sari (Lugade) and choli. Only old aged women do not put on the upper breast garment and wear the double-fold sari after their old tribal tradition. Tattooing too, is getting outdated Modern pattern of living was more observed amongst the Pardhans living in villages like Bori (Patan) and Ayata of the Kelapur tehsil and Matharjun and Mukutban of the Wani tehsil of Yavatmal District. These villages are closer to city and township where industrial impact is intruding. In villages like Pendhari, Weded and Andherwadi of Kelapur tehsil and Raipur, Isapur and Mudhati in Wani tehsil, the Pardhan people have still been following the rural life. These villages are distant and detached from town-ships and hence the cultural contacts and connections are less and rare so far as these poverty stricken people are concerned.

Being outlawed and disowned by their own tribal community and treated as lowest untouchables even by outlawed untouchables of the Hindu society, the Pardhans had hard times to earn their livelihood. They could hardly get one square meal on their earnings by means of their traditional profession (viz. hunt, collecting herbal medicines, preparing bamboo vessels and articles, singing mythology and ancestral history, and priest performance for the tribals etc.) They were and are still in a precarious pecuniary position. Especially in these and the recent past of hard economy, due to invading industrial development, when prices are spiralling higher and higher, these people, stricken by poverty, were nearly starving. They were, therefore, forced to forego their traditional occupation and had to take to new ones. Their outlawed, low social status and untouchability, denied them any other good employment. They were, therefore, compelled to conceal their caste and creed. They proclaimed and declared themselves as Gonds to seek a timely solution to the situation. They girded up their loins to fight a way out. Yet the Gonds could recognise them. They, therefore, singly and severally threatened one and all to murder, if any one attempted to disclose them by the caste. They even did not spare their own kith and kin from the community, if, even unawaredly, he were to do so. Circumstances constrained them to this conduct. They then abandoned their aboriginal assignments and took to labour of any kind. Being nomads they possessed no land. Yet they learnt and worked as labourers in fields and rural industries, and sundry sorts of labour, including the lowest menial one such as scavenging wood-mud work, carrying carcasses, chopping fuel-wood etc. Today they are in a little good economic position than before, but yet at the lowest end. Many of them have taken to field labour and corresponding concerns connected to agriculture. Some small number possess little lands of their own too, but a large portion of the Pardhan populace depends on labour for livelihood. Some others deal in liquor and money-lending also. They are intelligent and talented people and if appropriate opportunities are available to them, they can slowly and steadily though, improve their lot and come up by dint of their hard work and ingenious efforts.

With the abandoning of the ancestral tribal traditional occupations and duties, the Pardhans are fast forgetting their forefathers' faith, ancestral art, community culture, mythological, anthology and religious rites and rituals of which they were formerly custodians; this, so much so, that the Kingari the very instrument of their identity has almost been lost to them. The Kingari and the Pardhan were formerly inseparable associates– one being known by the other. A Pardhan must carry a Kingari with him and a Kingari player, must necessarily be a Pardhan only. But to-day, a majority of them do not know the Kingari and almost none knows to play on it. None of them is a priest practising rites for the community or a bard singing mythology and ancestral history of the tribe. None works as a social or religious advisor to the Gond community at any of their social, religious or matrimonial functions. On the contrary, they avoid Gonds out of the sheer fear for them. At present these duties are being performed by a small group of tribals known as 'Thoties'. It is curious enough and also amusing, that these very Pardhans, who are considered as untouchables and outlawed by the Gonds and other tribals, in their turn treat these 'Thoties' as untouchable and outlawed and keep no connections whatsoever (social, religious or matrimonial), with them. These 'Thoties' seem to be a group of Pardhans, who have retained their traditional tribal means of maintenance. The transitional Pardhans refrain from community connections with them, probably out of mere fear of unearthing unnecessarily their unwanted identity, which they have been cautiously and conscientiously concealing, to ward off the cruel calamities they had earlier experienced, and to improve their luck and lot by adopting and adhering to new ways and means of livelihood.

The Hindu surrounding has made such impact on their initial social institutions. Hindu customs have made inroads into their social life and have initiated introduction of new items of social life. It has intruded in their religious life too. Industrialisation, modernity and city civic culture are also, slowly yet steadily, stamping their society life. Some facts, observed by the author during even his surface survey of the society, may suffice to prove the proposition. Formerly they were accepting food and water from the caste Hindus but not from scheduled caste Hindus and even from some of the scheduled tribes. Now there is no such restriction with the only exception of the 'Thoties' whom they treat as full untouchables. Hitherto matrimonials were performed only within the clan and community and those too, following their saga system, strictly and rigidly. Now the restrictions have been relaxed. Marriage with sub-tribal or scheduled caste Hindu (e.g. Mahar, Mang, Chambhar etc.) is permissible. Wedding within the same saga was fully forbidden formerly, now such a one is not much objected too. Matrimonial with the mother's clan and saga, was also undesirable but now one may marry his maternal uncle's daughter. The tribal tradition of Pardhans was to perform wedding, during a particular period of the year, on "Gothan" a barren place at the village outskirts (reserved for cattle grazing) or under a secluded tree. Bride would go to the groom's residence for wedding. Ceremonials and rites would be done during late night and early morning before day break. At the actual wedding time groom wore the bridal ornaments. All these community customs are gradually ringing out and the reformed ones are riding in. Weddings now take place at common community place and or at bridal residence, even in morning, noon or evening, with all pomp and show after the Hindu fashion and no restriction of wearing bridal ornaments is rigidly followed. On the other hand, it is fast vanishing since younger generation is marching toward modernity, acquiring acculturisation. Ancestral wedding attires are also undergoing alternation, yeilding place to refined romantic robes, to keep pace with the reforms. Old ornaments and tattooing in women folk are also being abandoned and new ones after the local fashion are adopted. Thus many Hindu customary items have been stealing sanction in their social and cultural life.

The social surroundings and the situation of the soil wherein they have settled, have brought changes, not only in their social set-up but also in the region of religious life of the Pardhans. The rigid faith of the forefathers and rigid-rites of tribal tradition are being overtaken by new ones, which they have taken over, in recent times. Hindus ideas, ideals and idols have intruded inlets in their religious region, initiating and enuntiating intimate imitation of the Hindu life. Several local deities have stolen seats in their shrine by the side of their traditional tribal tutelary deities. Hindus Gods and Goddesses are honoured as holy, and wholly worshipped whole heartedly as wholesome to them. Santoshi Mata, Narasimha, Shri Krishna, Shiva, Devi Ambika, may be mentioned as a few new ones. On one occasion, the newly-wedded couple was observed offering an omen prayer to *Santoshi Mata* at their shrine soon after the wedding, to ward off ominous oncomings. In a certain village, the Pardhan populace was seen keenly participating, with due devotion and dedication, in the festival of the local presiding Hindu deity lord Narasimha, so much so, that a majority of them observed fast till the festive rituals were over and had their food only after taking 'Darshan' of the deity and offering pious prayer to it. In one of their Holi-festival songs, Hanuman has been seen to have honour of homage. Shiva and Parvati have had already a steady standing in their mythology and mythical legendary. (They much more resemble the tribal God Badadev and Goddess Tondyal of the Pardhans and the Pardhans pose and postulate that Shiva-Parvati are their tribal deities which have been later usurped and accepted by the Hindus as their own. The problem however, is a matter for the mythologist to research) They also allow allotting of Holi festival to Radha-Krishna. Thus the Hindu impact has impressed and improved their social, cultural and religious life. Though they are formally retaining the former frame firmly, the form is flirting with changing fashion of the day. They are at present semi-tribal and semi-Hindu.

To sum up, the Pardhans are talented and intelligent people. In historical past they had enjoyed high honourable status as pious priests, couragious and courteous courtiers, ministers and minstrels of mythology, brilliant bard-poets, who hoarded history of heroic happening and anthology of tribal ancestors. The cruel and crucial circumstances conspired to lead them to a nearly nude nomad life. They were obstinately oppressed and outlawed by their own tribals. Hence they are awefully afraid of unearthing their identity. They do not desire to disclose it, and declare their class, caste and creed, due to the fear of the former frightening experiences. It is rooted deep in their brain and brawn. They necessarily need an honest aid and helping hand of social workers, to uproot it from their head and heart. If they are freed from the fear, they can positively pursue the path of progress. Some few persons have risen high to political and social leadership, but they dare not declare themselves as Pardhans. Instead, they proclaim to be Gonds. That helps them to usurp the facilities and concessions granted by the Government to Scheduled Tribes. But this does not help them to raise their community from their slum status as its representatives. They have a class-consciousness but they cautiously conceal it, for the mere fear of the social suffering to which the society seriously succumbed. So the individualism is developing for personal progress but aggressive attempts for the uplift of community are absent. Social and political protection is a much needed element for the upliftment and progressive development of these precariously poverty-stricken Pardhans. Today they are a more backward class than any of the backward tribals. They have no education and they are mostly ignorant of the educational concession and facilities offered to the scheduled tribes. Even if some few percolate to them they would even evade them for fear of identity. These privileges are, therefore, being usurped by the Gonds, Kolams, Banjaras etc. of the Vidarbha Region. If political and social leaders afford them protection, and awaken their awareness to acquire the rights and privileges due to them, that would help to rouse these talented tribals to tread the track of learning once again, to uplift themselves to prior position of prominance. Once educated, they can brush off blind beliefs from their brain and fill it with faith for science and industrialism. Industrious, ingenious and intelligent as they are by nature, they would gradually develop rational, national and political consciousness. They would also feel zeal for forming a formal organisation, to persuade Pardhans to pursue their privileges for their proper progress. At present, they have no functional specificity which they can then decide appropriately for the individual and collective development. Their trend, towards tribal traditionalism is already tending towards transitional secularism. The more progressive they become, the more secular they will be to prove an asset to our secular nation than a liability as they are today for the country.

In free India, when all classes are enjoying freedom of speech, Pardhans are not free to speak for themselves. Fright forbids them to fight for freedom. Lurking fear is working harsh on their mind. It is a mass mental-malady and it requires to be readily remedied by the social leaders. It is a curse on them. Social sympathy and political protection, is the only course for its cure. Naturally, neat nursing by the National leaders is necessarily needed. Yesterday's outlawed and down-trodden 'Mahar's of Maharashtra have today risen to the status of Buddhist priests but the priest Pardhan of the yonder past is today only an oppressed outlaw and trodden down as unfortunate untouchable. What a paradox, an ironical feat of fate! Formerly, the proud protesting Pardhan had to be in hiding for fear of annihilation, by the advancing mass of the invaders, now he had held himself in hiding, though amongst people, for fear of humiliation, by the mass of the advanced tribal who evade them. This book may also draw attention of the social and national workers to this puzzling problem of the Pardhans. The author will feel amply rewarded, if effective efforts are made by them for the uplift of Pardhans, by redressing the afflictions they are subject to. They will surely pave the path of progress of these proud patriotic people, the Pardhans of the ancient vintage.

## REFERENCES

1. Kuppuswamy, B., *Social Change in India*, Vikas Publishing House Private Ltd., Bombay, 1972, p.43.
2. Kroeber, A.L., *Anthropology Today*. 1953.

3. Smelser, N.T., *Social Change During Industrial Revolution*, Chicago, University of Chicago Press, 1959, p. 43.
4. Eisenstadt, S.N., *Modernization: Protest And Change*, New Jersey Prentice Hall, 1966, p. 5.
5. Singh, Yogendra, *Modernization of Indian Traditions*, Thomson Press (India) Ltd., Publication Division, Delhi, 1973.
6. Epstein, T.S., *Economic Development and Social Change in South India*, The English Language Book Society and Manchester University Press, 1972.
7. Ferreira, John V., Oxford, *Totemism in India*, University Press, 1965, p. 144.
8. Srinivas, M.S., *Religion and Society Among the Coorge*, The Coorgs of South India, Oxford Clarendon Press, 1952, p. 30.
9. Kapadia, K.M., Rural Family Pattern: A Study in Rural-Urban Relationship, *Sociological Bulletin*, Vol. V. No. 2 September, 1956, p. 119.
10. Bailey, F.G., *Caste and Economic Frontier*, Manchester University Press, 1957, p. 92.
11. Desai, I.P., *Some Aspect of Family in Mahuva*, Asia Publishing House, Bombay, 1965, p. 71.
12. Epstein, T.S., *Economic Development and Social Change in South India*, The English Language Books Society and Manchester University Press, 1972, p. 316.
13. Dube, S.C., *Indian Village*, 1967, pp. 227-28.
14. Rama, K., The Origin of Ornaments: Being a Study of Kerala Ornaments, Pisharoti, *Man in India*, Vol. XI. No. 3 and 4 July-December 1931, pp. 268-274.
15. Pagdi, Setu Madhorao, *Among the Gonds of Adilabad*, Popular Book Depot, 1955, p. 74.

# Bibliography


Apte, V.S., 1958: *The Practical Sanskrit English Dictionary;* Edited by P.K. Gode and C.G. Karve. Vol. II. Prakash Parkashan, Poona, p. 1093

Bailey, F.C., 1957: *Caste and Economic Frontier,* Manchester University Press, p. 206.

Begdie, L.F.I.C.S. and Nelson, A.E., 1909: *Central Provinces District Gazetteers Chanda District* Allahabad, p.107.

Bhagwat, Durga, 1953: 'Bara-Deo: High God of Gonds', *Journal of the Asistic Society,* Bengal Vol. 7. No.2.

Bhandekar, P.L. and Wilkinson, T.S., 1977: *Methodolgy and Techniques of Social Research,* Himalaya Publishing House, Bombay.

Bhattacharya, Jogindar Nath, 1896: 'Gond Brahmans'. *Hindu Caste and Sect*, Calcutta, pp. 102-103.

Bodhankar Anantarao, 1964: *Gondi-Marathi Hand Book (Mar)* Part-I and II, Published by Director of Govt. Printing Press, Maharashtra State, Bombay.

Brown, C. and Russell, R.V., 1908: *Central Provinces District Gazetteers, Yavatmal District! A Descriptive,* Calcutta, p. 70.

Buradkar, M.P., 'Social Organization of Gonds' Unpublished Ph. D. Thesis, Nagpur University, Nagpur.

Buradkar, M.P., 1940: 'The Kinship Among Gonds' *Nagpur Uni-Journal.*

Buradkar, M.P., 1940: 'Totemism Among the Gonds' I and II, *Man in India.* Vol. 20 No.3-4, pp.114-143 & 268-269.

Buradkar, M.P., 1945, Gond Exogamy, *Journal of the Anthropological Institution,* Vol.1, pp. 48-58.

Buradkar, M.P., 1947: 'Clan Organization of Gonds' *Man in India.*, Vol. 27, No.2, pp.127-136.

Daltan, E.T., 1972: *Descriptive Enthology of Bengal*, Calcutta, p.282.

Desai, I.P., 1965: *Aspects of Family in Mahuva,* Asia Publishing House, Bombay, p.71.

Desai, I.P., 1965: *Some aspects of Family in Mahuwa. A Sociological study Jointness in a Small Town*, Asia, Bombay.

Dhebar, U.N., 1961: *Report of the Scheduled Areas and Scheduled Tribes Commission*. Govt. of India Press, Delhi.

Duncan and Mitchell, 1968: *A Dictionary of Sociology* Routledge and Kegan Paul, London.

Dube, Leela, 'The Gond Women', Unpublished Ph. D. Thesis, Nagpur University, Nagpur.

Dube, S.C., 1965: *Indian Village,* Allied Publishers Private Ltd. Bombay.

Dube, S.C., 1977: *Tribal Heritage of India,* Vikas Publishing House Private Ltd. Bombay.

Eisenstadi, S.N., 1966: *Modernization: Protest and Changes,* New Jersey Prentic Hall. p.5.

Elliott, Mabel A. and Merrill, F.E., 1950: *Social Disorganization,* 4th Edition, Harper and Row Publishers, London.

Elwin, Varrier, 1954: *The Religion of Indian Tribe*, Oxford University Press.

Elwin, Varrier (Pardhan), 1947: *Muria and Their Ghatul*, Oxford University Press. Indian Branch, Bombay, pp.13-14.

Elwin, Varrier (Pardhan), 1942: *The Agaris,* Calcutta, Oxford University Press.

Elwin, Varrier (Pardhan), 1950: *Bondo High Landers,* Oxford University Press, Bombay.

Elwin, Varrier (Gogia Pardhan Rajnengi Pardhan), 1946: *Myths of Middle India,* Bombay, pp. 496-498.

Enthoven, R.E. (Pardhan), 1922: *The Tribes and Castes of Bombay,* Vol.II. pp. 252.

Epstein, T.S., 1972: *Economic Development and Social Change in South India,* The English Book Society and Manchester University Press.

Ferreira, John V., 1965: *Totemism in India,* Oxford University Press, Bombay.

Firth, Raymond, 1957: *We the Tikopia.*

Ghode, R.N., 1977: 'A Sociological Study of a Tribal Community in Industrial Setting.', Unpublished Ph. D. Thesis, Nagpur University.

Ghurye, G.S., 1963: *The Scheduled Tribes,* Third Ed. Popular Press, Bombay.

Goode, W.J., 1966: *The World Revolution and The Family Patterns,* Free Press of Glenco, New York, p.6.

Govt. of India, 1931: *Census of India.* Vol.XII.

Govt. of India, 1955: *The Adivasis.* The Publication Division of Ministry of Information and Broadcasting, New Delhi.

Govt. of India, 1961: *Census of India*, 1961, Vol.X Part.V.B.

Govt. of India, 1961: *Census of India,* 1961, Vol.X Maharashtra. Part-V. A. Scheduled Castes and Tribes in Maharashtra.

Govt. of India, 1962: *The Advasis of Maharashtra,* Modern Review, Vol. III p. 397.

Govt. of India, 1971: *Census of India,* District Census Handbooks. Amravati, Chandrapur, Yavatmal.

Govt. of Maharashtra, 1974: *Maharashtra State District Gazetteers, Yavatmal District.* Second Edition, Bombay, pp. 207-208.

Haimandorf, Furer, Christoph Von, 1948: *The Aboriginal Tribes of Hyderabad.* Vol.III. The Raj Gonds of Adilabad; a Book I Myth and Ritual Macmillan & Co. London.

Haimandorf Furer, Christoph Von, 1951: *The Pardhans: The Bards of Raj Gonds.* Vol. 4 No.3-4. pp.172-184.

Haimandorf Furer, C. Von., 1979: *The Gonds of Andhra Pradesh*, Vikas Publishing House, Bombay, pp.24.

Hislop, Stephen Rev., 1866: 'Papers relating to Aboriginal Tribes of Central Provinces, Nagpur.'

Hiralal, R.B., 1922: The Aborigins of Central India, *Man in India,* Vol. II. Mar. & June I and II. pp.12-32.

Hivale, Shamrao, 1946: *The Pardhan of Upper Narbada Valley.* Oxford University Press, Bombay.

Hoselitz and Moore, 1963: *Industrilization and Society,* p.136.

Karve, Iravati, 1953: *Kinship Organization in India.*

Kapadia, K.M., 1956: Rural Family Patterns: A Study in Rural Urban Relationship. *Sociological Bulletin*, Vol. V. No. 2. p.119.

Kapadia, K.M., 1966: *Marriage and Family In India,* Oxford University Press, Bombay.

Kolenda, 1973: *Regional Differences in Indian Family Structure;* Quoted by Yogendra Singh in Modernization of Indian Traditions, p.179.

Kroeber, A.L., 1953: *Anthropology To-day.*

Kuppuswami, B., 1977: *Social Change in India.* 2nd Ed. Vikas Publishing House Private Ltd., Bombay.

Majumdar, D.N., 1950: *The Affairs of A Tribe,* Universal Publishing House, Lucknow.

Majumdar, D.N. and Madan, T.N., 1957: *An Introduction to Social Anthropology,* Asia Publishing House, Bombay.

Majumdar, D.N., 1944: *The Fortunes of Primitive Tribes,* Universal Publishers Ltd., Lucknow. *The Korwas*, pp. 37-45. *The Tharus,* pp. 66-68.

Mandeokar, Bhausaheb, 1966: *Kolam* (Marathi); Sewa Prakashan Amravati.

Mandeokar Bhausaheb, 1972: *Nandadeep* (Marathi) *Adim.* (Marathi) *Festivals and Ceremonies of the Pardhans.* Edited by Dr. Sarojinee Babar. Published by Lok Sahitya Prakashan Pune, p.127.

Masaram, Rushi, 1971: 'Typical Cultural References of Aboriginal Tribes' (Unpublished Articles in Marathi) Secretary Maharashtra Adiwasi Mandal, Nagpur.

Memoria, C.B., *Tribal Demography in India,* pp.24-25.

Pagdi, Setu Madhorao (Pardhan or Pradhan), 1955: *Among the Gonds of Adilabad,* Popular Book Depot, Bombay, pp.69-78.

Pisharoti Rama, K., 1931: The Origin of Ornaments: Being a Study of Kerala Ornaments, *Man in India,* Vol.XI No. 3 & 4 July-Dec. pp.268-274.

Reuter and Hart, 1935: *Introduction to Sociology*, McGraw Hill Book Co. New York 2nd Ed.9th Impression, p.143.

Ross, A.D., 1961: *Hindu Family in Its Urban Setting,* Oxford University Press, Bombay.

Russel, R.V. and Hiralal, 1916: Reprint 1975, *The Tribes and Castes of the Central Provincies of India.* London. Vol. I. II, III, IV. Pardhan: Vol. 1, p.397. Vol. 4, p.352.

Shashi, S.S., 1977: *The Gaddi Tribe of Himachal Pradesh: A Sociological Study*, Sterling Publishing Ltd., New Delhi.

Singh, Yogendra, 1973: *Modernization In Indian Traditions.* The Quotation by I.P. Desai, pp.117-178.

Singh, Yogendra, 1973: *Modernization of Indian Traditions,* Thomson Press (India) Ltd., Publication Division, Delhi.

Smelsen, N.T., 1959: *Social Changes During Industrial Revolution,* Chicago, University of Chicago Press, p. 43.

Srinivas, M.S., 1952: *Religion and Society Among the Coorgs: The Coorgs of South India,* Oxford University Press, p.30.

Stephen, Fuchs, 1973: *The Aboriginal Tribes of India,* Macmillan Co. of India.

Upreti, H., 1970: *Bharatiya Janjati (Hindi).* Bharat Printers, Jaipur.

Wilkinson, T.S., *Gotul School of the Muria Gonds of Baster: A Case Study of Village Ghotul*, Banglaore. ICSSR p.44.

# ILLUSTRATIONS

1. A Typical Pardhan Hut

2. A Pardhan Family

3. The temple of Lord Narsimha at village Anji. Tq. Ghantanji, Dist. Yavatmal

4. The idol of Lord Narsimha at Village Anji

5. A "Dhemsa" dance - the author on the left

6. A marriage being solemnised

7. A newly married couple performing religious rites on the raised platform. *Bohala* i.e. Altar

8. Fully married

9. Ashram School at Matharjun with students

# INDEX